THROUGH THE
SHATTERING GLASS

THROUGH THE SHATTERING GLASS

Cervantes and the Self-Made World

NICHOLAS SPADACCINI
AND JENARO TALENS

University of Minnesota Press
Minneapolis   London

The University of Minnesota Press gratefully acknowledges assistance from the
Program for Cultural Cooperation between Spain's Ministry of Culture and United
States' Universities toward preparation of this work.

Diagrams by Cesare Segre from *Poetics Today* 1: 2 (1980) and 2: 3 (1981) published by
Duke University Press. Reprinted with permision of the publisher.

Published by the University of Minnesota Press
2037 University Avenue Southeast, Minneapolis, MN 55414
Printed in the United States of America on acid-free paper

Library of Congress Cataloging-in-Publication Data

Spadaccini, Nicholas.
   Through the shattering glass : Cervantes and the self-made world /
Nicholas Spadaccini and Jenaro Talens.
      p.   cm.
   Includes bibliographical references and index.
   ISBN 0-8166-2140-3 (acid-free paper). —ISBN 0-8166-2263-9 (acid-free paper)
   1. Cervantes Saavedra, Miguel de, 1547–1616—Criticism and
interpretation.   2. Reality in literature.   I. Talens, Jenaro,
   1946–   . II. Title.
   PQ6351.S6   1993
   863'.3—dc20   92-14158
                                                     CIP

To Judy and Giulia

Contents

Acknowledgments

Some of the materials used in this book were published in previous form in scholarly series (notably Hispanic Issues) or as Introductions to our collaborative and individual editions of Cervantes's works that have been widely disseminated in Spain during the past few years. Nevertheless, here these writings have been recast in a new light, one that is summed up by the images of the "shattering glass" and the "self-made world." In this sense, one could say that everything has been rewritten. We might also add that in this writing we have been accompanied by many friends and colleagues. Among the former we wish to thank Gustavo Domínguez, director of Ediciones Cátedra of Madrid, who helped us to initiate our common adventure years ago and also provided permission to adapt here pages originally written for his Letras Hispánicas series; Michael Nerlich, who invited us to present our project in a graduate course that we co-taught at the Technische Universität Berlin in July 1990 while the wall (of reinforced concrete rather than glass) was literally crumbling down—the discussions with Michael and his research team (especially Sybil Dümchen) in the midst of those momentous political changes and the distractions of the World Soccer Cup were as fruitful as they were challenging; Jennifer Lang, who helped with the translation of several sections of the book and contributed her competent and enthusiastic help in the preparation of the final manuscript; Gwendolyn Barnes-Karol, who, with her usual reliability, translated a previous version of the first chapter when the book was beginning to take shape; Antonio Ramos-Gascón for his intellectual and personal support during some shared turbulent years; Laura Westlund, our copy editor, for her careful and impressive work, which allowed us to eliminate inconsistencies in the text; and Biodun Iginla, editor at the University of Minnesota Press, for the enthusiasm and understanding he offered us when we first discussed the possibility of submitting this book for peer review and publication. Time—with its way of marching on, oblivious to the weakness of human memory—has erased other names.

Finally, we wish to thank Judy and Giulia respectively for the patience with which they accepted frequent mental absences and obsessive conversations about Cervantes's writings during recurrent periods. To leave crazy people to their craziness is a loving way of giving understanding and support. This book is dedicated to both of them.

Nicholas Spadaccini and Jenaro Talens
Minneapolis, January 1992

Introduction: The Constructed Mirror; or, The World as a Text

Miguel de Cervantes Saavedra (1547–1616) wrote largely during the latter part of his life. After the appearance of his pastoral prose fiction, *La Galatea* (1585), and a brief engagement as a practicing playwright at the end of the sixteenth century, he is heard from again officially in 1605 when *Don Quijote I* is published in Madrid. All of his other works appear in print between 1613 and 1617: *Novelas ejemplares* (1613); *Viaje del Parnaso* (1614); *Don Quijote II* (1615); *Ocho comedias y ocho entremeses* (1615); and *Los trabajos de Persiles y Sigismunda* (1617).

Since most of Cervantes's known works were not only published but also, probably, composed or reworked toward the very end of his life, it could be argued that an analysis carried out on a single text or on texts belonging only to the same genre might, in some instances, be less productive than a transversal analysis that cuts synchronically across generic lines. Such an analysis is apt to single out orders of relations resting on what Jacques Dubois calls "the laws of the collective unconscious which leave their traces on the work and allow us to perceive the most socialized aspect of the message."[1] It also allows one to focus broadly on questions of poetics and discourses.

Midway between the two centuries, which encompass the periods of the Renaissance and the baroque, and immersed in one of the most decisive processes of historical change, in Spanish history as well as in the history of Western civilization, Cervantes stands at the crossroads of intellectual, social, religious, ideological, philosophical, and political struggles, from the Christian humanism of Erasmus, Juan Luis Vives, and their followers, to the conservative winds of the Counter-Reformation that were to isolate Spain from the mainstream of European life. His work embraces the contradictory forces on which it draws, and manages to construct upon them a dialectical view of the world that, in the final analysis, is at the very foundations of modernity. In a manner that is essentially dialogical, he carries out what is, perhaps, the most important work of discursive synthesis undertaken until that time. The effervescence and continual change that traverse Spain, from imperial expansion to the bankruptcy of the state, serve not only as a historical and cultural frame but are also inscribed, analyzed, and deconstructed through Cervantes's literary discourse. Thus, one might say that his exceptional circumstance achieves total expression. Compared to Cervantes, many of the major Spanish writers of his time appear to be inexorably fragmented and dated.

Cervantes's life comprises two well-defined stages. The first involves a heroic youth, which is characterized by a complete surrender to (a) guidelines of the Renaissance from a cultural point of view; (b) the great romantic adventure of the global and unitary man, who tends toward multidimensional activities (arms and letters) in his everyday life; and (c) the political ideals of the Christian and Spanish empire. The second phase is one of transition: the triumphant hero, who has achieved self-realization in accordance with his original aspirations as a soldier, returns to Spain hoping to receive a well-deserved reward and recognition. Misfortune strikes, however, as he is captured and taken to Algiers, where he is held prisoner for five years. During his captivity, which was marked by his four attempts to escape, he is said to have persevered in his former ideals, while experiencing an incipient awareness of the crisis that was affecting both the empire and the world of values that had shaped his youth. Such an awareness was to develop fully and rapidly upon his final return to Spain. The hero who had hoped for glory and rewards for the services rendered to his country now finds himself a mere survivor; the adventurer is forced to become a tax collector, and the man of high ideals must endure trials and prison, defending himself from accusations concerning the most wretched interests of his life. The ideals of chivalry imply the least adequate preparation for the tasks that a discharged soldier is forced to carry out in an unproductive society. Spain has neither room for its heroes nor the ability to feed them. Ironically, these two stages of Cervantes's life are interwoven with two facts that symbolize the change operated on the empire. As a soldier he finds himself involved in the Battle of Lepanto, which is the apex of an expansive cycle. But he also finds himself enveloped in the expedition of the Invincible Armada, the starting point of decadence. In this last adventure he participates not as a soldier, but as a wheat supplier.

The last fifteen years of Cervantes's life are focused on the task of giving a totalizing artistic expression to an exceptional wealth of experiences. His work reveals a veritable literary vertigo as he feverishly writes and publishes at the twilight of his life. The richness and complexity of Cervantes's writings cannot be connected univocally to the historical and literary circumstances in which they were produced, for there is no specular reproduction of the world, but a reflection about how, from where, and why the world is thought out and lived. While numerous efforts have been made to describe the writings in terms of a totalizing and closed world related to the history and culture of the time, such efforts have not yielded a "definitive" meaning of his work. This is not surprising because it is impossible to unify the three different discursive levels that interact in his writings. In effect, those writings speak about "reality" in three simultaneous and complementary ways—"reality as discourse," "reality of discourse," and "discourse on reality." Thus Cervantes's writings cannot simply be placed in *a* given position, realizing *a* given function, within *a* particular understanding of how literature *has to* work. In these cases the result has proven to be polemical. A wide range of interpretations exists (possibly no other writer in Spanish literature has been the object of so many and such disparate interpretations) and one might classify them along two different lines. The first attempts to define the conception of the Cervantine world, uniting it with the major cultural notions of the time: hence, the first Américo Castro (*El pensamiento de Cervantes*), for whom Cervantes's intellectual roots are to be found in the Renaissance; Arnold Hauser, who connects him to mannerism; Helmut Hatzfeld or Joaquín Casalduero, for whom Cervantes would be wholly a baroque writer. The second line of interpretation chooses a different approach, relying on ideology rather than on the conception of the world. One can point to the second phase of Américo Castro's work (*Hacia Cervantes* and *Cervantes y los casticismos españoles*), where Cervantes's ideology is defined as that of an Erasmian while his attitude toward life is linked to that of the "New Christians," or to Paul Descouzis, who characterizes Cervantes as a Counter-Reformation writer. Other scholars (Pierre Vilar and Francisco Olmos) have examined the relationship of the author of *Don Quijote* with the material conditions of his society, interpreting this relationship as an actively critical one, based on Cervantes's discrepant lucidity. One might also discuss the most generalized (and eclectic) solution: Cervantes or ambiguity, Cervantes or relativism, a Cervantes fluctuating between two poles of identical force and attraction—Renaissance idealism and baroque realism, spiritualism and Tridentine militancy. To define Cervantes may be extremely difficult, but it is a task that must be dealt with.

The various chapters that make up this book do not attempt to do the same. First of all we are not dealing with an "author" but with a "writing." Moreover, to *define* an author's work implies the acceptance of its existence as a closed object and an understanding of its analysis as a form of dissection. Our study moves in another direction and is essentially concerned with establishing a reading space from which to approach the work as an open and contradictory process, constructing as object *a proposal for the expression of possible meanings.*

Our work on Cervantine discourse is guided by two basic assumptions. First, there is the idea that in Cervantes's work an open rupture operates between the classical rhetorical universe that it claims to assume and the specular metaphor that serves as an epistemological foundation: art as an imitation of life and nature. Indeed, in Cervantine writings the writer's task is not to *return* to the so-called preexistent images of the real. If, as in the subsequent Stendhalian metaphor, a mirror exists that simulates walking through the path, it is never the world that is reflected in the mirror. This is so because in real life there are human beings rather than characters, fragments rather than totalities. Thus, only images and fragments can appear on the mirror's surface. The transformation of the image of a human being into a character presupposes an act of interpretation: we have to give meaning to what is nothing but a presence. In the same way, the idea of a totality, that is to say, of an interconnected whole, results from the creation of a hypothesis for articulating fragments. Thus the world, as a structured organism, exists as a corollary of said reflection; it is the very mirror that, feigning reproduction, constructs the path. Consequently, the latter does not come to us as a fact a priori but as the result of an observation, that is, an interpretation, or a construction. As such it is also discursive and, therefore, analyzable in terms of discourse. The so-called realism that guides Cervantes's writing is not a way of *representing* the world, but a manner of *showing* the system of relationships that constitute it. In Cervantes there is no contradiction or lack of coherence, so that disorder is not the result of a lack of order but a way of inscribing truth. Such is the double perspective assumed by the shattering glass and the self-made world, one that generates itself in the act of moving away from all metaphysical pretensions of totality. Emilio Orozco Díaz (1970, 1988) has pointed out correctly that mannerism and baroque were characterized by the use of variety and a plurality of themes in opposition to the rational principle of unity imposed by Aristotelian poetics. He argued that in mannerism this variety manifested itself in a disintegrating structure based on the idea of *composition*, but in the baroque the latter is substituted by the notion of *mixture*, in which elements blend together, losing their independent meaning and constituting a united whole in their variety. In *Don Quijote I*, Cervantes acts as a mannerist, but *Don Quijote II* is already a baroque structure that subsumes the mannerist composition of the first part. The metaphor of the mirror thus becomes the metaphor of a mirror constructed with the fragments of the classical shattered glass.

Second, and as a consequence of the former supposition, there is the idea of the metadiscursive nature of Cervantes's writing that is characterized by a sustained reflection on the *medium* that serves it as a discursive anchor. The conscious and continuous dialectics between *seeing* (the sharing action of confronting the external) and *looking* (the task of individualized construction of that exterior as a comprehensible expression) *leaves out* the problem of truth—the latter understood as something objective and absolute—by showing its lack of essence and the ideological order that constitutes it. Thus, rather than assuming the role of a compact mirror in which external elements might be reflected, Cervantes's writing seeks to *re*-construct this exterior from a conglomerate of fragments of the shattered mirror. Behaving like a kaleidoscope, the resulting world has the form of text and as such it may be read and analyzed; like the text it is mobile, fragmentary, and contradictory. The question of verisimilitude, which is a central issue in Cervantine writing, neither substitutes nor denies the truth. Rather, it inscribes it within a system of historical and concrete values that does not seek to make it relative but aims to connect it to a political, ideological, and social space that is responsible for its operativeness.

In stressing the dialogical nature of the texts—that is, the world as a discursive construction—Cervantes's writing avoids both the escapist formalism and the moralizing focus on content that were present in much of the production of his contemporaries. We are thinking here of the picaresque novel, the Lopean *comedia*, and the writings of Quevedo. The idea of the reader as an integral part of the process, no longer a part of reception but as a constitution of the discursive device, even seems to anticipate the "questioning" of the very notion of art that characterizes contemporary writing. To a great extent, this displacement—from traditional alternation between formal sources and matters of content—toward the problem of the medium provides the cast of modernity to Cervantes's writings.

This volume is the result of shared work on Cervantes spanning many years. It began with research undertaken for the preparation of several editions of Cervantes's plays and poetry and without a clear goal of becoming a book. In a certain sense we can say that the volume has been growing naturally, and that, once a common denominator was found in the fragments we had been writing, the idea of a book materialized and the fragments themselves dictated its structure. This is why our study deals with some global issues surrounding Cervantine writing without pretending to be all-inclusive.

While the bibliography on Cervantes is abundant, and usually of high quality, it is also the case that Cervantes's narrative, poetry, and theater are generally analyzed as specific and separate genres. Our dialogue had suggested to us the possibility of dealing with Cervantine writing as a kind of puzzle, where the borders between traditional genres could be dissolved. The mirror has usually been the metaphor for realism, but in Cervantes this mirror has shattered, disseminating a multiplicity of images that no longer reflect but re-*produce* reality, for as a new "Alice in no-where-land," it allows us to look at the world with the light of a candle when the candle is spent. Jorge Luis Borges once said that in reading Quevedo's poems he could not imagine a real person behind them, and that reading Cervantes, on the other hand, he could even experience the presence of a human body. For us, in effect, to deal with Cervantes is to engage in a living dialogue with "something" or "someone" who can speak our own language, and who can be our contemporary.

CHAPTER 1

Poetry as Autobiography

In his autobiography Robbe-Grillet, the chief exponent of the *nouveau roman*, made a surprising and, apparently, provocative declaration: "I have never spoken of anything but myself." The sentence points to a fundamental problem that has traversed contemporary theoretical discussions, namely, who speaks in a text, what a text speaks of, and from where it speaks. On the one hand, we know that the limits of our language are the limits of our world, that is, that we can *think* our relation with the real only in terms of discourse. On the other hand, when one speaks, it is impossible to not say "I." How, then, does one resolve what, in these terms, appears to be such an irreducible contradiction? How do we claim objectivity when we know that it is not possible to transcend our bodies, to feel with a skin that is not our own; to look with eyes that, for a moment, forget the untransferable place that our own history makes them occupy? How, on the contrary, does one narrate his or her own life with words that exist precisely because they cannot belong to anyone? As Lautréamont wrote, "These eyes are not yours. Where have you taken them from?" In one form or another, this vicious circle frames and traverses most contemporary writing. Its problematic, however, is not unique to this writing and, in large part, has guided the historical development of literature.

A paradigmatic case may be the discourse of lyric poetry, in which the frequent use of the first person does not necessarily imply the presence of an "I" that speaks of itself. Yet, the frequent absence of

1

anecdotal-argumentative support leaves bare procedures of composition and structure and allows one to analyze the traces that are no less real for being invisible. A life is drawn not only from what one tells of it, but also from what is silenced. A gesture, the choice of a certain perspective for approaching some matter, the predilection for an adjective, all tell more than a thousand anecdotes. In this sense Cervantes's poetic work can be seen as paradigmatic, despite the fact that it has not enjoyed much critical acclaim in literary history.

The work of Miguel de Cervantes is composed of three parts, which are well defined in their limits as well as in their function. He is not only the peerless prose writer and creator of a genre in its modern sense, but also the author who, together with Shakespeare, has managed to produce an entire literary continent. Second, he is a playwright who breaks his own paths, distinct from those of Lope de Vega. Finally, he is the poet who perseveres in a task that brings him nothing more than sorrows and none of the praise commensurate with his estimation of its worth. And if critics have been preoccupied with his novel, and have paid attention, though perhaps not enough, to his theatrical work, his poetry has not enjoyed the same fortune. The attitude toward this portion of Cervantes's work is particularly unjust, above all if, as we will attempt to demonstrate, we can see in it not only its substantive value as poetry (with respect to its original conception of poetic work), but also a small-scale model of his entire literary world. The constancy with which Cervantes applies himself to the unpleasant task of *writing verses* throughout his life would otherwise have little justification.

Cervantes begins his poetic adventures in 1569, at the age of twenty-three. The four compositions included by his teacher, Juan López de Hoyos, in his *History and True Tale of the Sickness, Happy Death and Magnificent Funeral Rites of the Most Serene Queen of Spain, Our Lady, Doña Isabel de Valois,*[1] are, indeed, the oldest of his works to have come down to us. In them, there are, as in all beginners, the marks of the teaching of his elders. At the same time, when read from the perspective of his later works, one observes what will become his fundamental tendency: the adoption of the *cancionero* lyric and the Italian model, a double tradition in which he inserts himself and that he then manages to transform. This function of playful craftsmanship—which will later make of him one of the great and original innovators—is what catches one's attention in his poetic work from the very beginning. Such work may be understood as a method on the one hand, and as *salvation of man by beauty* on the other. Both aspects are joined from the beginning, if we consider the simple comparison of texts that are so far apart in

time as the "Elegy" of 1569 and that which Dorotea and Clara hear
sung in *Don Quijote* (I, 43):

> He who always enjoys tranquillity in his state of being
>> and whose effect leads him to hope
>> and of what he wants, nothing is changed:
>>> It is said that one may have
>>> little confidence in he
>>> who enjoys and sees with
> limpid eyes good fortune. ("Elegy" vv. 133–138)

>> Sluggards do not deserve
> the glory of triumphs or of victory;
>> good luck will never serve
> those who resist not fortune manfully,
>>> but fall weakly to ground,
> and in soft sloth their senses all confound.
>> ("Don Luis's Song" 388)[2]

Nearly half a century of Cervantes's poetic activity compels us to
pay more attention to this work. That activity responds to a vocation
that was stated in the prologue to *La Galatea* (*The Galatea*): "by which
I can prove the inclination toward poetry that I have always had"
("para lo cual puedo alegar de mi parte la inclinación que a la poesía
siempre he tenido"), repeated only two years before his death in the
fourth song of *Viaje del Parnaso* (*Journey to Parnassus*):

> Since my tender years I have loved
> the sweet art of agreeable poetry and with it
> I will always try to please you.[3]

Some critics have taken this vocation for granted,[4] while the tendency of others to confuse poetry and verse and not to take into account
the same presuppositions with which Cervantes confronted his work
as a poet, have led even modern editors such as Vicente Gaos to say
that Cervantes "was not a born poet."

Cervantes's high esteem for poetry verges on religion (Schevill and
Bonilla 1922), but his relationship with poetry turns out to be somewhat ambivalent, for, with the exception of *Viaje del Parnaso*, he never
published a book of poetry. These facts, however, should lead us to
reformulate the matter of his poetry in other terms, without judging

the results of Cervantes's poetry from presuppositions other than those that he himself established. By so doing, perhaps we could break a long critical tradition, initiated in Cervantes's own time, that undervalues his poetic production.

The passages that follow cannot be taken literally, especially in an author who constantly uses irony and double entendre in his work. First there is the shopworn citation of the third tercet of *Viaje del Parnaso*:

> I who always strive and am vigilant
> to appear that I have the poet's wit
> that heaven didn't choose to grant me.[5]

There is also the sentence uttered by the Licenciado Vidriera in the novella by the same title: "I haven't been so foolish as to begin to be a bad poet, or so fortunate as to have deserved to be a good one" ("No he sido tan necio que diese en poeta malo, ni tan venturoso que haya merecido serlo bueno"). Finally, there are the allusions to poetry scattered throughout his works. Let us recall, for instance, the following statement from *Don Quijote* (I, 6): "That Cervantes has been a great friend of mine for many years and I know that he is more versed in misfortunes than in verse" (62) ("Muchos años ha que es grande amigo mío ese Cervantes, y sé que es más versado en desdichas que en versos"). Yet many other quotations that are not so often glossed would lead us to different conclusions. We cite three fragments from *Viaje del Parnaso*:

> Pass on, inventor rare, further advance
> With thy subtle design, and aid supply
> To Delian Apollo, of vast weight—
> Or ere the vulgar squadron comes to call
> E'en more than twenty thousand seven months old
> Poets, whom so to be are much in doubt. (Chap. 1, vv. 223–228)

> Mercy on us! What poetasters rise. (Chap. 2, v. 396)

> He said, Shall it be possible that in Spain
> There be nine bards with laureated crowns? (Chap. 8, vv. 97–98)[6]

One cannot take Cervantes's ironic statements seriously.[7] Rather, it is necessary to underline their humorous and sly character.[8]

For Cervantes, poetry was grounded in the cult of beauty so that a poem could not lower itself to the status of a commercial object directed toward a pleasure-seeking public. In *Don Quijote* (II, 16) he states that poetry should be kept out of reach of "the ignorant vulgar, who are incapable of recognizing or appreciating her treasures" (569). For this very reason, he considers himself a poet by avocation (*afición*) rather than by vocation (*oficio*). He states as much in *La gitanilla* (*The Gypsy Girl*) and in *Don Quijote* (II, 18). The distinction between avocation and vocation has supported those critics who have interpreted Cervantes's attitude toward poetry as being contrary to the normal work of the artist; as being a mere pastime. There is little substance to this view, however, for while Cervantes does not want to lower art to the daily vulgarity of a remunerable job, he never ceases to consider poetry as constant and tiring work. This exclusive attitude already is manifest in the fourth book of *La Galatea*:

> Despite the low esteem in which [poets] are held by princes and common people alike, they communicate with their intellects their lofty and strange concepts, without daring to make them known to the world, and in my opinion, Heaven should order the world in this fashion, because neither the world nor our maligned century deserves to enjoy such tasty repasts for the soul.[9]

A detailed analysis of Cervantes's poetry shows, as much from the point of view of his theoretical statements as from that of his concrete practice, that if we seek to discover his work, it requires us to speak of its articulation based on two presuppositions: consciousness and a search for balance. From the latter will come the elements of Cervantes's poetic scaffolding: (1) the objectification of lyric sentiment, and (2) the existence of shrewd talents that guide the compositional work. The preceptive zeal is evident throughout his extensive poetic career, but Cervantes possesses a poetics without a code, a theory rather than a normative program. His is a poetics that defends the principle of invention, provided that it does not result in the corruption of art in order to meet public demand, and provided that it does not violate the laws of reason. His rules of composition are flexible and variable. Thus, they are less evident than those of his contemporaries. His theory allows for the modification of what is established by the norms of verse, provided that such modification is submitted to a harmonic scheme fashioned by an intellect controlled by reason and in an analogical relationship with the natural processes of the universe. His theory of poetic expression concerns more a meta-aesthetic system of ideas than a treatise on poetic art. He can make a mockery of the rules, given their particular character, in contrast to the scope of the universals in which the poem operates and shows itself, and he can laugh at sterile erudition because of its apoetical nature. His rules of composition are consequently a habit of thought more than norms and orders. His critical scruples as well as his distrust of academic literary judgments derive from that habit. There is nothing but irony and humorous sarcasm behind the "Privileges, Decrees, and Regulations That Apollo Sends to Spanish Poets" in the Appendix to *Viaje del Parnaso*:

> The first essential is that poets be as well known for the slovenliness of their persons as for the fame of their verses.
>
> Also, should any poet say he is poor, that he instantly be credited on his word, without any other oath or verification whatsoever.
>
> It is required that every poet be of a mild and becoming mental habit, and that one should not look at stitches, albeit they appear in his stocking.
>
> Ditto, should any poet touch at the house of a friend or acquaintance, and should stay there for material sustenance, that although he swear that he has eaten, let it not be believed, save that he be made to eat by force, which in that case will be no great thing.
>
> Ditto, that the poorest bard in the world, though neither Adam nor Methuselah, may say that he is in love, though he be not so, and should give as the name of his lady, now styled Amaryllis, now Anarda, now Cloris, Phỳllis, or Filida, or Juana Téllez, or any other name at will, all may be done without asking reasons why. . . .
>
> Again, notify that he be not held for a thief who would appropriate others' verses, and pass them off for his own, whether in conception or in part, in which case he is as much a thief as Cacus.[10]

Likewise, we can say that humor and sarcasm are hidden behind the serious thoughts of the sick poet in *El coloquio de los perros* (*The Dialogue of the Dogs*), when he complains of the failure of his work even while he takes great care to respect "what Horace orders in his *Poetics*" ("lo que Horacio manda en su *Poética*"). If Cervantes's poetics is a habit of thought, his theory is a method of resolving specific artistic problems at a level that is superior to that of codified precepts. In this sense Cervantes associates poetry with life, which he likewise does not subject to precepts. Indeed, his artistic formula is applicable as much to the composition of a poem as to vital processes in general. That principle even appears to rule the world of military affairs, as he states in the first act of *El cerco de Numancia* (*The Siege of Numancia*) in Scipio's speech:

> If an army, however small,
> is subjected to military order,
> you will see that it shines like the bright sun

and achieves the victories it desires;
but if the army conducts itself with indolence,
although the world sees itself condensed in it,
in a moment it will be routed
by a more forthright hand and stronger heart.[11]

In *Cervantes's Theory of the Novel*, E. C. Riley noted that the origin of Cervantes's idea on the function of imaginative literature was one of "instructing while pleasing" (*instruir deleitando*). Cervantes reconciled this classical concept of the artistic with the antinomy inherent in the accommodation of neo-Platonic aesthetic ideas with a plan of life ruled by reason. León Hebreo, whom Cervantes had read and assimilated, according to Américo Castro and Francisco López-Estrada, had established a way of articulating this antinomic relation in his *Diálogos de amor* (*Dialogues of Love*). In the *Dialogues* Philo describes the method to grant to him, a bit paradoxically, first a poetic fiction, a Cabalistic meaning, and, later, a pedagogical function. This is, in principle, something apparently contradictory, but Hebreo saves the antinomy by assigning both elements to differentiated powers:

1. Hermetic, intellectual knowledge is grasped by "creative faculties suitable for divine and intellectual matters and a mind that preserves and does not corrupt the true sciences of those matters."
2. The matter of beneficial instruction (*provecho*) is assigned to three kinds of minds: (a) "the less intelligent can only take from poetry the story with the ornament and melody of verse"; (b) "the more intelligent can digest the moral sense, in addition to the story"; (c) "the most intelligent can digest, in addition to the story and the moral sense, the allegorical repast, not only of natural philosophy, but of astrology and theology as well."[12]

Cervantes's position does not differ much from that of León Hebreo. He reserves the knowledge of universals to a select few and assigns the "instruction while pleasing" to those not apt for the highest knowledge. In prose, this double purpose of serving everyone can be realized, even if everyone does not benefit in the same fashion by what is offered to them. In poetry, however, this realization is not possible because of its very high position in the scale of the harmonic. Poetry aspires to produce pleasure and a supreme good and, therefore, its use is forbidden to the "ignorant vulgar, who are incapable of recognizing or appreciating her treasures" (569) ("*ignorante vulgo, incapaz de conocer ni estimar los tesoros que en ella se encierran*") as we hear in Don Quijote's speech (II, 16:155).

For Cervantes, the fundamental objective of the poem is enjoyment in the contemplation of beauty. The poem's beneficial effect consists of enriching itself with the truth of this graciously received gift. That thought is similar to what is expressed in the treatises on Christian piety in the sixteenth century. One thinks, for example, of Fray Diego de Estella, who writes in his *Meditaciones devotísimas del amor de Dios* [*Most Devout Meditations on the Love of God* (1576)]: "He who says that he loves You and keeps the Ten Commandments of Your law only or chiefly because You give glory to him, should consider himself abandoned by that glory" ("El que dice que te ama y guarda los diez mandamientos de tu ley solamente o más principalmente porque le des la gloria, téngase por despedido della"). This thought coincides with that of Don Quijote when he speaks of his consecration to his lady Dulcinea (I, 31). There he speaks, in neo-Platonic fashion, of the transfer of concepts of universal courage from the sacred to the profane and vice versa.

According to these ideas, prose, as well as poetry, occasions responses in accord with a reader's specific sensibility. But the poem, in contrast to prose, also has the function of producing what is impossible for prose, namely, mental and spiritual therapy by means of the cessation of emotive processes. This kind of therapy is possible only for those who know how to interpret poetry. This pseudomystical position, of Plotinist derivation, is also characteristic of León Hebreo. From this perspective, we can understand the definition of poetry that Cervantes gives in *Don Quijote* (II,16), insisting that it is "made of an alchemy of such virtue that he who knows how to treat her will receive in turn the purest gold of priceless worth" ("es hecha de una alquimia de tal virtud, que quien la sabe tratar la volverá en oro purísimo de inestimable precio"). In Cervantes this vision of poetry as an exclusive artistic labor is joined by the consciousness of having both the creative genius and the technical competence necessary to convert this mental schema into verbal discourse. At the same time, he knows that not all of his poetic peers possess this virtue.

In effect, in the length and breadth of his poetic production, Cervantes shows himself to have mastered a fairly ample formal and metrical repertory, including troubadouresque, Italianized, and popular styles. Moreover, even his own variations within the fixed schemas are intricately woven and superimposed without ever privileging any of these modes of composition. A simple examination of his work shows not only technical and strophic variety, but also the balanced perfection with which it is employed. Examples of this perfection include his sonnets; the *silvas* that appear with the same ease and fluency in *Nueve canciones petrarquistas* (*Nine Petrarchan Songs*), fashioned from the news of the defeat of the Invincible Armada in 1588; the poem "A los éxtasis de Nuestra Beata Madre Teresa de Jesús" ("To the Ecstasies of Our Blessed Mother Theresa of Jesus") of 1615; and the ballads or *romances* that, together with those of Lope de Vega and Luis de Góngora, must have influenced the formation of the *Romancero Nuevo*.[13] If his peers considered his *romances* well made, the same can be said of his *zéjeles* and *villancicos*.[14] In short, Cervantes's formal range encompasses virtually all known varieties of verses and strophes used in his time.

The lack of predilection for one meter compared to another does not imply an eclecticism or indecision, but rather the clear conscience of an instrument for putting into practice what really matters: form, understood as composition, as configuration of all the elements integrated in the superior unity called a poem. Already in *La Galatea* this particular approach to the matter of meter appears, generically speaking, as a form in which the poetic material is embodied, the material that, in the last instance, determines the form and grants value to it. A clear example of this approach is to be found in the eclogue of the third book of *La Galatea*, when Orfinio reiterates in two successive instances the same theme with different versification.

> The fruit that was sown
> by my constant work,
> having arrived in a sweet season,
> with thriving destiny
> was delivered in my power.
> And no sooner had I succeeded in arriving
> at such incomparable ends,
> when I came to know
> the occasion of such pleasure
> to be of sorrow for me. (I, 219)

> To my sight there appeared
> an opulent lair full of a thousand riches;
> I triumphed in its conquest,
> and at the very time that fate
> showed itself most serene
> I saw it changed to black darkness. (I, 222)[15]

Likewise, this approach to meter can be seen when two octaves of the same eclogue, in the words of Crisio (vv. 223–238), appear reformulated as a sonnet, in the words of Cardenio in the first act of *La entretenida*:

> My slim and weak hope flies
> on feeble wings and although the flight
> rises to the zenith of the beautiful heaven,
> never will it attain the point to which it aspires.
> I come to be the dead ringer
> for that youth who left Crete's soil
> and, rivaling his father's zeal,
> propelled himself into the heavens.
> Melted by the amorous fire,
> my audacious thoughts will fall
> in the turbulent and cold sea of fear;
> but the violent courses
> forewarned by time and death,
> will not carry my name
> into oblivion.[16]

Meter and the combination of meters lose their determinate value so that the strength of the poem resides in the structural-compositional form and in the internal order of distribution of the poetic material. In this way the craftsmanlike artifice of the poet-writer is fundamental. And what counts for Cervantes, at the end of the process of writing, is fulfilling the lyric intention and the conceptual and technical harmony of the parts.

In the same way, the function of the acoustic in the poem is a problem of structure, so that its meter and prosody cannot be judged by the metric and prosodic norms of the Castilian poem, but from Cervantes's particular use of both in his form of conceiving the poem. The greatest attack on Cervantes's poetry has taken place nearly always in the territory of prosody, yet it is something that few critics have tried to explain.[17]

In prosodic terms, Cervantes's verse lacks acoustic value in itself. Its value is relative to the structure and function of the poem. The relation is not established between the voice and the phonic group, but between the architectonically elaborated thought and the phonic group that is rhythmically disposed and subordinated to the harmony of the concepts. This Cervantine characteristic comes from the enormous importance conceded to the voice that sings and is not limited to speaking the verse. Indeed, the phonological schemas of song do not correspond to those of spoken language. We cannot, of course, determine from a written text what its musical cadence would be, but in view of Cervantes's constant preoccupation with the form of rhythmically linking strophes, we could envisage the possibility that it would be (structurally speaking) repetitive and balanced.

Only in this fashion can one understand how a poem that fails prosodically to our ears may be considered pleasant and sweet within the work. The melody would lend the necessary acoustic harmony, so that it would correspond to the structural harmony. However, since neither all poems included in texts are written in prose, nor are the individual poems sung, it would be worth exploring what happens in these cases. Let us recall that in the years in which Cervantes initiates his poetic career, the matter of prosody was not part of metric theory. Herrera, in his *Anotaciones* (*Annotations*) to Garcilaso, complained of the strictures of rhyme in 1580: "As those who write in this genre of poetry know, this difficulty of rhymes, which disturbs many beautiful bits of wisdom; they cannot be recounted with so much ease and clarity" (68).[18] In that same year, Miguel Sánchez de Luna in his *El arte poética en romance castellano* (*The Poetic Art in Castilian Romance Poetry*) confronts the problem of the measured verse that sounds worse than unmeasured verse, and he gives it a practical solution:

> The poet should guide himself by sound more than by any other path; and for this purpose some composers usually sing what they are composing. . . . It is necessary that each composition have its melody. . . . When I was studying, my teacher read Virgil to me by chanting, because in that way, he said, one felt better the smoothness of the verse. He said that Virgil sung them also as he was composing them.[19]

Cervantes, who was very much a poet of the sixteenth century, would probably have used a melody to look for the fluency and smoothness of his verse. Cervantes's preoccupation with music has already been pointed out by Miguel Querol and by Adolfo Salazar, so that it is not too daring to think that the melody, in its specific concept of poetic composition, could make smooth and faint what to our ears seems harsh today. This manner of focusing on the problem had ceased to be the dominant one in the baroque period.[20]

Despite what has been said above, the use of a musical leitmotiv to overcome the formal pitfalls of prosody is not an excuse for the deficient acoustic qualities that many of Cervantes's poems may have. But that use explains how someone with so much facility for discovering the errors of others could compose verses that seem imperfect to us. Perhaps, in the long run, Cervantes himself might have come to think that, within these particular rules of composition without a code, the superficial, mechanical, and acoustic structure was something secondary to the global structure of the poem which was, in the final analysis, the fundamental consideration.

Cervantes structures his poetry with the precision of a painter, but the important thing for him is not the painterliness of verbal clusters, as Jorge Guillén perceptively noted with respect to Góngora, or the melody of sounds that thereafter become inlaid in words, as Valle-Inclán said of Valéry's "Le cimetière marin" ("The Marine Graveyard"). Rather, Cervantes is interested in the conceptual scaffolding that sustains the verbal clusters. And if the painterly aspect does not appear at times in a specific text, it is because he has decided truly to lay bare that structure, or scaffolding. Therefore, his procedures are of a global nature and attend to the ordering, cohesion, and intensification of the signified. This means that figures and tropes are nearly always secondary; they are resources of a cellular function and accessories to procedures of greater significance: correlation and reiteration, verbal play, the secularization of sacred themes, and the reformulation of the themes and fragments of others, as well as his own. These procedures allow him to say to the Cervantes of the fourth chapter of *Viaje del Parnaso* that he has always seen his poetry "dressed in spring color" ("vestida de color de primavera").

Cervantes's organizing model for his verse was, as stated earlier, a concept of harmony analogous to that of the natural processes of the universe. More specifically, we can allude now to the human body. Already in *La Galatea* he signals his concept of the rhythm of the art of poetry, the relation between the parts of the poem and between the poem and each part (that which some avant-garde theorists refer to as the great discovery of Baudelaire and that, in fact, dates back to Cervantes). He says in *La Galatea* that the natural correspondence of this relation is the human body:

> But just as physical beauty is thus divided into two parts, living and dead bodies, likewise can there be love of physical beauty that may be good. One part of physical beauty shows itself in the living bodies of males and of females, and this consists in that all the parts of the body are good in themselves and that together they all make a perfect whole and form a body proportioned in members and smoothness of colors. The nonliving beauty of the physical part consists of pictures, statues,

buildings, a kind of beauty that can be loved without vilifying the love with which one loves.[21]

It is a concept of the rhythm of beauty that Cervantes will apply not only to his verse production, but to his own novels as well. In *Don Quijote* (I, 47) he critiques the romances of chivalry in large part for lacking proportions:

> And even though the principal aim of such books is to delight, I do not know how they can succeed, seeing the monstrous absurdities they are filled with. For the delight that the mind conceives must arise from the beauty and harmony it sees, or contemplates, in things presented to it by the eyes or the imagination; and nothing ugly or ill proportioned can cause us any pleasure. What beauty can there be, or what harmony between the parts and the whole, or between the whole and its parts, in a book or story in which a sixteen-year-old lad deals a giant as tall as a steeple one blow with his sword, and cuts him in two as if he were made of marzipan? And when they want to describe a battle, first they tell us that there are a million fighting men on the enemy's side. But if the hero of the book is against them, inevitably, whether we like it or not, we have to believe that such and such a knight gained the victory by the valour of his strong arm alone. Then what are we to say of the ease with which a hereditary Queen or Empress throws herself into the arms of an unknown and wandering knight? (424–425)[22]

For this formal scheme to be a poem, it needs to be incarnated in a word that represents it. Poetic representation is, for Cervantes, a matter of configuration that subordinates meter and prosody to a structural balance (or to an imbalance motivated by an ironic or burlesque function that demands it) and the active disposition that demands it. Poetic representation orders and distributes elements at the same time that it binds them, with procedures more discursive than imaginative, in the poetic totality. The rhythm of beauty will be the lexicalized construction that enables the embodiment of what was only embryonic thought.

An emblem of the image that is offered to us by rhythm and representation is given by the "most beautiful damsel" of the poet-page in *La gitanilla*; by the nymph, "the universal lady" of *Viaje del Parnaso*; and by the tender damsel of the second volume of *Don Quijote*. Rhythm produces unity and representation produces clarity, while rhythm and representation combined produce harmony or consonance, the three characteristics of universal beauty, according to Thomas Aquinas (*Ad pulchritudinem tria requiruntur integritas, consonantia, claritas*). These three elements, in turn, motivate the image of a beautiful world condensed in the poem, in the same way that the beauty of the universe condenses it in the physical beauty of man. In the last instance, it is clear that Cervantes is looking for a beauty beyond the reach of man, because although the poem searches for perfection, it cannot be in itself perfect, as he already said in the fourth book of *La Galatea*: "the beauty of which I speak cannot be enjoyed perfectly and entirely . . . because it isn't in man's capacity to enjoy perfectly something that is beyond him and is not all his" ("la belleza de quien hablo no se puede gozar perfecta y enteramente . . . porque no está en mano del hombre gozar cumplidamente cosa que está fuera dél y no sea toda suya").

What the poem may contain is an approximation of the beauty contemplated by the poet. And that mental design both validates the "invention" and justifies, within Cervantes's work, the value given to the force of writing, shown as such in the very poem. When Cervantes is seen as an uncomfortable poet because he transmits to the reader the sensation of the painful effort that the writer seems to have experienced in shaping his verses, one points to another element of Cervantes's originality.[23] It is not a question of acting before the public eye, without artifice or *trompe l'oeil*, but one of implicating the reader in his sufferings.

The essence of this mental design would be the configuration structured in the thought of an image or a concept. It can be the mental design of a face, such as the one that Andrés requests of the poet-page in *La gitanilla*:

> Look, Clemente, the star-studded veil
> with which this cold night
> competes with the day
> of beautiful lights adorning the sky;
> and in this resemblance,
> if your divine wit perceives so much,
> that face figures
> where the utmost beauty is present. (vv. 108–116)[24]

Perhaps this is the reason why *La gitanilla* has been considered Cervantes's macrometaphor for poetry.[25]

Despite everything that has been said, it is indisputable that many of Cervantes's poems can be characterized as "bad." The problem of bad poems underscores the importance of Cervantes's adventure. The higher one aims, the greater the error if the target is missed. The emphasis on the mental plane is transformed sometimes into a wall against which the verbal achievement explodes. While the verses of Garcilaso, Herrera, Lope de Vega, or Góngora leave a mark on the eyes and ears, Cervantes seeks to impress our intellective capacity without entering through the senses. More than an error, this is a trademark. There exists in Cervantes a certain mistrust of sensible perception that shows itself with clarity in the *reductio ad absurdam* of the value assigned to the senses in Don Quijote's tale of what he has seen in Montesinos's cave (II, 23):

> I opened and rubbed my eyes, and saw that I was not asleep but really awake. For all that, I felt my head and my bosom to make certain whether it was my very self who was there, or some empty and counterfeit phantom; but touch, feeling, and the coherent argument I held with myself assured me that I was there then just as I am here now. (615)[26]

An example of the intellective, nonsensorial mechanism of his conception of structure as formal manifestation is in the following verses of the first book of *La Galatea*: "a thousand incomparable, indescribable charms / have made me fog to the amorous wind" ("mil gracias que no tienen par ni cuento / niebla me han hecho al amoroso viento"). These verses, which undoubtedly have a high affective level, perform their function within their context (the nine octaves of dialogue between Elicio and Erastro as a counterpoint to the verses that close the previous octave): "and other things I saw as I was blinded / have made me fuel for the invisible fire" ("y otras cosas que vi quedando ciego / yesca me han hecho al invisible fuego"). The syntactical and compositional parallelism (each verse is at the end of the preceding octave) puts two worlds into contact: that of the poetic shepherd, Elicio, who refers to "fuel," "invisible," and "fire" and that of the historical shepherd, Erastro, who refers to "fog," "amorous," and "wind." The worlds are related, harmonizing the universal (poetic) and the particular (historical) to sing to the woman they both love. It is not the isolated verses that count, but the verbal artifice of counterpoint that permits the figure portioned from the whole.

In addition to Cervantes's refusal to commercialize his poetry, this notion of poetry in the totality of the works, rather than in singular ones, provides a possible answer as to why he did not publish an independent book of poetry, except for *Viaje del Parnaso*. His entire corpus of poetic work is a kind of frame where he integrates his proposal as a poet. Thus, the intercalated poems are not really isolated "exceptions," but are part of the fabric of the prose in his narrative and of the verse necessary to the dramatic plan of his theater. If we extract the poems from his novels and plays, we decontextualize them and, as a result, they lose most of their meaning. In this manner, the poems integrated in *La Galatea* are not simple excursuses in the traditional fashion, but a form of inscribing his critique of the pastoral genre.

What is at stake in Cervantes's work is what could be defined as a kind of baroque integration, in contrast to the merely accumulative character of mannerism.[27] "The Song of Grisóstomo," for example, in *Don Quijote* (I, 14:181) [where Garcilaso's *Egloga tercera* ("Third Eclogue") is cited: "Let all together cry from my aching soul" (104) ("salgan con la doliente ánima fuera")], explains a suicide, whereas the narrative text in which it is inserted only speaks of the death of love. Even in single poems, his tendency to integrate genres is evident.

There is a truly paradigmatic example of this integration in the sonnet "Al túmulo de Felipe II" ("To the Funeral Casket of Philip II"). That boasting, which at the end of the poem visualizes what seems to be the neutral voice of the lyric poet, making of him a soldier and holding him responsible for as much as he says, has a great deal of theatricality. On the other hand, Cervantes does not seem to have much interest in conserving individual poems as discrete entities. Some of his compositions would end up being integrated, with few variants, in his works, whether narrative or theatrical. Such is the case of the "Epístola a Mateo Vázquez" ("Letter to Mateo Vázquez"), which coincides, with slight changes, with Saavedra's speech in the first act of *Los tratos de Argel*, and the case of some of the verses of Elicio's song in book II of *La Galatea*, which are reproduced in the same play:

ELICIO: It is so easy for my faint fortune
     to see bitter death
     joined with sweet life
     and see grief dwell where joy resides.
     Between opposites I see
     hope wane, and not desire. (*La Galatea*, vv. 43–48)

SAAVEDRA: In the fast track
       I see the hurried hours of fleeting time
       conspire against me with heaven,
         with hope left behind, not desire. (*Los tratos de Argel*, I)[28]

Finally, before speaking of *Viaje del Parnaso*, we would like to consider briefly Cervantes's tendency to quote his own works, as much as those of others, as poetic material. It has been said that as a poet he does not seem to have a "personal voice,"[29] or that he used entire verses of Garcilaso.[30] This is not so much a matter of a lack of originality, however, as of the deliberate search for the dissolution of the personal voice. In his poem "A los éxtasis de la Beata Madre Teresa de Jesús" ("To the Ecstasies of Our Blessed Mother Theresa of Jesus"), Cervantes includes three lines in which Garcilaso praises the Viceroy of Naples in his *Egloga primera* ("First Eclogue"):

> You who by working earned
> renown the world over
> and a rank second to none.[31]

Here he is not taking refuge in Garcilaso in order to hide his inexperience. The text is from 1615 and by then his apprentice years had passed. Perhaps the hypothesis could be put forth that with this citation, Cervantes achieved a certain impersonal generalization by neutralizing his voice among voices foreign to his, some of them incorporated from his own writings. This procedure would not be unique to his poems. Indeed, the imbrication of narrators in *Don Quijote* would likewise make the personal disappear behind the work, in order to resurface as the universal textual voice from that same work; for example, the character who reads the first part of Don Quijote's life is none other than the transcriber/adapter of a previous text of Cide Hamete Benengeli.

Cervantes neither cites sterile erudition nor does he wink at the reader. Such is also the case with *Viaje del Parnaso* (1614). Its date of composition, as well as its considerable length, seems to indicate the importance that Cervantes attached to this work. In ill health, involved with the production of the second part of *Don Quijote* and engaged in writing *Persiles y Sigismunda*, Cervantes might not have dedicated the time that was slipping away from him to a poem with the characteristics of *Viaje* if it were not because he sought to achieve something important and significant.[32]

While *Viaje* is not an essay in literary criticism per se, Cervantes humorously criticizes himself as a literary figure:

> "Oh you!," he said, who canonized
> the poets from the long list
> by indirect reasons and ways.
>
> Where did you hold, evil one,
> the sharp sight of your talent, so that

> though blind, you were such a lying chronicler?
> (Chap. 4, vv. 490–495)[33]

Cervantes's curious affirmation "by indirect reasons and ways" can be taken as a self-vindication, for, although the direct and fundamental thing to do was to speak of oneself, the primordial purpose of *Viaje* was to leave to posterity an autobiography vindicating Cervantes's function as a poet. And, in truth, the only sincere praise, without the clichés of the time, are the ones dedicated to his own work:

> He who doesn't value being a poet,
> for what reason does he write and proclaim verses?
> Why does he disdain what he most esteems?
>
> I was never happy or satisfied
> with hypocritical fastidiousness; I simply
> wanted praise for what I did well. (Chap. 4, vv. 337–342)[34]

The plot of the book could not be more Cervantine: (a) by means of memory, he leaves his country on an "ideal voyage," to cite the expression of Croce, and returns to the golden Italy of his youth; (b) the Spanish "prosaic" reality of the time in which writers have to survive is ironically pictured by means of the representation of a mythography—evasion and improbability being constant features of his style; and (c) by simultaneously doubling as narrator and character, he "leaves" himself. In this fashion, whether by his own means or by those of the god Mercury, Cervantes can say what he thought of his work and himself.

Having fulfilled these purposes, Cervantes extends the symbolic function of the poem to the métier of literature and converts *Viaje* into a mock epic of the illusions and vanities of the writer in a world where beauty and poetry have no place anymore. This is exemplified in the poet's blind zeal for glory, again uniting the particular and the universal. In some measure and without ignoring that *Don Quijote* is a work of greater substance, we could agree with Vicente Gaos that *Viaje del Parnaso* is a kind of *Don Quijote* in miniature and in verse. It makes clear that man usually judges himself to be greater than his own merits and in the process he is swept along by a chimera. His self-concept and, to a certain degree, his aspirations, surpass the real possibility of satisfying them. There is no trace of idealism in Cervantes's utilization of self-confidence, however. The ironic reference to mythology has a very practical significance. When, upon arriving in Parnassus, the character named Cervantes finds that Apollo does not recognize him, he tells the god about his own literary career, outlining its more important achievements. There is no vanity in this, just the expression of a need to succeed in order to avoid the jealousy and the lack of appreciation of his largely mediocre contemporaries.[35]

There is also another point of contact with *Don Quijote*. If *Don Quijote* mocks the romances of chivalry, *Viaje* parodies the mythological world of classicism that Renaissance authors had abused so much. If Don Quijote makes princesses of country girls and castles of windmills, *Viaje* brings the gods down from the Olympic pedestals and grants them human stature, submerging them in an atmosphere of caricature similar to that of Velázquez's paintings.[36]

The point of departure for the poem is the appendix to Cesare Caporali's *Viaggio in Parnaso*. Cervantes himself acknowledges as much in the first line of his *Viaje* as well as in the prologue to his *Novelas ejemplares* (*Exemplary Novels*). One can only point to other possible Spanish sources: Juan de la Cueva's *Viage de Sannio* (*Journey to Sannio*), 1585; a couple of *romances* of the *Coro febeo* (*Phoebean Choir*), 1587; and some older antecedents, such as *Infierno de los enamorados* (*Lovers' Hell*) or *El triunfete de Amor* (*The Triumph of Love*), by the Marquis of Santillana. In turn, Cervantes's *Viaje* was widely read in the seventeenth century. Republished in 1624, it inspired Salas Barbadillo's *Coronas del Parnaso* (*Crowns of Parnassus*), 1635, and Jerónimo de Cáncer's *Platos de las Musas de Salas* (*The Daily Fare of the Salon Muses*), 1640.

Even if this long poem has been fully accepted as an ironic expression of Cervantes's literary criticism, it has not been well received as a poem as such. Nevertheless, it is a kind of reassessment of his ideas about literature seen from the twilight of his career. *Viaje del Parnaso* is in fact the journey to that discursive continent that is literature.[37] From this point of view, *Viaje* does not imply a search for the "self" in the tradition of Virgil, but a way of discovering the uselessness of the search for perfection in some lost paradise of poetry. Parnassus, which is nowhere, has turned its back on daily life. Italy, the country where in his youth Cervantes found the greatness of the Renaissance, has by now been sterilized by Academies that clone classicism, using it not as a cultural model but as a simple repertory of prescriptive norms. Spain (or at least the Madrid where he lives) may not be a good place for a poet to be, but it is the only place Cervantes possesses. The task of the poet is to work immersed in his or her own time and country; to work not in search of fame but in order to achieve pleasure for self and others. In a Platonic tradition, Cervantes sees the poet as a repository of moral and collective responsibilities. This is why a country that does not respect poets cannot be well governed.

The utilization of the linked tercet in Cervantes's poetry has been criticized for its monotony and its failures. Yet, it seems to us that this kind of stanza, as used in *Viaje*, is not gratuitous; it was a question of putting all poets on the same level, of stacking them to show their extensive mediocrity. Thus, there was no better way of making them indistinct than by putting all judgments and clichés in the same verse and using a redundant stanza. From another point of view, Cervantes discovers in his symbolic journey that poetry has nothing to do with a Parnassus that has turned its back on the real world; the final sense of the poem will thus clearly entail an ethical reflection about what it means to write and to be, "socially," a writer. The "terceto" stanza is more appropriate to reflexive discourse than the "octava rima," which was usually employed by his more academic contemporaries when dealing with these topics.[38] To speak of Cervantes's error[39] is not to understand Cervantes's special constructive sense which, quite justly, characterized him as a "rare inventor."

Cervantes proclaims his truth and life despite the cold reception suffered at the hands of many of his peers. Yet the possibility that he would not be understood forced him to explain his own viewpoints and perspectives. Cervantes's linked narrative(s) of *El casamiento engañoso* (*The Deceitful Marriage*)/*El coloquio de los perros* (*The Dialogue of the Dogs*) and, especially, *Don Quijote* testify to his capacity for eluding the mix that was so common in the picaresque tradition: writing and explicit construction of the self. Unlike *Lazarillo de Tormes*, for example, Cervantes did not use the "true" story of his life to answer a question not answered directly. On the contrary, he wrote a kind of literary, "fictional" story to inscribe himself in the margins, as absence. For Cervantes, life is not conceived as anecdote, but as a way of living, thinking, and writing:

> To sing with such a harmonious and live voice
> that they think I am a swan and that I am dying.[40]

This is why the end of the journey shows us not a social image of an artist, but a rediscovered "human body," tired by movement and age:

> With this I left, and, full of spite,
> I looked for my old and dark inn,
> and I threw myself vanquished on the bed;
> for tiring is a day, when it is long.[41]

CHAPTER 2

Theater, Literature, and Social History

In 1615, a volume appeared in Madrid entitled "Ocho comedias y ocho entremeses nunca representados. . . . Los títulos destas ocho comedias, y sus entremeses van en la cuarta hoja" ("Eight comedies and eight *entremeses* never represented. . . . The titles of these eight comedies and their *entremeses* appear on the fourth page"). The volume's title is significant in that it returns to one of Cervantes's reflections in *Adjunta al Parnaso* (1614), where he indicates, perhaps ironically, that he had composed six comedies with *their* new *entremeses* (interludes) which he intended to print "so that one may examine slowly what transpires quickly and is dissimulated or not understood when represented [on stage]" ["para que se vea de espacio lo que pasa apriesa, y se disimula o no se entiende cuando las representan" (Ed. Gaos 1973: 183)]. The volume's title, therefore, also suggests an inseparable link between two dramatic genres: *comedia* and *entremés*.

The proven observations of Eugenio Asensio (1965: 25) in his seminal study of the interlude are perfectly applicable to Cervantes: "the history of the *entremés* . . . demands constant incursions into other literary fields from which it receives nourishment and renewal." Among the most prominent of those areas are *La Celestina*, the picaresque novel, well-known collections of ballads (*romanceros*), poetry dealing with ruffians and the underworld (*jácaras*), sixteenth-century comic theater, and the new comedy (*comedia*), as well as Cervantes's own literary creations.

21

In his one-act comic plays called *entremeses,* Cervantes engages in dialogue with the literature of his time as well as with his own writing. Hence, many of the socioliterary themes of *Don Quijote,* the *Novelas ejemplares,* and the *comedias*—themes such as marriage, lineage, money, honor, courage, madness, generosity, illusion/reality, and deceit/disillusion, among others—reemerge in his interludes from a perspective that assumes a peculiar kind of aesthetic distance.

A key to what might be called a comic-satirical vision is provided by Cervantes himself in the "Prologue to the Reader" of his *Ocho comedias y ocho entremeses* (Ed. Spadaccini 1982), where he speaks of the Aristotelian principle of separation of styles, thus managing to link the question of verisimilitude to a binding relationship between the style of those one-act comic pieces and the estate to which their character types belong:

> The verse is the very same that is called for by the comedies, which must be, of the three styles, the lowest, and the language of the *entremeses* is suitable for the figures that are introduced in them. (94)[1]

As obvious as this statement might seem to us today, it is not always sufficiently emphasized in the vast majority of studies dealing with Cervantes's comic pieces. These studies, with few exceptions, have highlighted their burlesque quality; their parodic figures, themes, and motives; their scenic language and theatricality; the singularity of their comic perspective vis-à-vis the multidimensional treatment of those same themes in *Don Quijote* and in the *Novelas ejemplares.* On occasion some of the plays have even been characterized as frivolous and immoral. And yet, despite the blindness generated by readings that are overly framed by generic conventions, it would not be difficult to argue that human conduct, as individual and as social being, is at the very center of a world constructed through the language of farce.

Because of these factors it becomes clear that any search for "exemplarity" in the *entremeses* may prove to be fleeting, unless one considers Cervantes's explicit reflection on the "propriety" of the language of those comic pieces: "it is suitable for the figures that are introduced in them" ("es propio de las figuras que en ellos se introducen"), and his implicit observation on the matter of separation of styles, a division, we might add, that is as applicable to his comedies as it is to his comic interludes.

It may be worthwhile to recall here Lope de Vega's statement in his playful manifesto called *Arte nuevo de hacer comedias en este tiempo* (1609), in which he observes that while his new way of writing plays effects a break with classical poetics, the old comedies and *entremeses* rely instead on a more rigid adherence to neo-Aristotelian principles. Thus, he speaks of

> the custom / of referring to the interludes as ancient comedies, / in which art still rules, / [and which are] characterized by a single action among low-class subjects, / for an interlude has never had a king as a protagonist.[2]

For Lope, then, the comic treatment reserved for the lowly subjects of the *entremeses* is determined by the estate to which those character types belong.

A rapid glance at the imaginary world of Cervantes's interludes allows us to focus further on Lope de Vega's cited verses and, most especially, on the idea that by virtue of his social position a king cannot be the protagonist of an interlude. Thus we see how in the world of Cervantes's *entremeses*, villagers and rich peasants appear (*El retablo de las maravillas, Los alcaldes de Daganzo*), as well as ruffians and depraved soldiers who move on the fringes of a society of orders and estates (*El rufián viudo, La guarda cuidadosa*); there are also lascivious women surrounded by impotent and cuckolded men (*La cueva de Salamanca, El viejo celoso*); then there are prostitutes and women of adventure and easy virtue (*El vizcaíno fingido*); opportunistic scriveners (*El juez de los divorcios*); and an entire gallery of identifiable socioliterary types, among them student hustlers, cowardly barbers, infatuated sacristans, brassy bawds, intriguing go-betweens, colorful Biscayans who mouth Spanish words in a syntax that makes them incomprehensible and thus laughable, and Old Christians who desperately seek to distance themselves from all traces of Moorish or Jewish blood.

With the exception of *El retablo de las maravillas* and *Los alcaldes de Daganzo*, Cervantes's interludes are located in an urban space and, as in *La Celestina* and the picaresque novel, the reader is allowed to enter a world populated by lowly figures who move about in the administrative and bureaucratic city of baroque Spain. That city, which is generally Madrid, offers them anonymity and, with it, the possibility for denial of, or deviation from, established norms (see the example of *El vizcaíno fingido* discussed below).

While not the case, as in the picaresque novel, of a conscious desire to transgress the limits imposed by an estatist society [the *pícaro*, as Maravall (*La picaresca*, 1986) has repeatedly reminded us, wants to "thrive" socially and economically and seeks to achieve his or her goal of attaining a privileged status through any means], many of the character types of the interludes, and most especially women, also instrumentalize the established system of values, thus usurping the very symbols of the dominant social groups. Hence, traditional values such as love and honor, or loyalty and generosity, are often used as objects of pleasure and rancor. This resentment has been tied to certain social transformations, especially to the separation between home and work, that, in the precapitalist society of the sixteenth century and the beginning of the seventeenth, were to transform women into objects of luxury.

In *El viejo celoso*, for example, in analyzing the awkward relationship and lack of communication between the sixty-eight-year-old Cañizares and his fourteen-year-old wife Lorenza, one cannot allude simply to the old man's "sin" of jealousy and glide over an implicit but essential fact: the reduction of the young woman to the level of chattel when she is forced by the precarious circumstances of her parents—who belong to a financially ruined nobility—to enter into a marriage contract without freedom of choice, for purely economic reasons. This theme, along with those of illusion/reality or deceit/disillusionment, is one of Cervantes's obsessions, one that reemerges, with different nuances, throughout his writings.

While six of Cervantes's *entremeses* are framed within an urban space, at least two have a rural setting: *Los alcaldes de Daganzo* and *El retablo de las maravillas*. In these plays, the representation of rural or village life is in burlesque contrast to the idealized image of the countryside that was being propagated in Lope de Vega's well-known comedies of the early 1600s. We are thinking here of plays such as *Peribáñez*, in which the idealized figure of the rich peasant is held up as a mirror to that "mass" and undiscerning public that frequented the public theater. It was a public that was likely to be captivated by, and identify itself with, the values embodied by the play's hero.

Among the values propagated by Lope de Vega's *comedia* of the early 1600s some were considered of primary importance, including honor, love within the same estate and in the framework of marriage, the simplicity of village life, and respect for a monarcho-seigneurial system whose ultimate legitimacy rested on the figure of a just king who protected the people from the clutches of a predatory nobility. One could cite, for example, some of Lope de Vega's well-known plays from this period, including *Peribáñez y el comendador de Ocaña* and *Fuenteovejuna*, in which peasants—especially those of certain economic means—identify with the values and interests of the absolutist monarchy. A case in point is *Fuenteovejuna*, where the peasant Estéban is first made to admonish a lecherous and predatory nobleman (or *comendador*) for the abuses committed against the villagers and later is made to advocate a type of absolutist monarchy that would limit the power of the nobles (Act II, vv. 1621–1631). Cervantes's burlesque treatment of rural values must be seen, therefore, against the cultural and political guidance of the baroque when attempts are made to co-opt the undiscriminating public (*el vulgo*).

In the interludes with a rural theme—*El retablo* and *Los alcaldes*—Cervantes engages in dialogue with the well-known topic of "scorn or contempt of court and praise of village life" ("menosprecio de corte y alabanza de aldea"). This topos had found fortune among several writers since the middle of the sixteenth century—one thinks immediately of Fray Antonio de Guevara and Fray Luis de León—and was to acquire significant propagandistic currency with Lope de Vega's monopoly of the public stage. Cervantes's *El retablo*, in which the rich, grotesque, and impotent peasants of Old Christian stock are paralyzed by racism and by an obsession for purity of blood, speaks to the debunking of an ideology propagated by Lope de Vega's theater in the early 1600s, in which the rich peasant's values are associated with those of the monarcho-seigneurial segments of Spanish society, while the peasant's interests are tied exclusively to the fortunes of the monarchy.

Against the commercial triumphs of the Lopean *comedia* on the public stage, Cervantes's voice struggles to be heard in print, relying on the discerning reader-critic for the construction of meaning. It is the latter who is able to follow the codes of his *entremeses* and to connect them to those inscribed in a less-constricted generic context such as that of the novel, for example. Thus, while Cervantes's villagers and peasants are indeed the subjects of a lowly genre—the *entremés*—the dialogue with Lope de Vega's official theater is unmistakable. With few exceptions, Cervantes's character types are troubled souls; they are comic and distorted figures who move within a grotesque and antagonistic arcadia where ignorance and false knowledge lead to impotence and chaos. Furthermore, as in the case of Don Quijote, the anachronistic "knight of the village," the peasants of Cervantes's interludes also belong to that "republic of enchanted men who live outside the natural order of things," according to the well-known observation of Martín González de Cellorigo (1600).

While generic exigencies and socioliterary precepts require that the lowly subjects of the *entremeses* be treated comically, such requirements do not transfer necessarily to the sphere of reception—especially in the act of reading. One could argue here that expectations change, depending on the medium of transmission of cultural artifacts and, of course, on the time, place, and definition of the receiver. Furthermore, the world of the *entremeses* unravels its own contradictions so that often, with double-edged irony, there emerges an implicit questioning of a system of values that had been eroded by economic and social transformations, and that the privileged groups of Spanish society had internalized as a threat to their interests from the first half of the sixteenth century.

Let us recall here that those transformations had manifested themselves in many ways, among them in the development and increase of money, whose valuation entailed a change in attitude vis-à-vis the world and society and which, in the form of salary, had also altered relationships among people (see the case of *La Celestina*). Other manifestations of change were the depopulation of the countryside and an increase in the urban population, much of which was poor and/or marginalized. Those changes were to stimulate a drive for personal betterment or access to privileges (*medro*) by those individuals and groups who felt excluded under the system of relationships allowed for by a society of orders and estates.

Maravall (*Culture*, 1986) has reminded us how the perceived dislocations effected by the demands of these groups were to elicit a strong reaction around 1600, thus intensifying the process of "refeudalization" that had been initiated in the previous century. He also argues that the repression and regression that followed were to effect a "strong jolt over consciences," leading to a broad repertory of tensions among different social groups: rich and poor, men and women, and so on. The net result of these dislocations and tensions was a reliance on the part of the poor on the only outlets that were often available to them: banditry, picaresque life, prostitution, and so on.[3]

While the picaresque novel can be said to represent the *pícaro's* spiteful reaction vis-à-vis a closed social and economic system, and the new baroque comedy (especially Lope de Vega's) has been thought to reaffirm the legitimacy of a monarcho-seigneurial system, the very structure of the *entremeses* suggests a state of continuous tension between the dominant society and those who withdraw psychologically, socially, or economically from its norms. Unlike the ritual denouement of the new comedy, in which any kind of social, moral, or political transgression is dealt with in a manner that results ultimately in the reaffirmation of the values and interests of the established monarcho-seigneurial order (we are thinking, for example, of the endings of such well-known plays as Lope's *El castigo sin venganza*, and Tirso's *El burlador*), the internal structure of the *entremeses* reveals a lack of genuine resolution of conflict. Even in those rare instances in which a resolution seems to exist, as in the case of *El rufián viudo*, it is nothing more than parody.

In *El rufián*, for example, the "wedding" of the pimp Trampagos and Repulida, his concubine, is witnessed and sanctioned by "his royal presence," who is none other than the king of ruffians: the legendary and mythical Escarramán, the subject of lowly and parodic ballads (*jácaras*) and lascivious dances. This particular scene in *El rufián* is a burlesque imitation of the customary intervention of the king in innumerable comedies of the early 1600s, in which the monarch as maximum authority and guarantor of social order usually intervenes to end disputes for the purpose of reestablishing, often through the contract and sacrament of marriage, the threatened social order (Kenworthy 1976: 28).

No serious study of Cervantes's *entremeses* can disregard their dates of composition, and, at the very least, every study can begin modestly with the dates of their publication. The year 1615 would seem to be the apex of Cervantine literary production, since *Ocho comedias y ocho entremeses nunca representados* and the memorable second part of *Don Quijote* appear in print within a few months of each other. Let us also keep in mind that two years earlier, in 1613, Cervantes's *Novelas ejemplares* had been published, to be followed in 1614 by his *Viaje del Parnaso* and, in 1616, a few months before he died, by the submission of his *Persiles* to a printer. All of these works were dedicated to the Count of Lemos, his patron, from whom Cervantes, in constant economic trouble, expected "financial help." If the dates 1613–1616 are highlighted here it is because during those three years Cervantes brings to light nearly his entire literary production, whose beginnings go back to 1585 with the publication of *La Galatea* and whose plenitude begins to manifest itself with the publication of the first part of *Don Quijote* (1605).

Available documentation would seem to indicate that the dates of composition of the *entremeses* coincide with those of *Don Quijote*, especially the writing of its second part. Furthermore, in the *entremeses*, official discourse is mediated by a whole series of conventions, by literary and folkloric motifs, and by the particular structure of each play. One might say that a reference point of discussion for Cervantes is the dominant ideology of monarcho-seigneurial Spain around 1600, a time when culture in general and the theater in particular, are mobilized as a reaction to a perceived social crisis that was brought about by changes in relations between individuals and groups during the expansive period of the Renaissance.[4]

Although the notion of "guided culture" can often seem problematic, especially in reference to the "guidance" that could be effected by the ruling segments of society through the public stage at a time when competing institutions sought to control the theater's sphere of operation (let us recall here that at various times in the 1600s the theater is prohibited), there is little doubt that Cervantes chooses the theater to engage in discussions related to broad issues of manipulation and control. Let us recall, for example, the centrality of the metaphor of the theater in Cervantes, and how the latter is, unlike Lope de Vega, constantly engaged in unmasking its illusion-making devices and the very mechanisms that enhance the possibility of manipulation, especially in the framework of the spectacle that allows for co-optation of the audience in the context of a nondiscriminating "mass" reception.

As a preliminary example we refer briefly to *El vizcaíno fingido*, a play in which the conventional baroque theme of deceit/disillusionment revolves around an attempt by young noblemen and prostitutes to deceive each other and whose exemplarity, therefore, can only be understood at the level of an audience that is edified through a latent message: the reality of the false habits and customs of city and courtly life. An analysis of the play's dominant discourse and its theme of deceit/disillusion underscores the existence of a perfect unity between them, as the "unmasking" of the prostitutes Cristina and Brígida by the idle young aristocrats Solórzano and Quiñones coincides with the state's attempt to deal with prostitution through legal channels: through the promulgation of the "law of carriages" in 1611 ("pragmática de los coches"). Ironically, while this law is enacted ostensibly to deal with the problem of prostitution, or the exchange of sex for money and favors, its ultimate aim is to reestablish privileges that were traditionally reserved for the nobility.

We see, then, that besides the unmasking of the so-called slyness, greed, or zest for lucre of the two prostitutes, what is ultimately targeted by the new laws is the prostitutes' usurpation of the language and symbols of the court. Thus the "carriage" that once symbolized status and was reserved for those who were born to a position of privilege, is now nothing more than a "prison" ("galera" 196) for a nobility that has been relegated to a state of impotence by the loss of its traditional function. No longer needed to fight and to protect, and with most in its ranks not in condition to assume the role of a power elite (Maravall 1979), that nobility now finds itself imprisoned by a life of comfort and leisure, by a thirst for luxury and extravagant consumption.

The subject matter and general theme of this farcical interlude preoccupied many of Cervantes's contemporaries, including the *arbitrista* Pedro Fernández de Navarrete, who was to say a few years later in his *Conservación de monarquías*:

And at the very least there should be a strict prohibition against any woman of ill repute to travel in a carriage . . . It is equally convenient that young gentlemen of rank should be prevented from riding in carriages, for such activity makes them lazy and they should, instead, follow the exercise of chivalry in order to comply with the obligations inherent in their rank . . . (528; our translation)[5]

The anachronism of these formal answers was not lost on Cervantes, who manages to represent these obsessions comically in his *entremeses* which, while following certain generic conventions, are ultimately the product of an imagination whose existential reality is inscribed within a frame of perceived social crisis in the beginning of the 1600s. Following this line of thinking, it would not be an overstatement to say that if *Don Quijote* (1605, 1615) projects the literary image of such crisis—a crisis identified in its time by liberal *arbitristas* such as Martín González de Cellorigo (1600) and Sancho de Moncada (1619) (see Maravall 1976)—the same can be said of Cervantes's interludes. Besides being "fifteen-minute playthings" ("juguetes de un cuarto de hora"), according to E. Asensio's definition (1970), the *entremeses* also allow the reader the possibility of questioning critically the very subjects that the *comedia* and the non-Cervantine *entremés* mask, not only through generic conventions, but also through the illusion-making devices of the theater and the ideological exigencies of the public stage.

Cervantes invites the reader of his printed text to reflect upon what has been read: "so that one may examine slowly what transpires quickly and is dissimulated or is not understood when represented [on stage]" ("para que se vea de espacio lo que pasa apriesa, y se disimula o no se entiende cuando las representan"). Apart from the irony implicit in the fact that Cervantes never got to see his *entremeses* produced on stage, it is obvious that our attention is directed to these pieces as literary texts and that the act of critical reading implies, more than a pastime, a reflection on human conduct as an individual and as a social being who is often marginalized by economic, intellectual, psychological, and social limitations.

The World of Cervantes's *entremeses*: Conflicts, Tensions, Marginality

It has been said, correctly, that theater is "the art of conflict" and that dramatic action emanates from conflicts produced among the characters—protagonists and antagonists—at a conceptual or vital level. In Cervantes's *entremeses* those conflicts have psychological and socioeconomic roots that tend to manifest themselves in an estrangement from certain social norms and, in some cases, in the inversion of ethical and moral values of dominant social groups. Finally, the dialectical process to which the dramatic action is submitted becomes truncated and, except for some illusory resolutions, conflicts tend to remain. The result is that beyond the ritualistic and predictable denouement—it is known that most of the *entremeses* end in festivity—the imaginary world in which those comic and distorted figures operate (unemployed soldiers; well-to-do and infatuated sacristans; rich and ignorant peasants; prostitutes; jealous, asexual, and naive husbands; rebellious women; and so on) is defined by a lack of order, by an assault on intelligence, and, in the final analysis, by its refusal to recognize logic and reflection.

It is well known that one of the central themes of baroque literature and theater is that of disillusion. At the hands of certain authors such a theme is contrived to expose the pretensions of those individuals or groups who aspire to usurp social symbols or roles that do not correspond to their position in a society of orders and estates. One might mention, for example, Quevedo's *La vida del Buscón*, in which the protagonist Pablos de Segovia suffers a "chain of misfortunes" ("desgracias encadenadas"), as he fails repeatedly in his effort to deny his bloodline (his inferior genealogy) and become a nobleman. At other times the theme acquires metaphysical or theological overtones. Thus, in Calderón's *La vida es sueño*, Prince Segismundo succeeds in reintegrating himself into the society from which he has been excluded by his father, King Basilio, after having learned a key lesson: that to live is to dream ("representar"). And in Tirso's *El burlador de Sevilla* the unbridled Don Juan is consumed by the fires of hell precisely because he has not managed to change in time by assimilating the same moral lesson. Hence the poignancy of the moral expressed in a song that serves as the work's thematic nucleus: "Those who know the power / of God's ways beware / there is no deadline that does not arrive / nor debt that goes unpaid" (vv. 2724–2727) and "While one lives in the world / it is unjust to say / 'a long time in me you're trusting' / repayment time being so near" (vv. 2732–2735).[6] Don Juan dies because of his arrogant affront to the social and moral order; for not carrying out his corresponding social function and for denying at the same time his own temporality.

The stoic-Christian philosophy expressed in Pablos de Segovia's reflection at the end of his *Vida* ["But things went worse (in the New World), as they will for anybody who thinks he has only to move his dwelling without changing his life or ways" ("Y fuéme peor, como v.m. verá en la segunda parte, pues nunca mejora su estado quien muda solamente de lugar, y no de vida y costumbres") (284)] and the Christian-Catholic philosophy represented dramatically by Calderón in the metaphors of life is dream, world is theater, reaffirm the primacy of spirit over matter and, in the final analysis, use the notion of disillusion at the service of an estatist ethic and ideology. Those ideological notions sustain a position that is resistive to change and is directed "against the new bourgeois socioeconomic structures" (Ynduráin 1974: 70).

In the anticomedies or Cervantine interludes the "spiritual" values associated with a mythical and medieval past are debunked and the theme of disillusion becomes secularized. With few exceptions, the character types who take center stage are defined by their marginality and by the continued tensions among individuals and groups with socioeconomic, psychological, racial, and sexual roots. Such is the case with marriage, a theme to which Cervantes returns repeatedly throughout his writings. In these works of "low style," marital relationships are entangled in judicial disputes (*El juez de los divorcios*); are projected outside legal boundaries (*El rufián viudo*); and, in some cases, lead to infidelity and adultery (*La cueva de Salamanca, El viejo celoso*). Those relationships are nearly always conditioned by specific socioeconomic realities that obtain even in those instances in which the woman chooses her future husband "freely" (*La guarda cuidadosa*). The fact is that in sixteenth-century society, with the tendency to separate home from work, the woman loses her initiative; she becomes an economic burden and, as a consequence of that situation of dependency, she falls under a man's yoke. In the words of Martín González de Cellorigo, "women are . . . costly" and are objects of luxury. It is also the case that women are affected by the Tridentine prohibition of secret marriage. The reforms undertaken at the Council of Trent (ca. 1563) reduce further women's previously limited options as their own fathers or husbands now have greater flexibility in converting them into objects of exchange. Cervantes dramatizes these issues in the *entremeses* as well as in most of his other writings, especially the *Novelas ejemplares* and *Don Quijote*. For the time being let us limit our discussion to the *entremeses*.

In *El juez de los divorcios* three couples and a man file for divorce before a civil tribunal comprised of a judge, a scrivener, and a solicitor. In the case of the first couple (a little old man and his wife Mariana) the wife complains openly about her husband's impotence, describing it as a torment that she can no longer bear. After twenty-two years of a sterile marriage she cries out for freedom of action and movement, identifying sexual repression with agony and death.

Mariana argues with melodramatic flair before the judge that suicide is preferable to her current marriage: "Your Highness, undo this marriage if you do not want me to hang myself" ("Vuesa merced, señor juez, me descase, si no quiere que me ahorque" 98). Her protests are aimed at the process of commodification to which she has been subjected since entering into the marriage contract at a very tender age, when her parents placed her "in his power" ("en su poder") in return for a "very good dowry" ("muy buen dote"). At this point the unhappy young wife points to the unfairness of the marriage contract, expressing a notion that is echoed by contemporary psychologists and sociologists who argue that marriage should be limited to a given number of years, with the possibility of renewal.

Within the framework of a theatrical performance or spectacle, the linguistic codes operate with other, nonlinguistic ones—thus enabling the director, through the mediation of the actors, lighting, scenery, and so on, to manage the performance and play to the expectations of an audience that is ready to recognize in Mariana the stereotype of a hysterical young woman. The discerning reader is engaged in a different type of operation; the reader is his or her own director, so to speak, who can well convert the character's words into notes of anguish and alienation. The reader can realize that possibility especially if able to "see slowly what transpires quickly"; to examine critically what is likely to be trivialized within the context of a theatrical performance.

The discerning reader can thus go beyond the burlesque tone of the *entremés*, reflecting upon the anguish or hell to which two incompatible beings are subjected by a society that seeks to preserve a marriage contract even as it works against a truly Christian marriage and the salvation of the individual. Hence Mariana's cry:

> In well-ordered kingdoms and republics marriage should be of limited
> duration and ought to be dissolved and reconfirmed every three years as
> is the case with contracts governing rents, and ought not last forever
> with the perpetual grief of both parties. (Ed. Spadaccini 1982: 98)[7]

In Mariana's reflection there is enunciated a longing for a greater degree of secularization in matrimonial affairs, and the reference to "well-ordered republics" may be an allusion to those "reformed" countries that, according to Ricote (*Don Quijote II*, 54), allowed for the possibility of living with "freedom of conscience."

In petitioning for divorce Mariana seeks to discover her own materiality. Hence her refusal to be subjected to social conventions and her pleas for freedom. When the old man proposes a division of their estate and a mutual withdrawal to the confines of a monastic life in order to "live in peace and in the service of God" ("vivir en paz y en servicio de Dios" 101), Mariana complains that she is healthy, "and with all of my five senses intact and alive" ("y con todos mis sentidos cabales y vivos" 101). Through the use of expressions taken from card games Mariana affirms the primacy of matter over spirit, thus abandoning all social conventions that are cruel and dehumanizing: "I wish to use [my senses] openly . . ." ("quiero usar dellos [de los sentidos] a la descubierta" 101). The judge listens to her complaint and, echoing the words of Pilate when he refuses to judge Christ, rejects the divorce for lack of cause.

The same judicial procedure is used with the other litigants who present their complaints to the court—an impotent and famished soldier and one Doña Guiomar; a surgeon and one Doña Aldonza de Minjaca; a laborer and his absent wife, a market woman—with similar results. The essence of the official decision is captured by the refrain that comes at the end of the song: "the worst concert is worth more than the best divorce" ("que vale el peor concierto / más que el divorcio mejor" 110). That refrain serves as the play's thematic nucleus and conventional denouement. Hence, neither the *vejete*'s sexual impotence, nor the noble soldier's sexual and economic insufficiency, nor the hate that exists between Doña Aldonza de Minjaca and the surgeon ("Lucifer"), nor the high-spirited and quarrelsome character of the laborer's wife-prostitute proves sufficient reasons for the judge to grant the divorce.

In spite of the scrivener's remark that the substantial conflicts between the litigants are unresolvable ["Who in the hell can manage to concert these clocks if the wheels are so disconcerted?" ("¿Quién diablos acertará a concertar estos relojes estando las ruedas tan desconcertadas?" 107)], no divorce is granted. The reason for the judge's decision is that marriage fulfills a stabilizing function within the social structure. The integrity of marriage as a social institution is, therefore, guaranteed by the state through its bureaucracy. Unlike the pre-Tridentine marriage, which could be entered into privately through an oral agreement, with only God as a witness, the post-Tridentine marriage was a more formal affair, involving the publication of marriage banns and greater public accountability. Hence the judge's bureaucratic decision: "It must be recorded in writing, and confirmed by witnesses" ("es menester que conste por escrito, y que lo digan testigos" 109) and his expression of hope "that all present will calm down" ("que todos los presentes se apaciguasen" 109).

The judge's "solution" was put forth by the solicitor in a remark that reveals, ironically, the parasitism of the bureaucracy as well as the immobilizing mechanism of the state:

Let everyone ask for a divorce, for when all is said and done, most of them will remain as they are, and we will have reaped the fruits of their quarrels and foolish nonsense. (109)[8]

Laws and legal recourses are part of a mechanism implemented by the state in order to prevent changes that are likely to destabilize the social order; the law is nothing more than a mechanism used to redirect forces that are unleashed against the interests of the monarcho-seigneurial segments of Spanish society. Within this context the regulation of marriage and its preservation becomes a central concern as changes would likely affect the transfer of property as well as the very basis of relations between social groups. The implications of such laws for women are many, not the least important of which is their continued bondage in marriage and the social death that results from such servitude.

Cervantes, whose marital misfortunes are well known, introduces a theme loaded with explosive potentiality within the burlesque frame of the *entremés,* knowing full well that reading activates codes that are quite different from those available to the spectator who is witnessing a staged performance. In this "monodimensional space" of the literary text the possibility of examining slowly [in print] what [on stage] transpires quickly, allows for a critical decoding of signs. Such is not the case with spectacle, whose space is bidimensional and whose statute is, therefore, one of absence rather than presence (Ruffini 1978: 34–35).

In *El juez de los divorcios* marriage as a socioeconomic contract and sacramental bond sanctioned by the state and the post-Tridentine church, is explored in terms of its controversial aspects. The seemingly harmonic and festive note that brings the play to closure is not in harmony with the internal dynamics of the piece: nothing has been resolved among the various couples who are imprisoned by sociopsychological and socioeconomic tensions. Only the outward manifestations of order remain intact: the bureaucratic mechanisms of the state and, of course, the conventional ending of the *entremés.*

Ironically, it is in the realm of the underworld where "marriage" functions without conflict and tension. There the union between men and women operates on the basis of instincts and interests, and the value system that rules those relations exists parallel to, and as a parody of, the system of values imposed by the privileged social groups. In *El rufián viudo,* for example, the pimp Trampagos laments the death of Pericona, his concubine, on whose prostitution his material sustenance hinges. No fewer than three prostitutes attempt to bring him out of his grief, promising him material rewards and loyalty in exchange for protection. Thus, the three declare:

MOSTRENCA: We have been born; no one has been made by God
to be unsheltered. I am worth little;
But in any case, I eat and dine, and my pimp
I keep dressed better than a figurine;
PIZPITA: I am small, Trampagos, yet I am big.
I have a will to serve you;
I have no pimp, and I have eighty amusing lies;
REPULIDA: I am yours; brand me
on these two cheeks.[9]

From the planctus of the first two verses "Oh Pericona, my Pericona! And of the whole council too!" ("¡Ah Pericona, Pericona mía, / Y aun de todo el concejo!") Trampagos alludes to the sexual and commercial value of his deceased nymph, the very value that the three prostitutes who are courting him attribute to themselves. These women are "savers" ("ahorrativas") besides, and the function that they seek to carry out in the service of Trampagos is both emotional and economic. Thus we see here how, within a structure defined by marginality, the society of ruffians is sustained by these women through perfect marriages.

The competition for Trampagos's hand is eventually won by Repulida and the union or "marriage" between the two is legitimized through the intervention of the king of ruffians, Escarramán, who "honors" them with lascivious dances. Here again one must differentiate between the literary text and its representations on stage; between the monodimensional linguistic space and the bidimensional space of spectacle; between presence and absence. In the words of Joaquín Casalduero (1951: 202), "the dancer enters, and while the wine flows, that satyr directs his steps toward the nymphs, and the elemental union of the man and woman is celebrated in a bacchanalian feast" (our translation). That union, which is made on the margin of all social norms, is defined by a lack of conflict while the bacchanalian feast energized by Escarramán, the mythical character of lowly ballads (jácaras), serves as a logical denouement to the matrimonial farce.

Thus far we have exposed the manner in which the character types of the entremeses are driven to operate outside the boundaries of social norms, and we have seen how, in the end, there is no reconciliation with society's norms. We have noticed how conflicts among individuals remain, and how the disillusion emanating from their relationships tends to have psychological and socioeconomic roots. We now wish to turn to the case of El viejo celoso, in which the issue of adultery is dramatized explicitly and implicitly, in terms of the sexual impotence and the perverse passion of jealousy of old man Cañizares, and in light of the tensions imposed on his marriage by certain socioeconomic realities.

In *El viejo celoso* a young wife feels imprisoned by social norms that reduce her to an object of luxury. When she is denied any semblance of a physical or moral relationship, she finds her escape route in adultery. The plot of *El viejo celoso* is very simple: Doña Lorenza was married to Cañizares, a rich, jealous, and impotent old man. The young wife's complaint is established in the first scene of the *entremés*: she is showered with gifts, money, and jewels, but has been deprived of the fruits of marriage. Her reaction in the face of this dehumanizing and alienating situation leaves no room for doubt:

> Of what use is all of this to me if in the midst of riches I am poor and in the midst of abundance I am hungry? (257)[10]

Wealth without love is a form of poverty, and marriage outside the context of a physical and moral relationship becomes a legal yoke; a relationship of dependence. Under these conditions marriage is far from being what the Erasmian humanist Juan Luis Vives (*De officio mariti* 1528) had referred to as "the legitimate union of a man and a woman for coexistence and community for life" (our translation; Spanish ed. Lorenzo Riber 1947: 1270).

The marriage between the rich septuagenarian Cañizares and the young Doña Lorenza is not a union entered into freely among equals for, according to Doña Lorenza, it was arranged and imposed by her family:

> Do you think I chose him, my niece? He was given to me, and I, as a young girl, was quicker in obeying than in contradicting; but if I had had so much experience of these things, I would have torn out my tongue with my own teeth before saying yes. (258)[11]

Doña Lorenza's sufferings are laid to the system of exchange that prevails in the urban world of baroque Spain, where money becomes an instrument of decisive economic power that controls relationships among groups and among individuals. The power exercised through the use of money in marital affairs is seen clearly in *El viejo celoso*'s most immediate source of inspiration which, according to Eugenio Asensio (1970: 26), was "Cervantes himself who was repeating along comic lines the history of the jealous Extremaduran Carrizales, who was rebaptized Cañizares" (our translation).

The exemplary novella *El celoso extremeño*, which antedates and inspires *El viejo celoso*, provides us with the psychological and socioeconomic profile of the old husband. In the novella (Ed. Sieber 1985), Felipo Carrizales is a nobleman who spent some twenty years in the Indies where, "aided by his industry and diligence, he managed to save more than one hundred fifty thousand *pesos ensayados*." Carrizales is a self-made man whose social mobility and economic well-being are clearly owed to his deals and transactions with others; to his mercantile activities. Such activities, particularly in the realm of retail trade, would have been unthinkable for a nobleman, lest he be tainted with dishonor and loss of reputation. Carrizales made his money in the New World, and upon returning to Spain at the age of sixty-eight, conscious of his wealth and advanced age, he decides to marry Leonora, a "thirteen- or fourteen-" year-old maiden, the daughter of nobility who had experienced economic reversals.

The narrator specifies that Carrizales "was by nature the most jealous man in the world" ("de su natural condición [Carrizales] era el más celoso hombre del mundo") and that apart from this he was given to generosity and liberality. The reader is told that Carrizales had awarded Leonora a dowry of twenty thousand ducats, and Carrizales himself states that with that amount of money, "more than three [women] of [his wife's] social standing could marry and be considered rich" ("más de tres de su misma calidad se pudieran casar con opinión de ricas" 132). Regarding Carrizales's relationship with his in-laws, the narrator relates that

> he gave them so many gifts that, although they pitied their daughter because of the sacrifices to which she was subjected [on account of being locked up by her jealous husband], they were assuaged with the many gifts that Carrizales, their liberal son-in-law, gave them. (105)[12]

In the novella, and implicitly in the *entremés*, marriage is a commercial transaction. The objects of exchange are money (or its substitute: gifts, offerings, and so on) on the one side and a young woman on the other. The result of that relationship, which is dominated by the husband's jealousy, is the young woman's adultery. Such an issue is treated not only in *El viejo celoso* but in the first of two versions of the novella *El celoso extremeño* as well.

Because of generic exigencies, the same plot appears in the two works with different approaches and techniques. Eugenio Asensio (1970: 27) rightly states that "in the novella Leonora's seduction develops slowly, gradually, supported by internal justifications, causal linkings, with the collaboration of both the environment and the servant's chorus. In the *entremés* the arduous problem of honor is resolved in a very brief dialogue with Cristina, the perverse young woman, and the adultery is consummated only with the assistance of the go-between Ortigosa." Asensio's conclusion is predictable: the *entremés* can aspire only to "jocularity"; it is nothing more than a fifteen-minute plaything.

Yet, if one goes beyond a reading marked by strict generic conventions; if one forgets to imagine momentarily the "spectacular" side of the text and the absent spectacle and instead connects the woman's utterances in this play to the voices of women echoing in other Cervantine texts, the reception is likely to change. Along these lines, Doña Lorenza's adultery in *El viejo celoso* and Mariana's petition in *El juez de los divorcios* may be seen as effects of certain socioeconomic and psychological realities that weigh upon women in their circumstances, while marriage is converted into a legal, bureaucratic, and repressive structure. Only in this way can one understand the disillusion and feeling of alienation that spring forth from Mariana's complaints and Doña Lorenza's sexual liberation as she rebels against the oppression perpetrated by the rich, jealous, and asexual Cañizares.

The jealous old man's impotence and sexual blindness are revealed in his dialogue with the go-between Ortigosa, to whom he says that "Doña Lorenza has neither a mother [matrix] nor a toothache" ("Doña Lorenza, ni tiene madre [matriz] ni dolor de muelas" 269). The lack of physical contact between Cañizares and his wife Doña Lorenza paves the way for the latter's rebellion, which is instigated by her servant Cristina and the neighbor Ortigosa. That rebellion ends in adultery as she locks herself in her room with a handsome young man, extolling her good fortune from behind the door, while her old husband listens with incredulity to the description of their lovemaking:

If you only knew what good fortune has fallen upon me! A well-disposed, dark-haired young man, whose mouth smells like a thousand citron flowers. (271)[13]

The description of the sexual act reaches an orgiastic pitch as old man Cañizares is told that "her flesh is shaking" (le "tiemblan [las carnes]" 271). The deception ends in physical aggression: at the precise moment when Cañizares seeks to enter the room, he is blinded with a basin of water (the same water used by Doña Lorenza to wash the black-haired gallant's whiskers). That trick facilitates the lad's flight and orients the piece toward a conventional denouement: when a constable, some musicians, and a dancer arrive Cañizares dismisses them, saying "my wife and I are now at peace" ("ya mi esposa y yo quedamos en paz" 273).

The adulterous act has been prompted by the old man's passion of jealousy and by the manner in which he treated his young wife—not with love, communion, and understanding, but as an object of luxury. The literary text allows the discriminating reader to inscribe this story in the larger text of Cervantes's discourse on love and marriage; on the other hand, a highly mediated staged performance played to the expectations of a nondiscriminating public (el vulgo) would most likely prevent such an inscription.

The theme of marital infidelity is common in the entremeses and is also dramatized from a comic-burlesque perspective in La cueva de Salamanca, where a husband's irrational behavior leads to his wife's adultery. Among the techniques used by Cervantes in this entremés are those of magic and false knowledge and that of internal duplication. Pancracio, the figure of the husband in La cueva, is little more than a foolish, manipulated marionette, whose misinterpretations of linguistic and visual signs also remind us of the well-known stereotype of the cuckolded consort of Lope de Rueda's pasos some fifty years earlier.

The initial manipulator and instigator of the dramatic action of La cueva de Salamanca is Pancracio's wife Leonarda. That role is later assumed by the student Carraolano when he is forced to resort to his ingenuity (his presumed magical powers) in order to mask the adulterous relationship between Leonarda and Reponce, the sacristan. In the beginning of the entremés, Leonarda plays the role of the respectful and submissive wife. Thus, when Pancracio is about to leave on a four- or five-day trip to be present at his sister's wedding in another village, Leonarda complains about his impending absence, shedding tears, sighing, and eventually fainting. The wife's performance proves so believable that the manipulated husband thinks of resorting to a conjuration in order to revive her: "I will utter in her ears some words I know, which have the capacity of reviving her" ("diréle unas palabras que sé al oído, que tienen virtud para hacer volver de los desmayos" 238).

Pancracio shows a certain predisposition toward magic and false knowledge, and his impaired judgment will not allow him to distinguish empirical reality from fantastic illusion. His flight from reality, like that of the peasant-administrators of El retablo de las maravillas (discussed later in this chapter), is anchored in an obsession that prevents him from recognizing all rational processes. In his case, the extreme attraction to magic transforms him into a victim, into a cuckolded husband.

The student Carraolano managed to find a room at the inn at the very time when Leonarda and her lover, Reponce the sacristan, along with Cristina and her friend Roque, the barber, were about to celebrate the departure of the ingenuous Pancracio with an orgiastic supper. When the foolish husband returns home unexpectedly, following a breakdown of the carriage in which he was traveling, Carraolano is forced to make use of his wit to get everyone out of the tight spot. The roguish student becomes a necromancer, a transmitter of forbidden knowledge punishable by the church through its enforcing arm—the Inquisition. He claims to have acquired that knowledge in the Cave of Salamanca where, according to the legend, the Devil taught science and evil arts.

The initial dialogue held by the deceiving student with the credulous husband paves the way for the burlesque and "theatrical" conjuration that makes it possible for "demons" to parade before Pancracio in the guise of the sacristan and the barber. The student identifies himself to Pancracio as the disciple of the Devil and possessor of magical and forbidden powers:

> STUDENT: The science I learned in the Cave of Salamanca from which I come, were it to be allowed without fear by the Holy Inquisition, I am convinced that I would eat time and again at the expense of my descendants, and, perhaps, I am not far off from using it . . . , but I am not sure if these ladies will be as secretive as I have been. (249)[14]

Pancracio is attracted by those powers and he is willing to risk everything, including being denounced to the Inquisition, on condition that he be allowed to "see" some of the effects of the "science" that, according to Carraolano, one learns in the cave. Pancracio's desire to verify the effects of forbidden knowledge is, in Pancracio's own ironic declaration, extreme:

> PANCRACIO: Don't worry about them, friend, do as you wish, for I will make sure that they keep quiet; and I am extremely eager to see some of the things that you say are learned in the Cave of Salamanca. (249)[15]

Pancracio's passion for black magic further diminishes his limited understanding and allows the dramatic action to come to a resolution: after the bookish conjuration of the student necromancer, the "demons" (the sacristan and the barber) leave the coal bin where they were hidden and Pancracio goes so far as inviting them to dinner.

As in the case of *El retablo de las maravillas*—where the quarter-master's intervention does not succeed in shattering the illusion of the magical tableau brought by Montiel (Chanfalla)—the reality of the internal performance is sustained. Pancracio is left irrevocably tricked and, wanting to acquire magical powers, he declares himself an apprentice of those very same "demons":

PANCRACIO: Let us go in, for I wish to verify whether or not devils eat, with a hundred thousand other things they say about them; and by God, they will not be allowed to leave my house until they have instructed me in the science or sciences taught in the Cave of Salamanca. (255)[16]

Although the socioeconomic roots of marriage are not explored in *La cueva de Salamanca*, the theme of matrimonial infidelity is inscribed within a consistent Cervantine perspective that makes the main responsibility of adultery fall upon the husband. In *El viejo celoso* adultery was the result of the sexual impotence and extreme jealousy of old man Cañizares and the reduction of his young wife to the level of chattel. In *La cueva de Salamanca*, on the other hand, the husband's deception is made possible by his blindness to superstition and false knowledge, and by his excessive credulity in demons and necromancy. In both cases the husband is victimized less by his wife's scorn than by a lack of capacity to operate within the realm of reason and common sense.

One could argue, of course, that generic conventions condition the emergence of the stereotype. Yet, it is clear that the Cervantine *entremés* subverts the conventions by inserting the reader—the discriminating reader or "lector mío"—in the communicative process. It is up to the latter to reflect carefully upon what is read; to make connections with other Cervantine texts dealing with men and women, love and marriage, fidelity and infidelity. Thus, beneath the jocular and festive rhythm of Cervantes's farces, through the eccentric dialogues of the character types, there lies a series of ideas about a society in crisis. It is also clear that some of the prevailing ideologies of the Spain of the early 1600s are represented in the texts, however indirectly, so that humor is also imbued with an ideological content.

The Representation of Urban Drama in the *entremés*: The Examples of *El vizcaíno fingido* and *La guarda cuidadosa*

From the first part of the sixteenth century there is the postulation of a causal relationship between city or urban life and the loss of ethical-social values. That relationship manifests itself in an attitude of individualism that ultimately leads to a form of anomie or a denial of norms. Thus, in his *Menosprecio de corte y alabanza de aldea* (1539), Fray Antonio de Guevara contrasts the solitude, liberty, and intimacy of rural life to the demands imposed upon the individual by urban life and the institutions surrounding it. For far from the familiarity and intimacy of village life, the individual becomes alienated.

The Spain of the beginning of the 1600s was indeed a rural society and "the cities, which were numerous and in the process of expansion, and not centers of industrial production, were essentially parasitic tumors of an agrarian economy" (Lynch 1972: II, 6). Those cities were centers of attraction and, according to texts of the time, true Babylons and "mother" to all: to the unemployed and the underemployed, to beggars and adventurers, to merchants and artisans, all of whom live side by side—even if only in a spatial and symbiotic sense—with those who live off bureaucratic positions or rents. Madrid stands out among the parasitic cities of baroque Spain because it is, after all, its political axis. The capital is distinguished from other urban centers by a service economy and by the production of luxury goods produced by artisans for the court's internal consumption.

In Madrid one does not work in productive activities and the norm is to live in idleness. The city has become a center of consumerism, particularly with respect to food and luxury items. According to a well-known text by A. Liñan y Verdugo (*Guía y avisos de forasteros que vienen a la corte*), in Madrid all social relationships are converted into theatrical appearances: "do not think that all that glitters is gold . . . , many of these courtesies are nothing but slyness: do not believe in regalia, or in graces, or in appearances, or in presence, or in exterior riches, if you do not know in what internal occupations they were gained" ("no se persuada que es todo oro lo que reluce . . . , y muchas de estas cortesías son socarronerías: ni fíe en galas, ni en gracias, ni en apariencias, ni en presencias, ni en riquezas exteriores, si no sabe los oficios interiores a que se ganaron" 105).

To the extent that all social transactions are conditioned by "exterior wealth (riches)," they constitute a possible subversion of the estatist order. It is a situation that the traditional segments of society seek to address through the promulgation of official decrees (that of the carriages in January, 1611, for example) and through other requirements as well, among them the ability to prove that one's riches were not acquired through ignoble occupations. The aim of those decrees and practices was to preserve or to reaffirm privileges traditionally reserved for the nobility.

El vizcaíno fingido and *La guarda cuidadosa* dramatize in burlesque fashion some of the tensions afflicting the bureaucratic city of baroque Spain in the first decade of the seventeenth century. Once again we must recall Cervantes's reflections in the "Prologue" to *Ocho comedias y ocho entremeses* (1615) and in *Adjunta al Parnaso* (1614), where reading is defined as a privileged activity that allows the discriminating reader to perceive latent messages. In *La guarda* and, especially, in *El vizcaíno* those messages deal with the false values of city and courtly life. In the city, where money conditions social relationships, life is defined not only by deceiving appearances but by other realities as well: unemployment, underemployment, prostitution, retail trade, idleness, and a general crisis of values.

One of the themes of *El vizcaíno fingido* is undoubtedly that of pretension, which encompasses the conduct of a womanizing silversmith, that of a constable who is open to bribery, the actions of two ambitious prostitutes, and the life-style of idle young aristocrats. The plot is simple enough: Solórzano, an idle and adventurous young nobleman, intends to play a trick on a certain Cristina, a well-known Sevillan nymph. After explaining to his friend and accomplice, Quiñones, that "this trick shall neither offend God nor damage the tricked woman" ("esta burla . . . ni ha de ser con ofensa de Dios ni con daño de la burlada" 193), he introduces himself to Cristina: "I am a courtier whom you do not know" ("soy un cortesano a quien vuestra merced no conoce" 198). In the presence of Cristina's friend Brígida he then praises the son of a friend of his, "a Biscayan, very gallant . . . somewhat of a jackass . . . very given to women" ("vizcaíno, muy galán . . . un poco burro . . . muy amigo de damas" 199) and proposes that they take advantage of his liberality:

> Here we'll skin him . . . like a cat; and to begin I bring your excellency this chain . . . , which weighs one hundred and twenty gold *escudos*, which you will take in exchange for ten *escudos* now, for I need them for certain little things, and [you] shall spend twenty more on a dinner this evening. (199)[17]

After having assured herself through a silversmith that the chain "weighs one hundred and fifty golden *escudos* of twenty-two carats" ("pesa ciento y cincuenta escudos de oro de a veinte y dos quilates" 203), Cristina hands over the ten gold coins to Solórzano and declares herself willing to take charge of the supper that evening. The outcome bears no surprises: following the appearance of the false Biscayan (Quiñones) in the nymph's house, Solórzano reclaims the chain, accusing Cristina of having substituted a false one, of alchemy, for the real chain made of gold (210–212). Cristina comes to realize that she has been tricked, but she cannot appeal to the authorities because of who she is: "if this business reaches the *corregidor* I am as good as guilty" ("si a las manos del corregidor llega este negocio, me doy por condenada" 211). Solórzano promises not to reclaim the chain if Cristina bribes the constable and sees to the promised dinner. The prostitute accepts the risky conditions although the supper will be more modest: "May heaven pay your excellency in full; I shall give the constable a half dozen *escudos*, and I shall spend one on the dinner, and I shall be in perpetual servitude to Sir Solórzano" ("Págueselo a vuestra merced todo el cielo; al señor alguacil daré media docena de escudos, y en la cena gastaré uno, y quedaré por esclava perpetua del señor Solórzano" 213). The two musicians and Quiñones enter at that moment. The musicians recite one of Quiñones's ballads about women's vanity and the *entremés* has a seemingly festive ending.

This conventional plot is circumscribed by a discourse that alludes to a degradation of concepts that originally concerned the sphere of noble life. Thus, in the first scene of *El vizcaíno fingido*, in a dialogue between Cristina and Brígida, a new decree concerning the use of carriages is linked to the implications of that law for prostitutes or "happy women" ("mujeres alegres") as well as for young noblemen who spend their time idly, "forgetting that there were horses and horse riding" ("sin acordárseles que había caballos y jineta" 196). Cristina connects the promulgation of the decree with the loss of nobiliary values, thus assuaging Brígida's worries that the decree was directed exclusively to women such as themselves.

Here we see how a topic that has currency in Cervantes's time is inserted within the frame of an *entremés* to be interpreted by the discerning reader who is aware not only of the generic conventions governing these comic pieces, but also of the broader debates surrounding the topic itself. Clearly, the decree concerning the use of carriages is an attempt to reestablish privileges traditionally reserved for the nobility. But that attempt also implies an awareness, on the part of those in authority, that a crisis of values exists and that something must be done to restore them. Cristina's rational explanation, supported in the metaphor "carriage = galley" (coche-galera), is a burlesque verbalization of that crisis:

From what I have heard, chivalry was in real decline in Spain, for young gentlemen sandwiched themselves in a carriage ten or twelve deep like meat pies and pounded the streets night and day, forgetting that there were horses and horseriding in the world. (196)[18]

The "carriage" is the "galley" where social estates and hierarchies are thrown into confusion; it is, moreover, a prison inhabited by the idle and effeminate young nobility that no longer shares the ideals and activities of its forefathers. Let us recall here that the nobility has lost its original function of fighting, which has passed to professional, mercenary armies, and that the higher nobility—for it was never monolithic—had become a power elite (Maravall 1979). The remark by the prostitute Cristina concerning official intentions in laying down rules for the use of carriages is both humorous and ironic. While praising the provision prohibiting the use of carriages by young noblemen— since without those "galleys" or "prisons" ("galeras") they could once again use their time profitably, training on horses, in accordance with their noble rank—she also suggests that the nobleman's ("caballero's") function of old to defend others by means of arms has been surpassed by the social and strategic realities of the militia of 1600, a time when, as is well known, war is fought among professional corps whose members are recruited from all classes. In the military strategies of the sixteenth and seventeenth centuries the infantry eclipses the cavalry, and the quality of the combatants ("caballeros") is superseded by the quantity of foot soldiers who are armed with pikes.

The military lexicon is usurped by Cristina in order to convince her friend Brígida that she is worrying needlessly over the possible effects of the decree on her work. Thus, when Brígida states with a certain degree of uneasiness that, "it is on condition that [carriages] not be lent, nor that they be used by any [prostitute] . . . you understand" ("es con condición que [los coches] no se presten, ni que en ellos ande ninguna [puta] . . . ya me entiendes" 196), Cristina succeeds in pacifying her:

> Let them punish us that way, for you should know, dear sister, that those who follow this war, are of differing views, as to which is better . . . , the cavalry or the infantry . . . , and it has been ascertained that the Spanish infantry outshines that of all other nations. And now we— the happy hookers—can display our gallantry on foot . . . , and even more so with our uncovered faces, giving those who serve us no excuse of having been deceived, for they have seen us. (196)[19]

Although prostitutes will no longer be able to conceal their false courtesy in the private space of the carriage, and will be forced to go through the streets with their faces exposed, ultimately nothing will change. They will seek out their customers on foot for, after all, in this war too, as in some of the great military encounters of the time, the infantry will prevail over the cavalry.

It is clear that the anachronistic attempt to restore an old system of values by means of a decree is doomed to failure. And while Cristina does not question traditional social hierarchies, she also knows that relationships among individuals and, implicitly, among groups are conditioned by exterior riches—by money. Thus she reminds Brígida with double-edged irony that "it was not right that a carriage should equalize those who were such and such with those who were not" ("no era bien que un coche igualase a las no tales con las tales" 197) and advises her with confidence to ply her trade on foot, displaying her wares with pride and ostentation:

> Arrange yourself with spirit and with tidiness, and with your Sevillan chiffon shawl, and your new slippers, and in any case with silver bows, and let yourself loose on the streets; that I will assure you that flies won't fail to be attracted to such a sweet honey . . ." (197)[20]

According to Cristina, appearances are kept up through the practice of ostentation which is likely to ensure that those who frequent the company of the "courtesans" will be precisely those "young gentlemen" (caballeros) who, prior to the promulgation and the decree (pragmática), "sandwiched themselves in a carriage . . . ten or twelve deep like meat pies" and "pounded the streets night and day" ("se empanaban diez o doce . . . en un coche" and "azotaban las calles de noche y de día" 196). That is to say, those same young gentlemen, having forgotten the old rituals of chivalric life and no longer trained in the proper riding of horses ("montar a la jineta"), will continue living idle, unbridled lives, subject to all sorts of social contaminations; they will continue to be rushed like "flies" to the sweetness and pleasures of good honey.

We know that the imaginary space of El vizcaíno fingido is that of the city and the court, where traditional values such as honor and virtue are replaced by a new ethic based on wealth and money. The figures who move about that space are defined by deception and pretension, which ultimately manifest themselves in idleness, luxury, and conspicuous consumption. All social relationships in this piece of low style can be said to be oriented along these lines and all of its characters are laughable.

While it is true that Cervantes follows Aristotelian precepts in the entremeses, thus establishing a correlation between style and estate, it is also clear that the young noblemen Solórzano and Quiñones are not spared a comic treatment. Apart from the syntactic distortions of the false Biscayan or Solórzano's pranks in fooling the prostitute with the chain of alchemy, what ultimately stands out is the breach that is opened between Solórzano's aim of swindling the Sevillan courtesan without going beyond the proper limits of a prank and the void of his own existence as a member of an idle class that has abandoned the nobiliary values of its ancestors. For Solórzano the moralist "pounds the streets" ("azota las calles")—if not in a carriage, at least on foot—with the aim of mocking a courtesan.

Within the framework of the play, the prostitutes and the young noblemen are engaged in a game of mutual deception, yet only the former end up being deceived. If one can speak, therefore, of exemplarity, or of some beneficial example to be gained from the prank, it is at the level of the discriminating reader who, from a privileged position, witnesses both the unmasking of the parasitic prostitutes as well as the conduct of young aristocrats who have abandoned themselves to a life of idleness and leisure in the absence of the ethical-social values of their forefathers. The "theater" or public space in which this comic, farcical drama unfolds is Madrid. The internal date of the work corresponds to 1611. The vehicle chosen by Cervantes to develop such an important critique of nobiliary values and urban life is the comic mold of the *entremés*.

Madrid is also the space of operation of the lowly and laughable character types of *La guarda cuidadosa* (1611), whose conflicts revolve essentially around the themes of marriage and money. Regarding marriage, Cervantes never loses sight of its economic aspects, but the theme of money is placed within a broader context of socioeconomic and political life: vagabondage and unemployment; alms and underemployment; work and service; food and consumption. Thus, in the world of *La guarda cuidadosa* there are various social types, including unemployed soldiers, beggars and peddlers, wage-earning sacristans, shoemakers who live from their work, servants yearning for comfort and luxury, and domestic employers from the middle levels of society.

A torn and tattered soldier ("vestido a lo pícaro") and a sacristan of modest economic means, who is defined in the stage directions as a "bad sacristan," are the main antagonists of the piece. The two covet a pretty kitchen maid (Cristina) who works in one of the well-to-do houses of Madrid. The contest between two suitors is a conventional literary topos and, as Eugenio Asensio (1970: 51) has pointed out with his usual acumen, "those who look for sources have been able to go back to Elena and María where the [relative] advantages of loving a cleric or a gentleman are debated" (our translation). What is of interest, nevertheless, is the way in which that traditional narrative thread is developed to highlight, in the comic language of the *entremés*, the tensions that affect the inferior strata of the society in the Madrid of

1611. Thus, along with the development of the figures of the tattered soldier and the infatuated, wage-earning sacristan, *La guarda cuidadosa* also highlights others whose lives revolve around anachronistic economic structures. Among those street people are a lad who begs for alms; a peddler (Manuel) who earns a living selling lace imported from Flanders and other products not manufactured in Spain; and a shoemaker (Juan Juncos) who seems to live from (semiartisanal) work. That is, in the Madrid of *La guarda cuidadosa*, productive work and manufacturing activities are scarce while there is at the same time an increase in consumption.

The lowly figures of *La guarda cuidadosa* fit within the thematic and plot boundaries of the *entremés* and help lead it toward a logical conclusion: the rejection of the soldier for being out of touch with reality since his claims do not comply with the situation of his indigence, and Cristina de Parrazes's decision to contract marriage with Lorenzo Pasillas, the wage-earning sacristan. The young girl's "free" choice is backed by the master and the mistress of the house: "Well choose whomever pleases you . . . Eating and marriage must please oneself rather than others" ("Pues escoje . . . , el que más te agradare . . . El comer y el casar ha de ser a gusto propio, y no a voluntad ajena" 189) and is supported by economic considerations: in matters of nourishment and luxury Cristina has certain aims and the one who can satisfy her desires is the sacristan and not the soldier. Marriage thus has economic roots: marriage and a full stomach go hand in hand.

The debate between the debunked man of arms and the ridiculous man of letters is produced on the basis of insults and develops by means of expressions taken from a card game:

> SOLDIER: Well come here, under-sacristan of the Devil.
> SACRISTAN: Well there I go, Geneva's queen.
> SOLDIER: Very well; jack and queen; we only need the king to win the game [and come to blows]. (171–172)[21]

At the outset the debased representatives of arms and letters engage in a duel of words. The soldier scorns the sacristan; he is utterly confident that personal merits acquired in the war will make him triumph in this game of love. With that certainty he dedicates a love note, written on the back of an official recommendation ("memorial") extolling his own merits in war to the "nearly holy" hands (174) of that "image" (186). He is convinced—as he tells his rival—that "if this young woman has corresponded so highly to your miserable gifts, how will she correspond to the great ones I have given her?" ("si esta mochacha ha correspondido tan altamente . . . a la miseria de tus dádivas, ¿cómo corresponderá a la grandeza de las mías?" 173). The sacristan mocks the soldier's claims because he perceives that those claims are not backed by economic means. To those memoranda, which are barely worth four or six reals (174), and to the false hopes offered by the twisted heir of the *miles gloriosus*, who awaits a position of patronage in the kingdom of Naples, the sacristan answers with concrete gifts:

> I gave them one of these boxes of quince, a large one, full of slices of hosts, as white as the driven snow, and with it four candles, also as white as ermine. (172)[22]

The antagonists belong to different worlds. The soldier, anachronistic and half mad, appropriates the codes and values of the old nobility that privileged personal honor gained in battle, at the service of His Majesty, the King. That same code is applied to love—hence the laughable usurpation of the language of courtly love: a kitchen maid is transfigured into a deified beloved. The sacristan, on the other hand, knows perfectly well that the heart and hand of a kitchen maid cannot be won with pure rhetoric, or false courtesies or outlandish promises, but only through the practice of an occupation that can provide her with economic well-being. The contrast between the antagonists is telling:

> SOLDIER: Young woman, look at me; look at my graceful demeanor; I am a soldier, and hope to be in charge of a castle; I have a spirited heart; I am the most gallant man in the world; and by the thread of my little suit you can find the skein of my gentility.
>
> SACRISTAN: Cristina, I am a musician, even if only of bells; no one surpasses me in adorning a tombstone or in draping a church for solemn festivities; and these occupations I can well exercise as a married man and earn my bread like a prince. (189)[23]

Earning one's living through the practice of an occupation (unproductive and humble as it may be) is preferable to unemployment and to the soldier's empty rhetoric.

The debate between the two rivals thus becomes a burlesque duel. The stage directions clarify the meaning of this scene: "The vice sacristan Pasillas comes armed with a plug from an earthen jar and a very rusty sword; with him comes another sacristan, with a morion and a stick, with a fox's tail attached to it" (184).[24] Lorenzo Pasillas and Grajales, his grotesque companion, confront the soldier ("la guarda cuidadosa"), and the verbal sparring is about to explode in blows and lashes. It is the typical scene of an *entremés* in which an exchange within a different generic framework might have led to potentially tragic consequences among characters of noble rank but degenerates here into the level of farce. No one dares to strike the first blow. Action is replaced by gesture; fear takes the place of courage. The scene becomes guffaw for the audience.

The lowly conflict that has exploded between the suitors is "resolved" after the intervention of Cristina's master who suggests that she choose her future husband. The soldier's claims of his so-called merits acquired alongside generals on the field of battle are dismissed outright; they have no tangible value for the young servant or the master: "Up to this point," says the master, "the relations you are giving are of no interest to me" ("Hasta ahora—dice el amo—ninguna cosa me importa a mí estas relaciones que vuesa merced me da" 183). Thus, when Cristina de Parrazes chooses Lorenzo Pasillas, the sacristan, for her husband, the master proposes that they celebrate "the engagement by singing and dancing" ("el desposorio, cantando y bailando" 190). The "debate" between the two aspiring husbands has come to an end. The soldier has lost the kitchen maid's heart because he has only empty pieces of paper ("memoriales") at his disposal. His precarious economic situation is dramatized when he detains Juan Juncos, the cobbler, in the doorway of the house where Cristina works. According to the stage directions, the shoemaker "enters with a new pair of small slippers in his hands" ("entra con unas chinelas pequeñas nuevas en la mano" 179). The soldier asks for the slippers, offering in exchange "a toothpick made from Bishop's weed, a sash, and a magnifying glass" ("una biznaga, una banda y un antojo"), which he intends to redeem within a couple of days. The cobbler, as a "poor artisan" who lives from his work, dismisses the value of those articles. He rejects the soldier's proposition, telling him, with (sly) irony:

> Although I am a cobbler, I am not so discourteous as to want to strip your excellency of your jewels and gems. Your excellency should keep them, for I will keep my slippers, which is what suits me best." (180)[25]

The soldier's disillusion leaves no room for doubt: social relationships, among individuals and among groups, are now based on money. Affective life depends on economic considerations. Hence, the starving soldier's reflection: "Valor is no longer valued / Because money is now esteemed / For a sacristan is preferred / To a broken lay soldier" ("Ya no se estima el valor / Porque se estima el dinero, / Pues un sacristán prefieren / A un roto soldado lego" 190–191). In the Madrid of 1611 (the internal date of La guarda cuidadosa) the soldier realizes that he is disconnected from history, as he did not distinguish between past and present, between appearances and reality.

As in the case of most of Cervantes's *entremeses, La guarda cuidadosa* cannot be dismissed as a mere "fifteen-minute plaything," for its comicality incorporates a critique of certain prevailing values and ideologies. That critique is either displayed openly or through voids and absences. In either case there is a pointing to a crisis of values that is ultimately anchored in the concepts of social and economic crisis.

The Representation of Village and Rural Drama in the *entremés:* The Examples of *El retablo de las maravillas* and *Los alcaldes de Daganzo*

One of the characterizing traits of Cervantes's writings is polyphony, and the *entremeses* are no exception. By polyphony we refer to the plurality of discourses that are interwoven in those comic texts that engage in dialogue with Cervantes's own literary writing as well as with different poetic texts of the late sixteenth and early seventeenth centuries. Eugenio Asensio was the first to point out this characteristic with reference to *El rufián viudo*. Following the ideas propagated by M. Bakhtin in his study of Dostoevsky's poetics, Asensio (1970: 34) suggests that *El rufián viudo* "stands out among Cervantes's other *entremeses* for its literariness, that is to say, for its saturation of parodies and its references to poems and genres in vogue at the time" (our translation). The dialogical character of that *entremés* is all-embracing and references to other literary creations are numerous: Quevedo's ballads about the ruffian Escarramán; Garcilaso's eclogues; the mythological allusions and *cultismos* of Góngora's poetry; the Senecan tragedy; and many of Cervantes's own texts, among them *Rinconete y Cortadillo, La Numancia,* and *La Galatea.*

These observations regarding the polyphonic quality of *El rufián viudo* can be extended, to a certain point, to the majority of Cervantes's *entremeses,* even if not all of them are distinguished by the same degree of literariness. Thus, for example, although *El retablo de las maravillas* and *Los alcaldes de Daganzo* may not include concrete burlesque references to other contemporary texts, the distorted and grotesque images of the village and rural world that emerge from the respective structures of those theatrical texts suggest a dialogue with the commonplaces propagated by writers of poetics, novelists, and poets of the Renaissance such as the *locus amoenus* topos, the myth of Arcadia, the Platonic idealism of love, and the numerous interpretations of Horace's *Beatus Ille.* At the same time, those grotesque images function as counterpoints to the idealized, propagandistic images of the *comedia* (especially that of Lope de Vega) during the first part of the seventeenth century (1608–1615).

As a playwright, Cervantes returns to the tradition of village fools and comic peasants of the first generation of dramatists of the sixteenth century. Thus, when he identifies himself with the old way of writing plays, and with the principle of verisimilitude, he is specifically thinking about authors such as Torres Naharro and Lope de Rueda—especially the Rueda of the *pasos* to whom Lope de Vega also refers in his *Arte nuevo de hacer comedias* (1609) when he suggests that his "new comedy" has replaced the "old comedies," that is, those *entremeses* that adhered to neo-Aristotelian principles.

Cervantes's attitude vis-à-vis the new theatrical practice fomented by Lope de Vega expresses reservations that, going well beyond the issue of adherence or lack of adherence to traditional poetics, are directed toward the question of the social function of art and the role exercised by the creator of fictions. Thus, vis-à-vis a theatrical practice that he considers alienating, Cervantes reclaims a priority for the poetic text. If Lope de Vega submits his comedies to the demands of the marketplace and the exigencies of an undiscriminating audience (Lope had stated in his *Arte nuevo de hacer comedias en este tiempo* that "those who now write them according to rules / die without fame and reward" ["Que quien con arte ahora las escribe / muere sin fama y galardón"]), Cervantes orients his interludes toward a demystifying function. For that reason, in 1615, he opts to publish his dramatic works instead of turning them over to theatrical producers. Cervantes sees "the effect of the economic infrastructure on artistic values and the artist's integrity" (Johnson 1980: 250–251) and his dialogue with Lope de Vega and the public theater of his time may be read as an attempt to problematize those issues.

The differentiation that Cervantes establishes in *Adjunta al Parnaso* (1614) between "seeing slowly" and witnessing what "transpires quickly," that is, between an active, critical, and intellectual participation in the production/consumption of plays and the passive, superficial reception to which those artefacts are subjected by spectators who receive a mediated product, refers precisely to what occurs when a text goes from the domain of the artist's imagination (and that of the reading subject) to that of the people of the theater who convert the artist's product into a performance. The dramatic piece in this last case is transformed into a propagandistic vehicle that operates on the senses in order to "strengthen the collective ideology and fortify the established system of distribution of social powers which must have felt threatened" (Maravall 1972: 36).

Thanks to the respective studies by José Antonio Maravall (1972) and Noël Salomon (1965), we are now able to better assess the theater that emerged from the culture of crisis called the baroque, a historical period in which, according to Maravall (*Culture*, 1986), we have early manifestations of "mass" culture, a time when culture is also a "guided," "conservative," and "urban" phenomenon. Salomon (1965: 808), for his part, was to highlight the importance of the theme of peasant life in the theater of Lope de Vega, placing the emergence of the figure of the dignified and honorable peasant around 1608–1610.

It seems clear that in the early 1600s the theater is a vehicle for sociopolitical propaganda and, as such, attempts are made to incorporate the peasant into the monarchical-feudal order. That attempt coincides with an economic and social crisis, and, as Maravall (1972) specifies, the development of the rural theme in the *comedia* of this period may respond more to sociopolitical factors than to economic considerations. The *comedia*'s interest in the rural world would be to foment the socialization of an attitude of support for a traditional society, a hierarchical, aristocratic society that is fundamentally agrarian in nature. That is why the peasant theme occupies such an important place in Lope's theatrical production as well as in that of his contemporaries, and why the theme of the *labrador* achieves such a representative value. At that time there is revindication of honor on the part of rich peasants. That claim is interpreted both by the economists who write about the agrarian crisis around 1600, and by some of the playwrights of the establishment in the period 1608–1615.

Among Cervantes's *entremeses* two deal with rural and village life, and one of them—*El retablo de las maravillas*—dialogues brilliantly with those comedies of the beginning of the seventeenth century where the peasant's sense of honor is embodied in his wealth as well as in the racial (and racist) concept of purity of blood. That is, in the *Retablo* the rural theme is brought into focus from a burlesque angle and the object of laughter is precisely that minority segment of rich peasants that seeks to insert itself in the system of privileges. As an example of the latter, let us allude briefly to one of Lope's well-known pieces—*Peribáñez o el comendador de Ocaña* (1610?)—whose composition precedes *El retablo* by a few years and which seems to have caught Cervantes's critical eye.

In *Peribáñez* a conflict arises between a Comendador and a peasant, his vassal, and there is also an allusion to tensions between well-to-do peasants and the lowly rural nobility of the *hidalgos*. The play's denouement is already foreshadowed in the second act: when the Comendador de Ocaña begins to pursue Casilda, the wife of Peribáñez, the latter anticipates the fateful consequences of the lord's lack of social responsibility: "Enough that the Comendador should solicit my wife; / that he should take away my honor, / even while he should be giving me honor. / I am a vassal, he is my lord, / I live under his protection and defense; / and if he thinks of taking away my honor, / I shall take his life away" ("Basta que el Comendador / a mi mujer solicita; / basta que el honor me quita, / debiéndome dar honor. / Soy vassallo, es mi señor, / vivo en su amparo y defensa; / si en quitarme el honor piensa, / quitaréle yo la vida" [Act II, vv. 697–704]).

The peasant seems to be aware of two types of honor: one of a feudal order, bound to a hierarchy of classes (and, therefore, exterior to itself); the other intrinsic and joined with the idea of purity of blood. One of the Comendador's servants refers to this second dimension of honor, relating it, at the same time, with Peribáñez's wealth and the moral power that he can exert on his equals because of their esteem for him:

> Peribáñez is a peasant from Ocaña, / an Old Christian and rich, a man held / in great esteem by his equals, / and if he wished to rise now / in this town, he would be followed / by all of those who plow the fields, / for he is, though a peasant, a very honorable one. (Act I, vv. 824–830)[26]

Peribáñez is not bound to the Comendador as a serf, but as a vassal. Since that type of relationship was possible only in the seigneurial tradition, the implication is that "the rich peasant is capable of lofty sentiments" (our translation; Maravall 1972: 89). Such is, in any case, the image emphasized in the play's denouement. Peribáñez justifies the killing of the Comendador to the king, Enrique el Justiciero, backing that justification with an allusion to his purity of blood: "I am a man, / though of peasant caste / of pure blood, and never / stained by Jewish or Moorish blood" ("Yo soy un hombre, / aunque de villana casta, / limpio de sangre, y jamás / de hebrea o mora manchada" [Act III, vv. 947–950]), and later with a reference to his recently acquired honor as a captain: "For after all [the Comendador] gave me a valiant squad of one hundred *labradores* / And I left Ocaña with them with the title of captain" ("En fin, de cien labradores / me dio [el Comendador] la valiente escuadra. / Con nombre de capitán / salí con ellos de Ocaña" [Act III, vv. 985–988]). In this tragicomedy, the peasant is thus defined by his wealth, by the purity of his blood, and by his rise to the military estate.

In *El retablo de las maravillas*, the rich, honest, and distinguished peasants of the *comedia* are turned into laughable figures. Theatrical heroes such as Peribáñez, capable of dignity and honor, enter the domain of farce, becoming manipulated "spectators," or marionettes. A sociohistorical reading of the text clarifies its dialogical dimensions: Cervantes's invective becomes a satire against the minority group of rich peasants "whose juridical and political aim" (in exploiting the journeymen and fighting against the low rural nobility) was "to enter into the ranks of aristocracy" (our translation; Molho 1976: 151). That is, around 1612, in an *entremés* composed without hopes of "fame and reward," in a piece bound for a reading audience, Cervantes converts into laughter the pretensions of a few rich peasants who lay claim to a bloodline that, according to Molho (1976), is "inoperable . . . not conducive to the prestige of effective power such as the one exercised through income and rent, a bourgeoislike nobility, which, while disdaining trade, accepts dealing in land, without renouncing its feudal prerogatives, as a usurious financial capital" (151).

The image of the laughable peasant of *El retablo* is an inversion of the one promoted by those dramatists of the establishment who compose their plays between 1608 and 1615. Moreover, it also contrasts with the model presented by economists who write about the agrarian crisis around 1600. While the former convert the rich peasant into a theatrical hero worthy of dignity and honor in a society of orders and estates, the latter turn him into a social-political paradigm capable of resolving the country's economic crisis. In Cervantes's *entremeses* these images are subjected to a demystifying process. The character-spectators of *El retablo* (Gomecillos, the licentiate; Juan Castrado, *el regidor*, and his daughter, Juana Castrada; Benito Repollo, the mayor, his daughter Teresa Repolla, and his nephew Repollo; and Pedro Capacho, the scrivener) are ridiculed for their rustic pretensions, for their alienating obsession of "legitimacy," and for the illusory character of the power they have acquired by means of wealth, which has given them access to the town's council. In the case of the mayor and the *regidor*, the irony is cutting, as they represent "an independent rustic property, which, while still independent, is threatened in its independence" (Molho 1976: 149).

The structure of *El retablo* is governed by the grotesque claim of lineage on the part of the rich peasants. That obsession for legitimacy bears obvious socioeconomic and ethical-moral ramifications. On one hand it implies a grotesque eagerness for having access to privileges; on the other hand it carries with it a subversion of the humanist concept of virtue—a concept that is deeply rooted in Cervantine thought: the idea that each person is "the son of his own deeds."

In *El retablo*, two fibbers and an accomplice (Chanfalla, his wife Chirinos, and Rabelín, the boy "musician") arrive in a town with the intention of cheating the country bumpkins. To accomplish their scheme, they rely on the ignorance, vanity, and socioracial prejudice of the rich administrator-peasants of the village. They play upon the credulity of their audience, which is blinded by an obsession for legitimacy. Chanfalla, the "author," introduces himself as a descendant of sorcerers and wizards: "I, my dear ladies and gentlemen, am Montiel, the one who brings the Marvelous Tableau" ("Yo, señores míos, soy Montiel, el que trae el Retablo de las maravillas" 219). By means of a parodic allusion to the figure of the enchanting wizard and manipulator of magical objects (Montiel), the origin of *El retablo* is established, along with the conditions necessary to see it:

> [The Tableau] was fabricated and composed by the wise Tontonelo (Fool-foonelo) under so many parallels, courses, heavenly bodies, and stars, with such trades, characters, and observations, that no one can see the things that are shown in it if of the converted race, or if not begotten through procreation by parents united by legitimate matrimony. (220)[27]

An atmosphere of magic and superstition serves as a background to the illusory representation that Chanfalla and Chirinos seek to accomplish through verbal magic. Thus the wonders of Tontonelo's puppet theater will depend on the power of language, which, in turn, is anchored in the anxieties of a group and in the madness of a collectivity. From a social point of view, it is well known that impurity of blood and illegitimate birth represent two key obstacles to privileges in an estatist society. Moreover, they are obstacles that also preclude access to employment. In *El retablo* the "commonly used illnesses" ("tan usadas enfermedades"), according to Chanfalla's irony, contribute to the blindness of the audience that witnesses Montiel's magic tableau:

> Those who are afflicted by these two commonly used illnesses, should forget about seeing the things never seen or heard of from my tableau. (220)[28]

Bastardy, or the lack of purity of blood, alludes to the illegitimacies of birth and lineage. Moreover, they function, at the same time, on two levels: "that of the individual's socialization, that is, his position in the social and socioeconomic system of his experience, and that of his psychic being, which is conditioned by its insertion in the triangle of the filioparental relationship" (our translation; Molho, 1976: 164–165). Within that scheme, the rich, integrated, and virile peasant of the rural dramas of Lope and some of his contemporaries, becomes a character-victim; a "spectator" manipulated by the mystifying practice of the fibbers and their boy accomplice. The figure of the rich villain is inverted and, therefore, demystified. The rich, peasant-administrators of *Retablo* are impotent, in spite of their wealth that allows them to sponsor a theatrical function in one of their homes. That impotence is revealed in moral and physiological terms and underscores a total paralysis vis-à-vis any kind of creative activity. That impotence encompasses the social and economic realms, for apart from representing a class that does not invest its capital in commercial activities, the peasants of *El retablo* are neither the "sons of their parents," nor "sons of anyone," nor are they the "children of their own deeds."

The "spectators" of the magic tableau brought by Montiel (Chanfalla) are blinded by their own anxieties of legitimacy, by the intimidating language of Chanfalla and Chirinos, who play on those anxieties, and by the disorienting "sounds" of Rabelín. Out of fear they manage to "see" the wise Tontonelo's puppets that parade before them following the conjuration of the enchanting wizard (Montiel). They "see" what exists only in their fears and, consequently, in the manipulator's creation: first there is Sansón, the blind and symbolically "castrated" Jew of the Old Testament; then there is the bull of Salamanca with its penetrating horns, followed by a handful of chewing and phallic mice that are direct descendants of those raised in Noah's ark; then comes the regenerating and fecund water from the river Jordan; two dozen (rampaging) lions and bears who raid beehives (figures of heraldry) that, at the same time, represent virility; and finally there is Herodías, the figure of the New Testament who replaces here Salomé, her daughter, as a protagonist of "castrating" dances.

The villagers' belief in *El retablo* reaches such a pitch that Benito Repollo's nephew breaks into the linguistic space to "dance" with Herodías, "whose dance gained as a prize the head of the Precursor of life [John the Baptist]" ("cuyo baile alcanzó en premio la cabeza del Precursor de la vida" 232). The substitution of Salomé, the daughter, for Herodías, the mother, acquires, according to Maurice Molho (1976), a significant value, since the dancer is "a woman who is defined . . . by the very trait of her maternity, a phallic mother, seductress and castrator of the son, who, upon entering the dance, approaches the prohibited spectacle" (211). The only character who does not manage to enter into the illusory world of the theater within the theater (in the space created by the manipulating skills of the mystifiers and the villagers' anxiety) is a quartermaster who visits the village to request lodging for "thirty men (of arms)" (233). When Juan Castrado (*el regidor*) attempts to bribe him with the castrating dance of Herodías, we witness an act of demystification: "QUARTERMASTER: Are these people crazy? What devil of a young woman is she, and what dance, and what Tontonelo?" (235)[29] The quartermaster is unaware of the criteria necessary to be able to see the tableau. He cannot vouch for what he does not see. But his humanity (materiality) does not succeed in disillusioning the obsessed villagers, who continue to believe (with the partial exception of the cowardly and grotesque Governor-poet, the licentiate Gomecillos) in the reality of the wizard Montiel's (Chanfalla's) fiction and in the concepts of legitimacy that Chanfalla and Chirinos had advanced as requirements to see their magical performance.

It is clear that the play's denouement does not bring about any resolution of conflicts. The villagers accuse the quartermaster (*furrier*) of being a *converso* ("He is one of them"), using ironically the bastardized version of an expression taken from the gospel according to Saint Matthew: "De ex il[l]is es." The quartermaster, in turn, after calling the townspeople peasants and "good-for-nothing Jews" ("canalla barretina") takes out his sword and starts fighting with them. With the exception of the boy (Rabelín), who ends up receiving a beating at the hands of the effeminate Benito Repollo, the mystifying fibbers have succeeded in controlling their enchanted audience. In the words of Chanfalla:

> The happening has been extraordinary; the Tableau's virtue remains intact, and tomorrow we can show it to the town; and we ourselves can sing the triumph of this battle, saying "Long Live Chirinos and Chanfalla!" (236)[30]

This work of low style, which is undoubtedly the most perfect of Cervantes's *entremeses*, deals with a substantial and profound issue that, from the historical perspective of 1612, may be identified with the crisis of the minority group of rich peasants. The grotesque image of the impotent peasant in this *entremés* is Cervantes's response to the myth of the integrated peasant, which is propagated by the rural dramas of the period; it is the inverted figure of those rich peasants of the *comedia* who reclaim dignity and honor and even manage to enter into the ranks of aristocracy (see Peribáñez and the children of Juan Labrador, the protagonist of Lope de Vega's *El villano en su rincón*). Cervantes's lesson comes to the heart of the matter as it satirizes the obsessive notion of lineage and reaffirms implicitly the humanist notion that true honor does not emanate from purity of blood or from one's name or coat of arms, but from one's actions: "each is the son of his own deeds" ("cada uno es hijo de sus obras").

El retablo may engage in dialogue with the myths, beliefs, and escapisms identified with the idealistic literature of the sixteenth century—the *locus amoenus* topos, the theme of the *Beatus Ille*, the motif of Arcadia, and so on—and the propagandistic incorporation of those motifs in the new theater of the early 1600s, but what makes the *Retablo* relevant to today's readers is the elevation of the theme of legitimacy to a universal dimension: prejudice and false consciousness do not allow one to distinguish between reality and appearance, as prejudices predispose one to see what does not exist objectively. Racism is a blindness that induces men to live as if enchanted, outside of the natural order of things. The rural and village drama of *El retablo* is, in the final analysis, a human drama. Beyond the fun poked at Lope de Vega's rural dramas is an important message to be gathered by the discriminating reader.

In *Los alcaldes de Daganzo* (1610?) there is an anticipation of the Cervantine satire of the peasant-administrators who base their raison d'être on the myth of the purity of blood. In that *entremés*, as in *El retablo de las maravillas* (1612), the satire is carried out through a dialogical language that, apart from directing itself toward a demystification of the village refuge of the noble shepherds and poets who "flee" the worldly noise of the court, points to a conflictive arcadia that contrasts with the rural world invented by the new comedy near the end of the first decade of the 1600s.

In *Los alcaldes*, the literary background and folkloric material are inserted within a context of historical immediacy; that of the jurisdictional conflicts between the feudal lords and the village mayors. The backdrop chosen by Cervantes for his comic piece—that of Daganzo— could have had certain resonances for a reading public that was predominantly aristocratic and urban, and that had come to know the juridical work of Castillo de Bovadilla (1597). This treatise, which was widely circulated at the time, tells how the Count of Coruña, feudal lord of Daganzo, refused to confirm some judges chosen by their vassals because they were deemed incompetent. It seems that the Count was involved in two disputes in the Chancillería de Valladolid and the second time his decision to invalidate the election of the "ordinary judges" of Daganzo was approved: "for the lord of vassals who has the right to confirm the election, also has the right to know the defect and inability of those elected" ["porque al señor de vasallos, a quien compete el derecho de confirmar la elección, pertenece también conocer del defeto e inhabilidad de los elegidos" (Bovadilla 70–71)].

In *Los alcaldes* there is a clear allusion to the tensions that exist between lord and vassals due to the juridical prerogatives of the former not to confirm an election if he can prove "defect and inability" of the chosen. Estornudo, the scrivener, refers to this same situation when he announces the aim of the meeting of Daganzo's town council:

> And let it be known that we shall name judges
> For next year, who should be such
> That they will not incur the calumny of Toledo,
> But that they will be confirmed and found to be fit,
> Such is the reason why we have met. (146)[31]

The village vassals must choose judges who are acceptable to the lord who lives in the city of Toledo. The examining committee is composed of Estornudo, the *escribano*; Pesuña, the *bachiller*; and Algarroba and Panduro, the *regidores*.

In the initial dialogue of the *entremés* a comic contrast is established between the two *regidores*. Algarroba is educated, pedantic, and somewhat roguish ("zocarrón"); Panduro is illiterate, clumsy, and inept. The laughable traits of Panduro are immediately made evident by his linguistic transgressions (his use of the uncultured "sayagues" language) and his lack of adherence to all rational processes: "Sit back at ease; for everything will go smoothly / if it is willed by the holiest of heavens" ("Rellánense; que todo saldrá a cuajo. / Si es que lo quiera el cielo benditísimo" 143). Algarroba pokes fun at Panduro's simple-mindedness and lack of sophistication: "Whether or not [heaven] wishes is what's important" ("que quiera, o que no quiera, es lo que importa"), but when Panduro denounces him for such an impertinent and blasphemous remark ["Algarroba, your tongue is slipping! / Speak carefully" ("¡Algarroba, la lengua se os deslicia! / Habrad acomedido y de buen rejo")], Algarroba first defines himself in terms of his purity of lineage, untainted by *converso* blood, and then reaffirms, ironically, his belief in God: "I am a good Old Christian all the way, / and I believe in God without any doubt" ("Cristiano viejo soy a todo ruedo, / Y creo en Dios a pies jontillas" 144).

The theme of purity of blood and purity of thought serves as an introduction to the examination scene that begins after the burlesque description of the four candidates by Algarroba. According to him, Juan Berrocal is distinguished by his wine-tasting abilities; Miguel Jarrete for the way he hunts birds; Francisco de Humillos for knowing how to repair shoes "like a tailor"; and Pedro de la Rana for having a good memory, especially when it comes to the lyrics of an anti-Semitic poem—"the verses of the ancient and famous dog of Alba" ("las coplas del antiguo y famoso perro de Alba"). Algarroba mocks the entire process of selecting officials in Daganzo, underscoring at the same time the villagers' ignorance and the importance of selecting qualified judges. For that reason he proposes that "those found to be up to and able / for such a task, that they be given / a certificate" (" al que se hallase suficiente y hábil / Para tal menester, que se le diese / Carta de examen" 151). According to Algarroba, there is such a scarcity of good judges, especially in small towns, that qualified people would be well rewarded.

> To such a town can a poor man arrive
> that they would weigh him in gold; that nowadays
> there is nearly always a lack of judges of quality
> in small places. (152)[32]

Algarroba seems to say both in earnest and in jest that the peasants are intellectually unable to perform the work required of an administrator of justice. Judges "of quality" ("de caletre") are scarce in Castilian villages.

The four candidates who file before the examiners are all peasants of Old Christian stock. They belong to a world where all knowledge is suspicious and dangerous. Humillos, the first candidate, is proud of the fact that no one in his lineage has learned to read for, after all, knowing "four prayers" ("cuatro oraciones") and being "an Old Christian" qualified one not only to be mayor but to discharge the highest posts of political power ("I dare to be a Roman senator"). Jarrete, the second candidate, although hardly knowing how to read, bases his candidacy on knowing how to use a bow and arrow, on "preparing a plow fearlessly" ("calzar un arado bravamente"), and on "branding calves" ("herrar novillos") rapidly. The third candidate, Berrocal, believes he can be mayor because he can distinguish among sixty-six wines. Rana, the fourth, seems to be the only exception to the rule. He makes up for the lack of a formal education with common sense and political savvy. Thus, if chosen for the position, he promises to reject all bribes and to resist the abuse of power. He also promises to temper justice with pity ["I would be well-bred and restrained, / In part severe, but not harsh" ("Sería bien criado y comedido, / Parte severo y nada riguroso")] and not to insult the accused ["I would never dishonor the wretched one / brought before me by his crimes" ("Nunca deshonraría al miserable / que ante mi le trujesen sus delitos")].

Among the peasants of Daganzo, Rana stands out for his common sense, although his notion of justice does not always partake of "the natural goodness that obligates one to judge the offender with consideration and humanity" ("la bondad natural que obliga a enjuiciar al reo con miramientos y humanidad"). Thus, when some gypsies enter the room of the town council to entertain those in attendance with songs and dances, Rana is the only villager who shows distrust and prejudice against them: "Are they not gypsies? Well careful that they not steal our noses" ("¿Ellos no son gitanos? pues adviertan / Que no nos hurten las narices" 162). In spite of his negative and prejudicial attitude toward the gypsies, Rana is characterized by a political sense that might be defined as secular: his response to the stern sacristan ("mal endeliñado," according to the stage directions) who has come to chastise the town council for its lack of austerity ["Is this the way a town is governed, in this damn time, / Among guitars, dances, and good times?" ("¿Así se rige el pueblo, noramala, / Entre guitarras, bailes y bureos?")] aims toward a separation of religious and civil powers:

> Tell me, wretched one, what devil
> is heard through your tongue?
> Who allows you to criticize justice?
> Are you going to govern the Republic?
> Stick to your bells and to your work;
> Leave those who govern alone,
> for they know what to do better than we. (168)[33]

The intervention of the gypsies, followed by that of the sacristan, serves to postpone the election of the judges until the next day. Pesuña (the *bachiller*), Panduro (the *regidor*), and Jarrete, the candidate, declare that they will vote in favor of Rana. Algarroba does not commit himself. Humillos simply says that Rana will change once he has gained "power" ("la vara"). What is ironic is that Rana's election will not resolve the conflict that exists implicitly between the peasant-vassals of Daganzo and the lord who lives in Toledo, and who must confirm the results of the elections. We must bear in mind that the aim of the meeting of the town council of Daganzo is to elect "judges" and that, with the exception of Rana, the candidates are all "incompetent."

Except in the case of Rana, whose portrait of the judge reminds us of Don Quijote's advice to Sancho when the latter goes out to assume the governorship of Barataria, the vision of the peasants is essentially grotesque and anticipates the Cervantine invective against the minority group of the rich peasants of *El retablo de las maravillas*. The world of *Los alcaldes* is a closed, antagonistic world and represents a psychological space opposed to knowledge, reflection, and all capacity to think and question.

Cervantes's *entremeses* are defined by their dialogical relationship with the new art of writing and producing plays that is institutionalized in Spain at the beginning of the 1600s under Lope de Vega's theoretical-ideological impulse. Vis-à-vis that theater, which tends to reflect social myths, and "in which the established reality is supported ideologically" (Maravall), Cervantes's *entremeses* opt for a critical and demystifying attitude toward prevailing and official ideologies. In these comic pieces or plays of "low style," the observations of the artist and those of the discriminating receiver of his product are directed toward those vital and social areas that are rarely explored by the so-called new comedy of the early 1600s. In the *entremeses* those very areas are explored through laughter, which provokes an inversion of the images propagated by the vehicles of official culture. We might also say that it is precisely the opposition between reading, on the one hand, and the witnessing of a staged performance, on the other, that provokes in Cervantes's discourse the necessity to inscribe the "stage" in the written page, that is, to transform theatricality into narrativity. The latter problematic will be explored in the next chapter, and will be introduced through a theoretical discussion of the semiotics of drama and theater.

CHAPTER 3

On Theater as Narrativity

Adieu public theaters, honored
by ignorance, which I see extolled
in one hundred thousand pieces of recited nonsense.

Adiós teatros públicos, honrados
por la ignorancia, que ensalzada veo
en cien mil disparates recitados.
  Viaje del Parnaso (vv. 124–126)

I

It has been said that languages have no meaning, and that it is people who make them signify. This assertion by the Italian linguist Tullio de Mauro (1970) has two essential implications: (a) that what is signified and its discursive anchors (metaphor, symbol, allegory, and so on) exist not a priori, but as a result of an operation. In this sense, the notion of referent does not refer as much to what is real but to reality that, in turn, refers not to a fact but to the system of values of an interpretation; (b) as a corollary of the previous implication, there is the presence of someone real who can only be inscribed in language as a symptom, that is, as an absence.

This twofold plane, in which the problematic of discursive typologies and their ties with daily reality is articulated, is often overlooked by literary theories in general, and by semiotics in particular. This is because, in seeking to establish their method as science, these theories have left out what they consider to be secondary meanings, which have to be studied, if at all, only a posteriori, through that sort of parasite of the denoted known as connotation. In this line of thinking there operates a double closure that, within the term "connotation," mixes connotation itself and symptomatic meaning, even though the latter is not strictly discursive since it is not reducible to the realm of meaning.

As indicated by Augusto Ponzio (1974), this displacement can be seen even in Saussure, for whom semiology is (or should be) the science that studies the life of signs in social life; however, almost simultaneously with this declaration, Saussure's concrete practice, imposed by his theoretical paradigm, should develop an analysis of the sign of a binary and mental type, in which, obviously, the pragmatic and historical aspects are relegated.

It may also be useful to point out here how semiotics, in spite of its claims of autonomy, has continued to depend on paths opened by linguistics. As the latter approached pragmatics, semiotics overcame its complexes and began to focus on the domain pointed to by Charles S. Peirce: meaningful processes, in which any thing or act, by entering into those processes and by meeting the minimal indispensable conditions of meaning, acts as a sign.

It is from this perspective that a semiotic approach to the theatrical phenomenon can operate; because, if semiotic analyses have managed to fail dismally in an area, that failure has manifested itself in the realm of semiotics of theater, despite the undeniable attraction theater offers as an object. There is not only the matter of the structural complexity of its discourse, but also, above all, the intricate relationship that is produced in time between words and gestures, literature and stage.

One of the ways of reconsidering this situation is through the elaboration of a theoretical discourse that would tend to reconstruct dramaturgy, as a specific means of assuming what we might define in terms of theatrical "language." There, in a global vision of that language—immersed in a specific time and in intertextual connection with other discursive supports—lies the possibility of reactivating the relationships among theatrical sign, dramatic text, and spectacle, on the one hand, and the relationship between spectacle and spectator, on the other. In short, the notion of discourse as performance and the notion of performance as discourse, while related, possess different statutes and different functions.

It is not accidental that one of the intense preoccupations of modern theorizations of theater is the status of theater as a differentiated artistic discourse. A semiotic approach would stress the existence of two types of signs, in accordance with their respective means of realization: the dramatic work (what is written) and the performed work (what is staged). As a written text, the work is established by a framework of verbal signs that include linguistic, literary, and cultural codes. As performance, its framework includes other kinds of signs related to corporeal expression, color, lights, sounds, scenery, costumes, makeup, and so on. The privileging of one category over the other in hierarchical value leads to what Jean Alter (1981: 113–119) defines as a double fallacy: a literary fallacy and a performing fallacy.

For the former, theater must be confronted solely as literary text. The result is its reduction to a particular genre of literature. The latter, which is more common and popular, relates theater exclusively to performance, thus reducing it to a particular genre of spectacle.

It is evident that many performances do not necessarily possess a previous written text; it is also true that in the history of theater a great number of works exist that were originally written to be performed, but nevertheless were never brought to the stage. For that reason the argument cannot be reduced to those terms.

Theater, as a social practice, comprises both elements—text and performance—and the crux lies in how to confront those two different moments of the same articulated process without considering the text as a mere implicit project for performance, or the latter as a mere transcription of the text on stage. The problem is not irrelevant because we usually must study the history of theater from written texts, as a fixed and accessible shadow of a much more complex ephemeral act.

Nevertheless, to the extent that theater is not literature—although included in its fabric—literary analysis of the so-called dramatic text is not a part of the global analysis of a work—as a work of theater itself—but a falsification of it. The phenomenon is not, however, gratuitous, and reasons may be found that justify, at least, the existence of that misunderstanding. Marco de Marinis (1982: 24+) has analyzed this problem in a pertinent manner. According to the Italian semiotician, the situation of privilege and superiority bestowed upon the literary text (when it exists) with respect to its spectacular transcodifications—of which the text would be a kind of invariant or deep structure—brings about three types of consequences of necessary differentiation:

a. *The confusion between virtual and real performance.* It is assumed that the former tends to reconstruct the staging virtually inscribed in a given text, thus establishing an equivalence between the aforesaid reconstruction and the reconstructions of one or more real performances, which, according to this notion, would be nothing more than actualizations of the former.

b. *The precedence, in performance, of verbal components over nonverbal ones.* Such nonverbal components include lighting, stage designs, props, tone of voice, costumes, characterization, body movements of the actors, and so on.

c. *The restriction operating on the theatrical performance so that it becomes the subclass "staging of written dramatic texts."*

This is not an attempt to deny the legitimacy of a semiotic of the dramatic text, but rather to underline a difference that critical approaches to the history of theater, especially in the field of Hispanism, tend to ignore. The arguments that would explain this widely extended misunderstanding may be reduced, following de Marinis, to three main reasons. Two of those reasons are of a specific nature and the other is of a more general type:

a. The written text is the only component of performance that is present and persistent for the critic; the rest of the components, as is well known, are ephemeral and nonpersistent.

b. The linguistic model, taken metaphorically as an analytical paradigm, has been used indiscriminately. This has led to a privileging of the literary work, over which the model obviously had greater operative viability.

c. What in Lotman (1970) is a structural model is transformed into an explicative one when the notion of verbal language as a primary modeling system—and, therefore, as the most powerful semiotic device of all—is endowed with the capacity to translate all conveyable content through nonverbal semiotic devices. Such a theory is maintained by Hjelmslev (1943), Benveniste (1969), and Prieto (1970), among others, and has been questioned by Umberto Eco (1976), who argues that there still exist "semiotic" devices capable of covering areas of the general semantic space that the spoken language does not always manage to reach, and, from another perspective, by Halliday (1975).

If the dramatic text is not an invariant or deep structure of performance, as proposed by Steen Jansen (1968) through the analysis of *Andromaque,* and later theorized by Marcello Pagnini (1970), one wonders to what extent semiotics can resolve what seems to be an unresolvable problem. Julia Kristeva (1969), Tadeusz Kowzan (1969), Antonio Tordera (1978, 1979), and Jean Alter (1981), among others, have tried to find a solution for scenic signs, considering them to be analyzable through their linguistic inscription in the literary text. Kowzan proposes that the move from the literary to the scenic level does not change meanings, although signifiers may indeed change. Kowzan's position relativizes the problem but does not solve it. According to his hypothesis, through the signifier/meaning pair semiotics would be able to account for the dual nature of the art of performance: formal autonomy versus a dependence on content, a dependence understood as relating to the literary matrix.

This notion implies a definition of the dramatic text as a metatext a priori, so that, in both a logical and temporal sense, the spectacle would be an "after" in relation to the written text, an "after" toward which the written text tends and about which the playwright, when writing, may only formulate hypotheses or proposals of a more or less prescriptive nature. For this reason, as an analytical model, Kowzan's thirteen systems of coexistent signs in theatrical performance are founded, according to de Marinis, on a basic ambiguity: although the signs may vary as signifiers, they may be analyzed by focusing on their meaning which, being constant, is inscribed in the dramatic text in the form of an implicit or explicit stage direction.

De Marinis concludes by saying that it is necessary to individualize, in metalinguistic connection, two pairs of terms whose lack of differentiation is largely responsible for the aforementioned misunderstandings: (a) dramatic text/virtual production(s), and (b) spectacular metatext/real production(s). From a given dramatic text (that is, from a metatext a priori) only virtual productions—the only ones dealt with by the dramatic text—may be claimed through the metatextual channel. Real productions, on the other hand, constitute the object of the spectacular metatext, a posteriori. The diversity and incommensurability of both metatexts are based on the diversity and incommensurability of their respective *text-objects*: (a) a proposal for staging, and (b) the staged performance. Even if one were to assume that the whole literary text were respected in a given performance without manipulations, cuts, or transpositions, the permanence of the written word in the staging would be nonexistent, despite the appearance of being the only thing that remains (de Marinis 1982: 36+). Jean Alter, on the other hand, affirms that

> theatrical experience indicates . . . that some texts visibly are more resistant to transformations than others, yielding fewer variations in performances. If theatrality lies in the potentiality for transformational processes, insuring both the permanence and the renewal of theater, then such texts may be said to have a low theatrality index . . . Conversely, a heterogeneous text, with disconnected episodes, equivocal characters, unspecified geographical and historical circumstances, no evident structures beyond some general theme, incoherent chronology, etc., will easily accommodate partial transformations which need not extend farther than directly associated units. The free creativity of the director enjoys greater opportunities. The text has a high theatricality index.

For Jean Alter, then, the greater or lesser theatricality of a dramatic text lies in its open and, in a certain sense, little systematized structure. Some film directors also seem to think along these lines. In the history of the classic cinema of Hollywood, for example, there appeared to exist a rule requiring the production of works by minor authors, following an unwritten law that said that only a bad film could result from a good novel or a good drama, and a good film could materialize from a bad novel or a mediocre drama. There is no lack of examples, indeed, to justify such a drastic principle, even if it does not seem very serious to argue theoretically over such empirical bases. Nevertheless, Orson Welles's *Macbeth* is significantly and structurally different from Polansky's *Macbeth*, and both, in turn, are different from the *Macbeth* produced for the Royal Shakespeare Company by Trevor Nunn, with Ian McKellan in the leading role. Peter Brooks's *Marat/Sade* has nothing in common with Giorgio Strehler's *Marat/Sade* or the *Marat/Sade* of Adolfo Marsillach/Francisco Nieva. Does that mean, perhaps, that the respective works of William Shakespeare or Peter Weiss are texts so little structured to have allowed the freedom that exists behind such varied and often contradictory productions? We do not think so.

On the other hand, if, according to Bakhtin (1981), closure and structural systematization are characteristics of the novel as a genre from its very beginnings, does Jean Alter's proposal mean that theatricality is opposed to narrativity? Or that the scarce possibility of multiple transformations is directly related to the consideration of the dramatic text as a novel? The abundant stage productions in contemporary theater of works that are explicitly narrative would deny that hypothesis.

It appears to be clear, then, that a performance is not the actualization/translation of a written text upon the stage. Rather, it is a new text produced through the articulation of a multiplicity of different codes. What serves as a point of departure (a text, written or not, theatrical or not) is only one code among others, and it is not always the most important.

In any case, the problem remains unresolved. If it is true that a play may be read as a written text, what is the difference, then, between a novel and a play? Such is the dilemma facing those who attempt to explain dramatic productions such as those of Cervantes, who is one of the most difficult examples for historians and semioticians of theater. Since we cannot speak of a "residual text coming from a spectacular text" (de Marinis 1982), given that Cervantes writes knowing full well that his plays will not be staged in his own time—and, therefore, he does not fix his text either a priori or a posteriori, but rather *on the margins* of the performance—it is necessary to establish from what model and through which discursive formulations one can analyze his theatrical work.

It is well known that, with the exception of some of Cervantes's early plays, most of them were not performed on stage during his lifetime. This fact has provoked a whole series of sociological and historical explanations, though rarely from the standpoint of theatrical theory. When the latter has been taken into account, the explanation provided has often been too obvious to have credibility: vis-à-vis the successful model proposed by Lope in his *Arte nuevo de hacer comedias en este tiempo* (1609),[1] Cervantes's efforts were deemed partial failures. Similarly, as in the case of his poetry, the shadow of Cervantes the novelist seems to have condemned Cervantes the playwright to a lesser role. Yet, Cervantes was not a narrator who simply made forays into other genres; he was a much more original poet and playwright than he is often given credit for. The fact that in theater as well as in poetry his approaches had neither the success nor the acceptance that accompanied his novelistic adventure does not alter the existence of original proposals.

It seems somewhat odd that a writer with Cervantes's critical capacities should be incapable of seeing his own failure and should insist, until the very end of his life, on defending works accepted by no one. On the contrary, it makes sense only if he was defending a different epistemological position regarding the hegemonic theatrical and poetic discourses in his time and not just his own personal work. In that "difference" which—as far as theatrical practice is concerned—we might define in terms of *theater as narrativity*, lies, in our opinion, the historical importance of Cervantes's theater.

II

Cervantes's attraction to theater becomes evident not only from his early activities as a playwright in the last quarter of the sixteenth century, but also from his theoretical reflections concerning the state of theater in general, and the *comedia* in particular, in the beginning of the 1600s, that is, during the period in which the new comedy (*comedia nueva*), which is identified with Lope de Vega, is institutionalized in Spain as the result of a series of factors and changes. Foremost among them are: (a) the establishment of regulated and licensed companies; (b) the monopoly of guilds in matters of performance; (c) the establishment of permanent theaters in most of Spain's urban centers; (d) improvements in stage materials; and (e) the production en masse of the plays of Lope de Vega and his so-called school for a public that is sociologically heterogeneous, although characterized by a large degree of ideological homogeneity (Canavaggio 1977: 13+; Shergold 1967: 143–208).

The large-scale commercialization of theater contributes to Cervantes's marginalization as a playwright. His theater incurs a first displacement as a result of the conditions of production and the means of diffusion of the new comedy. That displacement is exacerbated by its lack of adherence to a vision of the world shared by the so-called new playwrights, by the professionals of the stage, and by the public that attended the theaters known as *corrales* (Canavaggio 1977: 14; Salomon 1965; Maravall 1972). Cervantes is thus forced to seek alternative solutions. One of them is the diversion of his plays toward the private sphere of reading.[2] His theoretical reflections on the theater of the beginning of the seventeenth century and his practice as a playwright are the keys for understanding that process of displacement that begins toward the last decade of the previous century.

As in the case of the novel, Cervantes has a great deal to say about the construction, transmission, and reception of plays. His reflections are supported by a solid conviction: around 1600 the dramatic text has become a "marketable commodity," so that its construction or structuration responds less to the exigencies of classical precepts than to the expectations and lived experiences of the new people of the theater and their audiences (Spadaccini, "Writing for Reading," 1986).

The most important commentaries on theater put forth by Cervantes are found, precisely, in his later works, that is, in texts published—and, probably, written—between 1605 and 1616, the period in which Lope de Vega had already assumed his "comic monarchy." The reflections themselves are attributed to various Cervantine characters and, in some cases, to Cervantes himself. Among the most salient texts in that respect are *Don Quijote* (1605 and 1615); *Adjunta al Parnaso* (1614); the Prologue to *Ocho comedias y ocho entremeses* (1615); *El rufián dichoso* (1615); *Pedro de Urdemalas* (1615); and *Los trabajos de Persiles y Sigismunda* (1617).

Most of Cervantes's plays—especially his later ones—are introduced in the contextual circuit of the *new art* and function as partial responses to the new poetics that was institutionalized in the imagination of the new professionals of theater and in certain sectors of the audience of the *corrales* at the beginning of the seventeenth century. The poetics of that new theater is summarized in Lope de Vega's famous *Arte nuevo de hacer comedias en este tiempo*,[3] in which, despite the burlesque references to "the common [nondiscriminating] audience" (*el vulgo*), he points out the impact of the latter on those who operate in the commercial circuit of the *corrales*. That is, in earnest and in jest, he alludes to the effect of that "jumbled popular mass" on the process of structuring, selecting, and staging of the dramatic texts, as "it allows itself to be carried away by passionate comings and goings, without reason, without an intellectually and objectively elaborated rule."[4] The power that the new audience supposedly exerts on the professionals of the theater (performers, authors, playwrights, and so on) serves as a pretext for the substitution of the old models for the new ones.

Lope's manifesto mixes two notions of the receiver which in Cervantes are distinguished, if not explicitly, at least in the practice of his writing: (a) *public*, that is, the heterogeneous and real receiver of the *corrales*, and (b) *spectator*, that is, that same audience transformed into a homogeneous horizon as it takes on, as its own, the model proposed by a given form of theatrical discourse. Thus, it is not the public that imposes its taste, but the spectator. To the extent that the spectator, as construction, comes directly from a model proposed from above, what Lope does is to hide himself behind his own creations in order to legitimize a standpoint whose existence is his responsibility, rather than that of his creations. For Cervantes, on the other hand, although the public as a heterogeneous collective cannot be changed, as a spectator it may well be. The problem, therefore, is not one of sociological structure, but one of a discursive nature. Demand may be altered by affecting the supply. It is here that the Cervantine displacement is located in relation to Lope's model.

Already in the first part of *Don Quijote* (I, 47-48) Cervantes enters subtly into the polemics surrounding the new comedy. He does so in a dialogue between the Canon (el Canónigo) and Pero Pérez, the priest, the very one who had burned Alonso Quijano's books of chivalry. Following a detailed critique of the preposterous books of knight-errantry, the Canon concludes that the authors of those texts flee "from verisimilitude and imitation, in whom consists the perfection of that which is written" ("de la verosimilitud y de la imitación, en quien consiste la perfección de lo que se escribe" 565). He admits, furthermore, that the undiscriminating common reader of those books—the "desvanecido vulgo"—neither understands "the precepts alluded to" (568), nor is interested in them.

Although he may have had a certain interest in finishing the writing of a book of knight-errantry, the Canon does not do it, and the basic reason is underscored in his comments concerning the new comedy:

> But most instrumental in making me drop the task of finishing it, even
> from my thoughts, was an argument which I drew from the comedies
> that are being played nowadays. For I reflected: if those now in fashion,

the fictitious ones and the historical as well, are all, or most of them, no-
torious nonsense, monsters without feet or head; and if, despite that, the
crowd enjoy seeing them, and approve of them and reckon them good,
when they are so far from being so; and if the authors who write them
and the managers who put them on say that they must be good, because
the crowd likes them like that and not otherwise, and that the authors
who observe a plan and follow the story as the rules of drama require
only serve to please the three or four men of sense who understand
them, while all the rest are left unsatisfied and cannot fathom their sub-
tlety; and since these managers add that it suits them better to earn their
bread from the many than approval from the few—such would have
been the fate of my book after I had scorched my eyebrows studying to
keep the rules I spoke of: it would have been love's labour lost. (427–
428)[5]

The Canon ends up saying that works composed according to rules
or artistic demands (i.e., those that adhere to the old poetics) find
themselves at a disadvantage the moment they attempt to enter the
commercial book circuit, or, by implication, the spectacular space of
the public theater in the case of comedies. The reason is that editors
and booksellers as well as theater impresarios and actors are less interested in art than in financial rewards. In the case of the books of
chivalry, those practical considerations would come to condition the
very structuration of the texts as well as the criteria necessary for their
publication: "For they all [the books of chivalry] seem to me more or
less the same, and there is no more in one than in another" (424).[6]
What is involved, therefore, is the reproduction of a model that has
met with a successful reception among consumers.

In the case of the new *comedias*, the Canon's criticism is aimed at
the theater companies themselves, or against those few licensed groups
that control the acquisition of dramatic texts, thus influencing their
composition and the very process of their transformation into spectacle.
Hence the Canon's indignation: "It is not the fault of the undiscerning
audience who asks for nonsense but of those who don't know how to
perform other things" (our translation).[7] It is not merely a question,
therefore, of an absolute, a priori incompatibility of art with the tastes
of the common, undiscerning "mass" public; it is also the establishment
of the idea of incompatibility in the minds of the new professionals of
the stage, whose interest in "earning a living" leads them to caution,
diffidence, and, ultimately, mediocrity.

In his *Arte nuevo*, Lope defends his new way of writing for the stage,
alluding to the expectations of the undiscerning public (*vulgo*) which,
he says, do not arise out of reflection but out of "habit." This kind of

audience was prone to accepting whatever the playwrights and professionals offered them, even comedies that did not follow the norms of their first inventors (Plautus, Terence, and so on). Lope comes to say implicitly that he could well have adhered to another type of theater, had the situation been different:

> But since I finally found that comedies
> were in Spain at that time
> not as their inventors thought
> they would be written in the world,
> but as many barbarians treated them
> who taught the vulgar ones their crudeness,
> and so they were introduced in such a way
> that those who write them now following rules
> die without fame and reward, for,
> among those who lack its light,
> custom weighs more than reason and power.[8]

In the poem Lope seems to rationalize his switch to the new way of writing for the theater by insisting on the predictability/expectations of the common public, or *vulgo*, whose taste, according to him, was oriented fundamentally toward action and spectacle:

> For considering that the bile
> of a seated Spaniard is not tempered
> if in two hours they don't perform in front of him
> from Genesis to the Final Judgment,
> I find that, if to please is the goal,
> the best means are those that achieve it.[9]

Clearly the problem is not that Lope abandons all classical principles or that Cervantes follows them slavishly. Rather, one is confronted with two different attitudes vis-à-vis the practice of public theater at a time when the playwright has lost control over the product of his work. According to the Canon's complaint in his conversation with the priest Pero Pérez in *Don Quijote*, the crisis of the public theater is most evident at the moment when the dramatic text is turned into performance at the hands of actors who only know how to represent nonsense (I, 48).

What can be gathered from these commentaries—reflections that, in general, agree with those put forth in other works by Cervantes—is that the composition of comedies now depends more on the expectations of a new audience and on the mediation of a few stage professionals, who are poorly prepared both technically and intellectually, than on the imagination of the playwright, an imagination that in the previous era was tempered by the strictures of classical poetics.

It is important to remember here that the weight of classical poetics had been lifting for some time, especially as the commentators of the Italian *Cinquecento*, Francesco Robortello in particular, move from a poetic perspective to a rhetorical one that begins to emphasize persuasion over aesthetic pleasure. With this change the locus of privilege shifts from the rules—the work of art is seen more as a collection of elements than as a unit—to the response that the work will produce in the receiving audience.[10]

There is no doubt that both Lope and Cervantes understood the new uses of the public theater. They also had undoubtedly differing notions of the playwright's role around 1600. Lope composes hundreds of dramatic pieces—individually and in collaboration—for specific companies, in whose hands they were to come alive through performances. Cervantes, following some earlier experiences in theater around 1580, writes a few more pieces and relegates them to silence until 1615, the date of publication of *Ocho comedias y ocho entremeses, nunca representados*. In essence, one might say that, given the context of the public theater in the beginning of the 1600s, Lope de Vega writes to have his plays performed, while Cervantes, on the other hand, finds himself obliged to address his texts to the reader.

Referring to the printing of the *Novena Parte* of his comedies, Lope confesses in the *Prologue*: "I did not write them with this urge to [print them] nor did I write them so that the ears of theater would be transferred to the censorship of private rooms" ("No las escribí con este ánimo [de imprimirlas] ni para que los oidos del teatro se trasladasen a la censura de los aposentos").[11] Cervantes also alludes to the different possibilities of reception between two kinds of texts: one that is read and the other that is heard in the context of a public performance. In *Adjunta al Parnaso* (1614), he focuses, precisely, on the conditions of reception marked by the private and solitary reading of the dramatic text on the one hand, and its communal and public act of performance in the *corrales* on the other. In a dialogue between Cervantes and Pancracio, a distinction is made between "viewing slowly" and "[seeing] what passes quickly before one's eyes" ("ver de espacio" "[ver] pasar apriesa"), that is, between the critical, and thus active, intellectual participation of the reader in his or her confrontation with a text and the acritical and passive reception of the spectator who receives a mediated product within a framework of collective expectations:

PANCRACIO: And do you have some [comedies]?
MIGUEL: I have six, with six other interludes.
PANCRACIO: Then, why are they not performed?
MIGUEL: Because neither do the producers look for me, nor do I seek them.
PANCRACIO: They probably don't know that you have them.
MIGUEL: Yes, they do, but since they have their own servile poets and they do well with them, they do not look for complications. But I aim to get them printed so that one may see slowly what happens quickly and is dissimulated or not understood when they are performed. And comedies have their seasons and times as do songs.[12]

The new theater tends toward alienation. The monopolistic situation that has been created around the licensed companies implies that those groups also respond to interests and pressures that guide them—to some extent—in the selection of plays and, subsequently, in the way in which those dramatic texts are converted into spectacles. In the process of stage performance any kind of contradiction inherent in the structure of the written text may be concealed. Furthermore, even in those cases in which the performance text might have remained "faithful" to the written text it is probable that the undiscerning audience (*el vulgo*) would not succeed in grasping those tensions. The playwright has conclusively lost control of his product. His work is subjected to a series of mediations that function within an economic infrastructure (that of the public theater) and in the presence of sociopolitical pressures (those of the state and the church). That theater, which is oriented toward distraction and persuasion, is a vehicle of sociopolitical propaganda, a creator of myths, which attempts to "strengthen collective ideology as well as the system of distribution of social powers which must have been regarded as being threatened" (our translation).[13]

This does not mean that Cervantes is opposed to novelty and progress. His commentary that "comedies have their seasons and times, as do songs" ("las comedias tienen sus sazones y tiempos, como los cantares") seems to suggest that "the flavor and pleasure that are perceived in things" ("el gusto y sabor que se percibe en las cosas") (*sazón*)—in this case those of the comedies that are fashionable in the *corrales*—are subject to change. The use made of those comedies will change over time and, consequently, his own plays will also be acceptable "at an opportune and favorable time" ["en ocasión oportuna y favorable"

(*Diccionario de Autoridades* 469a)]. Meanwhile, he addresses his works to his kind of reader (*lector mío*) who knows how "to view slowly" while continuing to be a virtual spectator.

One might say that the very structure of Cervantine comedies reserves a privileged space for the reader. His works prove to be more complicated than those of Lope de Vega, and require a more active and intellectually alert participation on the part of the receiver. Vis-à-vis the new Lopean comedy which is anchored in conditions of rapid movement and unity of action, Cervantes complicates the development of dramatic action by means of parallel episodes, thus approaching what has been called a "mental" or "conceptual" unity between plot and episode.[14] What has been said of the structure of *Persiles* can be applied perfectly to several of Cervantes's comedies (*La entretenida*, for example) inasmuch as "the sudden shifts from main plot to an episode which analogically reenacts it . . . the sudden intersection of main plot and episode, are all . . . techniques analogous to the ways in which the composer of a fugue develops contrapuntally the episodic variation of the main subject, allowing its entry simultaneously with one or another episode" (Forcione 1970: 145).

It seems ironic that, for practical reasons, Lope is closer to Aristotle (*Poetics*, Chap. VIII) than is Cervantes on the question of *unity of action*. Thus, thinking of the new public, Lope rejects the episodic plot:

> Let one take note that this topic
> have only one action, making sure
> that the story not be episodic,
> that is, inserted with something else,
> that it deviate from the original intention
> nor that a part that could destroy the whole
> may be taken from it. (vv. 181–187)[15]

It also happens to be the case, however, that thinking of that same public, Lope ignores *unity of time* (and *place*), and discounts the burden of Aristotle's *Poetics* on the new playwrights and their audiences:

> One should not heed that it transpire
> in a revolution of the sun, even if it is Aristotle's advice,
> for we no longer respect him
> when we mix tragedy
> with the low and humble comedy. (vv. 188–192)[16]

The "mass" audience that frequents the *corrales* does not see beyond plot or enter into the subtleties of precepts and/or contradictions. As in the case of the books of chivalry, theater also "allows the ignorant, undiscriminating public—*el vulgo*—to come to believe and to consider as true the many stupidities that are represented" ["da ocasión que el vulgo ignorante venga a creer y a tener por verdaderas tantas necedades como contiene" (*Don Quijote I*, 47)], or, as Lope will state in his *Arte nuevo*, the "undiscerning public" of the theater does not differentiate between the actor and the character whom he incarnates:

> For we see that if by chance an actor
> plays a traitor, he is so odious to all
> that what he goes to buy, they will not sell to him,
> and the vulgus flees when they see him;
> and if he is loyal they lend to him and invite him,
> and even noblemen honor and love him,
> they seek him out, they regale him and acclaim him. (vv. 331–337)[17]

For that reason, around 1600 one cannot speak of verisimilitude as a universal and immutable principle, but rather it becomes necessary to reconcile that principle with the lived experiences of those "enchanted men" who, in the opinion of the Utopian political thinker Martín González de Cellorigo, "seem to live outside of the natural order of things";[18] it is an audience that does not distinguish clearly between the world of theater and the theater of the world; between the dramatic illusion carried out on the stage by a few actors and the disillusion that articulates daily life.

III

In a book on the public theater in Spain and England during the Renaissance, Walter Cohen, although not focusing specifically on Cervantes's theater, traces an interesting map of the ideological, economic, and social background of the time which may aid us in understanding the problem at hand.[19] For Cohen, the Spanish as well as the English theater presents a special kind of synthesis: a "native popular" tradition and one that is learned and neoclassical. This fact, along with relative cultural homogeneity, reinforced by the absolutist state, allowed the political superstructure at first to support and later to control public theater.

Although Cohen clearly considers that the synthesis of the shepherd and the comic servant of Latin comedy—anticipating Lope's *gracioso*—required the institutional establishment of the public theater, his analysis nevertheless combines two concepts that are important to differentiate: *popular* and *populist*. In that sense, to assert that the public theater was a contradictory institution—although made up primarily of artisans—does not necessarily mean that it was internally popular, even if the forces of the political elite affected it externally. The existence of proverbs, plays on words, or the return to the minstrel legacy of the ballads in the works explains the popular nature of the audience, rather than the popular nature of the works. We must make a distinction between the notion of the audience as a real totality and that of the audience as an ideological construction, which is elaborated by theatrical discourse, projected onto the former, and finally assumed by it in a subliminal manner.

Indeed, if the main genres at the end of the sixteenth century were romantic comedy and national history—genres that complemented the adaptation of the aristocracy to the social and political changes—they were so inasmuch as they represented two different but articulated ways of manipulating social reality, by offering sentimental, literary and fictitious escapes from problems that were never resolved in daily life. *Fuenteovejuna*, for example, can hardly be analyzed as a revolutionary proposal, in spite of the fact that an abducted and beaten woman and a tortured member of the low peasantry represent rebellion. The solution arises from the goodness of the monarchy, whose authority and, more important, whose political and social implications, are never questioned.

History can serve as a source of plot even though it may be used to project an idealized notion of the past (for example, the times when everything was different). Cohen asserts that when history is pastoral—marking analogies between past and present—the solution implies, at the same time, interclass relationships and the intraclass conflict established between aristocracy and monarchy. Although this may be true for Lope de Vega, it is not necessarily applicable to Cervantes's case. *El cerco de Numancia*, for example, may hide class struggle on the level of plot and propose social unity. But at the level of structure, the insertion of explicitly unreal characters—inasmuch as they are allegorical in a realistic context—such as Spain, the Duero River, and so on, underscores the fictitious aspects of their referential universe. It has been emphasized on numerous occasions that, to the extent that History is only known through texts that are referred to as historical, it must be analyzed in terms of textuality.[20] In fact, as Hayden White (1978) has pointed out, historical texts are literary artifacts. For Cervantes History is never an argument for authority because it does not represent the truth; it is simply another kind of narrative, subjected to the manipulations of the historian/narrator. As Borges has written,

"We have dreamed the world. We have dreamed it resistant, mysterious, visible, ubiquitous in space and firm in time; but we have allowed in its architecture tenuous and eternal interstices of nonreason in order to know that it is false" ("Nosotros hemos soñado el mundo. Lo hemos soñado resistente, misterioso, visible, ubicuo en el espacio y firme en el tiempo; pero hemos consentido en su arquitectura ténues y eternos intersticios de sinrazón para saber que es falso").[21] Revealing the rhetoric of theatricality, Cervantes offers theater as theater, that is, theater as an interpretation of reality. His theater never claims to be a substitute for reality or to be reality itself, as in Lope. A kind of *Verfremdung avant la lettre* exists. Perhaps this explains the Cervantine resignation in the face of the lack of attraction of his plays at that particular moment in the Spanish theatrical scene. A similar case, as far as the approach is concerned, can be found in Calderón's *La vida es sueño*. The apparently metaphysical solution (life *is* a dream) does not agree with the knowledge possessed by Segismundo in the last scene of the play about his own role as a fictitious dreamer, a role imposed upon him through means that are far from metaphysical. Indeed, the Calderonian enunciation subverts the apparent conservatism of the utterance of the plot. Thus, we may attempt to explain the unusual case of Cervantes—that of a playwright who was marginalized because of his radical proposals—not only in abstract ideological terms but in ideological-discursive ones, which are, in this case, theatrical.

Perhaps it would be useful at this point to return to the underlying relationship between the Cervantine narrative and theatrical practices. Edward H. Friedman has done so in "Perspectivism on Stage: *Don Quijote* and the Mediated Vision of Cervantes's *Comedias*." In the first part of his essay, Friedman tries to demonstrate how, in stressing the distance between the signifier and the signified, the narrator of the *Quijote* destroys the myth of objectivity—the "singular point of view" of the picaresque that was defined by Carlos Blanco Aguinaga as *dogmatic realism*—substituting it for the discovery of the power of multiple vision or *dialectical realism*, to use Blanco Aguinaga's words.[22] The flow of exchange that occurs among *historian* (Cide Hamete), *narrator/translator* (Cervantes), and *reader* (Don Quijote as a character who reads his own life in the second part and, at the same time, Don Quijote as a symbolic inscription of the act of reading on the part of a real receiver outside of the text) would erase, according to Friedman, the line that separates reality as "truth" from novel as "lie" (fiction); these two manifestations are, in fact, operating on the same level, as discursive products: "Representation and perception are orchestrated acts that bring the realities of the writer and the reader into the fiction and make the fictitious analogues of reality in spite of themselves" (76). Consequently, Friedman concludes, "*Don Quijote* is metatheatrical, in the sense that the world is a stage for the recreation of fiction" (76).

Although the use of the term *theatrical* is metaphorical and, therefore, is not specifically appropriate for our purpose, we also follow the same line of argumentation, but for different reasons.

If we analyze the pragmatic development of medieval production of literary texts, we can see that artistic artifacts were not written to be read, but to be heard. The traditional division between theatrical and literary objects, as we understand it today, is relatively new, and their distinction is usually related to problems of a pragmatic level—act versus object. In fact, it has very little to do with the aforementioned period, in which a great number of writing practices are comprehensible only in terms of theatricality, inasmuch as their realization never took place for the private consumption of a reader but rather for an audience integrated in an oral public performance.[23] The discursive trajectory did not pass from page to eye but from mouth to ear.[24] Private reading only made sense to those few people who had access to the libraries of the monasteries, for most of the population was illiterate.

If this is true, we may argue that, for some, narration was the way to reproduce by different means theatrical acts with their inherent problems: political, ideological, and, especially, economic. It is interesting to recall how, in the prologue to his *Exemplary Novels*, Cervantes underlines, with pride, his originality in inventing a new genre. He knew that his notion of narrativity was different.

Cervantes's self-consciousness about his originality may be explained through certain theoretical consequences related to the aforementioned economic problems. When one confronts a classical theatrical text—Shakespeare, for instance—and attempts to analyze the function of certain passages that do not have much dramatic logic, such as seemingly gratuitous excursuses, or moments without action, one can attempt to justify such passages in various ways, from the moralizing will of the author who makes use of the occasion to intercalate an example or a sermon, to someone's desire to appear learned by inserting quotes of mythological or bookish references within a context that does not need them. Although this certainly may be true, in theatrical terms this may be explained in a simpler and less obscure manner. If a play has, for example, forty characters and a company can only rely on a considerably lower number of actors, it becomes evident that some of these actors must perform more than one role. Many of the literary passages that would seem expendable find, then, a practical justification for their existence: to allow, without interrupting the performance, the possibility of changes in costume, makeup, and so on, so that the actor may reappear in the following scene incarnating a different character. One must bear in mind, then, the possibility of seeking alternatives in terms of discourse.

Mikhail Bakhtin (1968) has shown how the novel arises from popular manifestations of the carnival. Novel and comedy, as genres detached from the norms of classical rhetoric, were, in a certain sense, confused. When Tirso de Molina, for example, refers to the Cervantine novellas he calls them "comedies." The problem, then, is rooted in the relationship between two traditional generic types within the same discursive structure. In a summary of the previously mentioned book, Walter Cohen (1986: 14) states the following:

> Feudalism influenced medieval theater negatively. The parcelization of sovereignty, a result of the absence of centralized political power, limited the extension of aristocratic authority over communal agriculture, ecclesiastical organization, and urban settlements . . . Historically, earlier medieval popular agrarian theater . . . was succeeded first by high medieval learned church drama . . . then . . . the simultaneously popular and learned urban religious plays gave voice . . . to the counterhegemonic, emergent, postfeudal ideologies.

If theatricality operated not only on the so-called plays, but also on production now considered as literary, we may consider the possibility that theatrical discourse survived in the novel, as a special form of performance. On that point we will base our line of argumentation.

Cesare Segre (1980, 1981) has explained the relationships and differences between theater and novel according to the following diagrams:

for novel (A)
for theater (B)

(A)

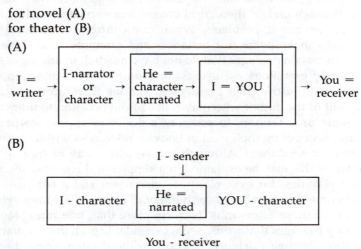

(B)

In A, "the subject of the utterance addresses himself to the receiver, reader or listener, through the possible mediation of an *I*-narrator or an *I*-character-narrator; it is he who relates in the third person the vicissitudes of the characters (*HE*). The first-person utterances of the characters are referred from within third-person diegesis realized by the subject of the enunciation, its sender" (96).

In B, "any mediation of the *I*-narrator or character-narrator is eliminated. The text in its substance is made up of the statements of the various *I*-characters; these may embrace, in diegetic form (*HE*-narrator), the narration of events offstage. In short, *I* is superimposed on *HE*, whereas in narrative *HE* is superimposed on *I*. The relationship between an *I*-sender and a *YOU*-receiver is veiled, although the possibility remains—particularly in the prologues and epilogues, in choruses and in asides—that there be direct communication between an *I*-character and a *YOU*-receiver (the public)" (96).

In Cesare Segre's argumentation it appears, as an undeniable truth, that, in theater, all mediation between an *I*-narrator and *YOU*-receiver is eliminated. Implicit in this assertion is the consideration that theater is speech in a pure state, without the obstructing intercession of a controlling presence. Cervantes's case proves that things do not function in such a simple way. If we analyze his *Exemplary Novels*, we will find an apparent absence of a narrative frame as a characteristic trademark. The tradition of *The Thousand and One Nights*, *The Decameron*, or *The Canterbury Tales*, indicates that a collection of stories required a kind of framing story in order to justify its union as an articulated whole. Cervantes, for the first time, in an explicit way,[25] discovers something that would not be theorized until much later: that the order of discourse may, in itself, constitute a story.[26] The arrangement of the *Exemplary Novels* is not, therefore, gratuitous, but rather defines a story (*in absentia* as an utterance, but *present* as an enunciation). This arrangement—in carrying out the function of the narrative frame—defines a point of view that indicates how to read. Consequently, in occupying a symbolic space, absent in the text but present as an articulation in the network that establishes it, the point of view assumes the role of the *I*-narrator. This forces us to insert a variant in Segre's outline:

(A)

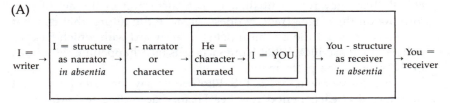

(B)

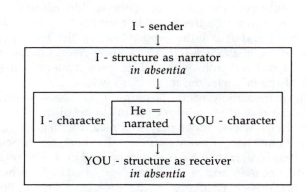

I - sender
↓

I - structure as narrator
in absentia
↓

| I - character | He = narrated | YOU - character |

↓

YOU - structure as receiver
in absentia

Discourse functions in this way in Cervantes's theater and in the *Exemplary Novels*. We might ask, then, why the last novella in the collection is a dialogued text.

It is important to indicate that *El coloquio de los perros* is, simultaneously, a theatrical composition (in terms of medieval theatricality) and the bond that marks the global discursive network. To some extent we may consider this short novel—which occurs during the dream of ensign Campuzano in *El casamiento engañoso*—as a theatrical novel. It is a kind of comedy in which the physical action of the events is substituted by mental action, that is, the development of the character's knowledge of life and the world. There are no characters who are defined psychologically as in Shakespeare, or events that occur through characters who are defined only as supports for the action as in Lope de Vega. What exists is the abstraction of discourse as stage.

This is the same attitude adopted by Cervantes with respect to poetry. Under the influence of León Hebreo's thought, poetic rhythm and musicality cease being auditive (as in Lope) or visualizable (as in Góngora); poetic space is a mental space.

Thus, *El cerco de Numancia, El rufián dichoso,* and *Pedro de Urdemalas* use their respective historical referents to transform them into discourse. The citizens of Numancia, for instance, would not confirm, as Friedman asserts, that "history will resurrect them" (Friedman 1986: 80). Rather, they represent their own resurrection in the act of performing on the stage. Tragedy does not stage the future, that is, what we might consider the mythical belief in a reward with which History will pay their sacrifice. What Numancia tells us is happening right now, in the now of the performance.

Cervantes seems to say, as T. S. Eliot would say centuries later about tradition, that each period rewrites History according to its own interests and needs. History only endures as an articulation of interpretations that one may accept or argue about and not as a past reality—that is, as something that occurred and is, consequently, true.

This position implies, on the one hand, an active role for the receiver; a role that contradicts that of the passive "undiscerning common audience" produced and generalized by Lope de Vega's model of the new comedy. On the other hand, it also implies a different typology of actor.[27] For this reason Cervantes returns to the printed text, in hopes of better times to come for his proposals. If it is true, as Friedman states, that Lope has an undeniable influence on Cervantes's theater, it is to the extent that the latter is written directly against Lope's model.

Nevertheless, the problem of the relationship between novel and theater remains unresolved. Indeed, if the novella, or the novel, can be a substitute for the act of performance by means of its own theatricality, why, then, write for the stage?

If we go back to the previously cited dialogue between Pancracio and Cervantes in *Adjunta al Parnaso*, we will see that the Cervantine line of argumentation is radically opposed to that adduced by Lope in the *Prologue* to his *Novena Parte* of the comedies, where he states: "I did not write them with this urge to [print them], nor did I write them so that the ears of the theater would be transferred to the censorship of private rooms" ["No las escribí con este ánimo [de imprimirlas], ni para que los oidos del teatro se trasladasen a la censura de los aposentos."]

Both Cervantes and Lope emphasize, as the main characteristic of the printed text, its different horizon and finality; however, Lope, with a clear subliminal displacement, does not set the performance against the written page, but rather contrasts the "ear" from the "eye." He speaks, as a result, of two differentiated oppositions: (a) performance/text, and (b) rapid consumption (ear)/slow consumption (eye).

Lope is concerned with the second opposition, for although the ear avoids a return to the text, the eye does not, as it allows the reader to examine what is being read, and, consequently, to be critical. It is not coincidental that Lope should define "reading" in terms of censorship—the "censorship of the living rooms." In contrast to Lope, Cervantes prefers a slow consumption of the text to the fleeting reception of the performance, and explains in his dialogue how and why. For our purpose the method used by Cervantes to force a critical gaze is more important than the reasons for doing so.[28] Cervantes does not write "so that one may read slowly," but rather "so that one may view slowly."[29] His words, then, clearly separate two different attitudes before the act of reading: (a) the first one is based on a spatial development in time (theatricality)—it is not by chance that he underscores the relationship between comedies and songs; (b) the second one is based on temporality as a condition for the production of mental spaces, that is, traditional narrativity in a strict sense.

Cervantes obviously sees theater for what it is: a system of performance and, at the same time, an apparatus that produces action, time, and meaning through a time imposed on the audience from moment to moment. In addressing his comedies to readers, as possible coproducers of meaning, he avoids the psychological pressures inherent to public reception and, consequently, the mediation imposed by the structure of theater as institution.

The displacement used to transform a "text for the stage" into a "theatrical narration" eliminates the possibility of reducing reading to the accepted canon of theatrical performance. The *comedias* and *entremeses*, therefore, cannot be examined in relation to the norms of established "genres" because Cervantes subverts key elements of their respective poetics.

Pedro de Urdemalas is possibly the work that most directly confronts these problems. Conscious of the fact that the power of the medium is overwhelming, precisely because the audience of the open-air theaters neither reflects upon that power nor sees the snares and tricks upon which it is built, Cervantes turns his comedy into a kind of self-reflection of theater as performance, using that reflection not only as a plot, but inscribing in his textual space the impossibility of a passive posture on the part of the spectator. Thus, focusing his attention on the illusory nature of theater, he shows the medium in counterperspective. To the extent that the existing theater companies, which employed the standard Lopean model, do not appear to offer guarantees for staging the subversive role that his own model proposes, Cervantes prefers to seek an alternative in the realm of discourse, substituting what is but a guide for a spectacle with a narrative of the spectacular.

IV

This Cervantine awareness of the state of comedy in the beginning of the seventeenth century is clearly inscribed in *El rufián dichoso*—which was apparently written later than the *Quijote* of 1605—at the beginning of the second act, in a dialogue between two allegorical characters, Curiosidad and Comedia. Modern critics have attempted to find in those verses a certain change in the Cervantine notion of theater, "some proof of the evolution of the tastes and habits and an acknowledgment, at least partial, of the practice of new comedy" (Friedman 1981: 217).

It must be stressed, however, that although *El rufián* follows various conventions of Lopean *comedia*, its divergences from what they seem to mean are even more substantial, since, both in theory and in practice, the dramatic text deals in a playful manner with the problematic of the new Lopean art. The cited dialogue alludes to the cliché of the primacy of use over art, and reiterates once again that the authority of the old canonical theater and of the playwrights themselves is now in the hands of the professionals of the stage as well as in those of the consumers of those texts that have been transformed into public performances. The new comedy succeeds in maintaining a certain artistic integrity—"I have left out part of them / and I have also kept some" ("He dexado parte dellos / y he también guardado parte")—but it is also true that playwrights no longer follow the lessons of the classical rhetoricians:

Seneca, Terence, Plautus
and other Greeks known by you.[30]

Moreover, those changes had immediate repercussions on the stage. Thus, for example, the new emphasis on action and visual elements was due to the need to show the audience where those events take place. Hence, the abandonment of the Aristotelian unities:

I now represent a thousand things
not narrating, as before,
but with facts, and it is therefore necessary
to change places:
and since they happen
in different parts,
I go there where they take place,
sorry for the nonsense.
Comedy is now a map.[31]

Comedy is a map and, as such, it privileges the *effect of reality* over the *effect of performance*:

The listener cares little
if in a moment I should move
from Germany to Guinea
without leaving the theater:
the mind is light.[32]

The audience of the new theater, the "common, undiscerning audience," suffers from mental blindness (it does not know how to "view slowly" what "transpires quickly" on stage before its eyes). It is an audience co-opted by visual images and magic formulas, which tend to strengthen social myths and fortify the established system of distribution of power. It is the same audience that was attuned to the performance of innumerable hagiographic plays ("comedias de santos"), a genre with which *El rufián dichoso* has been hastily associated by critics.

V

El rufián dichoso is characterized by unitary structure and action, but we cannot conclude that "his [Cervantes's] head may argue for the classical type of plays but, his heart, rejecting the academic approach, seems to be with the productions of that 'extremely successful talent of these kingdoms' ('felecísimo ingenio destos reinos'), whom commentators identify with Lope de Vega. His enormous toleration saves him from siding with one particular faction in the polemics of the dramatic aestheticians" (Wardropper 1955: 221, 219).

In our opinion, it is not a matter of alliances with one group or another regarding dramatic precept. The central issue is another: upon the introduction of the dramatic text in the public sphere of stage performance in the beginning of the 1600s, the play's meaning is related to the horizon of expectations of a public that, in Cervantes's opinion, is contemptible to the extent that while sociologically heterogeneous, it displays a certain ideological homogeneity as spectators. For that reason Cervantes neither writes a hagiographic play according to contemporary norms, nor attempts to sell his works to producers ("autores") who might have them performed on stage.

El rufián dichoso, and, in general, all Cervantine theater, lends itself to a more problematic reception than do contemporary comedies, and, unlike those dealing with hagiographic topics, which follow the formula proposed by Lope in his *Arte nuevo de hacer comedias*, its very structure seems to preclude the possibility of a closed dramatic universe. Cervantes the playwright seems to aim more toward the limits of the new comedy than toward an assimilation of the ideas prescribed by Lope's manifesto (Canavaggio 1977: 446–449).

At first glance *El rufián* apparently follows the itinerary of a typical hagiographic play, that is, the dramatization of the idea that even the greatest sinner may achieve salvation if he or she repents. This repentance is based not only on devotion and faith—both qualities present in Lugo's heart since his unbridled youth—but also on charity.

Upon close reading one realizes that Cervantes's text moves away from this model of hagiographic drama as practiced by Lope and his followers (Canavaggio 1977: 434). In the first place, the protagonist, Cristóbal Lugo, does not conform to the stereotype of that theater, which Karl Vossler (1965: 55) characterized as an essentially passive man:

> The holy man is *vas electionis* or *medium divinum* and, because of this, not very susceptible to self-love or to sensual, mundane, and lowly interests. In comedy, the true holy man usually plays more of a theatrical and representative figure than a dramatic character, for in his (or her) stead there act divine forces: a guardian angel, or Our Lady, or the Child Jesus or some other agent. (Our translation)

Unlike those men devoid of a "reflexive conscience," Cristóbal Lugo and other Cervantine characters (Pedro de Urdemalas, for example) possess a "methodical doubt about the conditions of their existence" which connects them with the problematic search for their novelistic protagonists (Canavaggio 1977: 450).

Furthermore, unlike the protagonists of the contemporary hagiographic plays, Cristóbal Lugo is characterized by a personality divided between insolence, an inferiority complex (for being the son of an innkeeper), and violence, on one hand, and generosity, loyalty, and devotion (to the souls of purgatory) on the other. Lugo, in the same way, manifests a "plan and a still indecisive existence, but he seeks to act with moderation in contact with reality" (Canavaggio 1977: 436). This scheme—and, with it, certain victory—crystallizes following his rejection of the "stacked deck of cards" to test God's mercifulness:

LOBILLO: I will give you a set of cards
       that are stacked, with which you can clean him out
       without leaving him anything.

LUGO: The means you choose take too much time.
       Another way I know of getting there.
       I swear to God the Omnipotent
       that, if I should lose them now,
       I shall become an outlaw. (vv. 1012–1019)[33]

His plan of existence implies challenges, but his search will culminate in the affirmation of his critical independence and free will:

LUGO: I am alone, and I wish
       to search only within myself

even if the waves should impede it,
the waves where I am afraid to shipwreck.
I swore that if I lost today
I would become an outlaw:
a clear and patent error
of a blind fantasy. (vv. 1150–1157)[34]

Although the terms of his decision have been presented by Lagartija ["either be a ruffian or be a saint" ("o sé rufián o sé santo")], Lugo's decision is taken independently, away from divine intervention.

Before we begin a more detailed analysis of *El rufián* it is important to mention that, as a playwright, Cervantes does not limit himself to representing conflicts or to structuring plots in the manner prescribed by *Arte nuevo de hacer comedias*:

> In the first act register the event,
> tie the happenings in the second,
> so that up 'til the middle of the third
> hardly anyone can judge where it will end.
> (*Arte nuevo*, vv. 209–212)[35]

> After dividing the plot into two parts
> make the connection from the beginning
> until the pace slows down,
> but do not permit a solution
> until it gets to the last scene,
> for, if the vulgus knows the ending,
> he who waited three hours facing the stage
> will turn his face and shoulders toward the door,
> for there is nothing else to know but the denouement.
> (vv. 231–239)[36]

If *El rufián* does not follow this dramatic formula, it is because, among other reasons, it is not addressed to the "common undiscerning audience," but rather to that ideal receiver, who is prepared intellectually to contribute his or her own codes of reception/production of meaning. It is to that typology of the spectator that Cervantes anticipates the strategy of composition of his work and the thematic progression that it will have throughout the three acts:

One of his free life,
another of his serious life,
another of his saintly death
and of his great miracles. (vv. 1293–1296)[37]

If the Lopean formula is shunned and there are no surprises, it is precisely because of a search for a contextualizing critical reading, one that incorporates a whole series of factors: the comparison of the dramatic text to the written sources that narrated, with propagandistic aims, the legend of Lugo's conversion, and, in particular, his saintly life in Mexico; the discriminating reader's consideration of the *Rufián's* divergences from a dramatic subgenre with which it is ironically identified—the hagiographic play; the "reading" of the text within the problematics of the New Art; the differentiation between written dramatic text and the performance text; and, in the background, its connections with all of the Cervantine texts that discuss the theory and practice of theater and the playwright's role in the first decade of the 1600s in Spain. That discreet "reading" of *El rufián* cannot be carried out by the undiscerning audience of the *corrales*, since, like any demystifying reading, it implies a rational position vis-à-vis the myths propagated by a system of power.

The deconstruction of the hagiographic play begins in the very first act of *El rufián*. There, the image of the protagonist is outlined by means of an accumulative process that emphasizes his psychological and social characteristics (Canavaggio 1977: 250). Thus, Cristóbal Lugo is not represented as a mere criminal who waits for divine grace to complete a process of conversion. The same delinquent is revealed in dialogue as a problematic figure and, although his conversion may seem initially unlikely, his "reflexive conscience" explains the possible motivations for his decision.

The first act is characterized by a sequence of seven consecutive scenes concentrated in two days. Each of those scenes emphasizes the capacity for conflict that the protagonist carries within himself and the way in which that essential element of conflict is shown in his confrontation with the values and laws of the prevailing society.

The initial conflict lies in Lugo's humble and lowly origin, in the way in which his genealogy affects him in his desire to "be someone," and in the confirmation that he is only respected for being the servant of Don Tello de Sandoval, the inquisitor. The latter, according to a bailiff, "rules the city," and Lugo's fortunes ride on the inquisitor's coattails; he is untouchable because of his master's power.

> There is no justice
> that will dare touch him out of respect [for the master].
> (vv. 44–45)[38]

The same idea is reiterated through the words of the constable, which are heard by Lugo himself: if he is not taken prisoner for his crimes, it is because of his master's power:

> We'll leave without pinching, and you can thank
> your master, for on my word as a gentleman,
> I don't know how this business would otherwise end. (vv. 51–53)[39]

This revelation proves disconcerting for the ruffian, and from that moment on Lugo, disillusioned, decides to gain control of his own fate, rejecting not only the burden placed on him by his humble genealogy ["Let my father be happy in his humble and lowly occupation / that I shall be famous in the exercise of mine" ("conténtese [mi padre] en su humilde y bajo oficio, / que seré famoso en mi ejercicio" vv. 79–80)], but the authority of his protector as well.[40] His new attitude of "rebelliousness and self-assertion" (Zimic 1980: 97), is manifested beyond the Sevillan underworld as he will transgress the authority embodied by Don Tello de Sandoval in Seville, in order to challenge the walls of the city of God:

> That they should respect me only for my master
> and not for my own sake, I don't understand this marvel;
> but I shall make a shout come out of me
> that will go beyond the walls of Seville. (vv. 73–74)[41]

Lugo's cry culminates in the individual's defined convictions that he has a say in his own destiny:

> I am alone, and I wish
> to search only within myself
> even if the waves should impede it,
> the waves where I am afraid to shipwreck.

This sudden change in Lugo cannot be explained in terms of abstractions. It is not convincing to argue, for example, that it is a consequence of a given Counter-Reformational ideology that would come to privilege, on the one hand, faith over good works, and, on the other, the devotion to the Cross, or the Virgin, over charity toward one's fellow man. The assertion that "Lugo is predestined for martyrdom"

(Marrast 1957: 79, 96–97) is not convincing either. It is important to bear in mind that the text, as verbal structures, contains its own codes that will be interpreted in accordance with the experiences and expectations of the audience. A reading of the text implies, at least potentially, a critical understanding of other texts, a relationship with other systems of meaning or social and discursive norms. Thus, if on the one hand it is true that language is not neutral and always originates from a frame of reference and from an exploration of possibilities, for the same reason the act of reception cannot be neutral either.

To that ideal receiver, or "my reader" ("lector mío"), to whom Cervantes addresses his *Ocho comedias y ocho entremeses, nunca representados,* one attributes the potential capacity to distinguish between *El rufián* and those other texts with which it engages in dialogue: the well-known chronicles dealing with the life of Cristóbal de Lugo in Mexico and the model of the contemporary hagiographic plays, that is, those devotional works propelled by Tridentine Catholicism in its effort to propagate faith, as well as the parochial interests of the monastic orders and guilds. If that type of "Catholicism multiplies the works of devotion more than those of charity,"[42] it is because charity implies a dialogue of the individual with the "other," and an awareness of the lack of equality in the assignment of roles in the theater of the world.

Regarding the Cervantine text, Lugo's conversion in Seville can only be explained in its dramatic context. This is suggested subtly by the text itself when, through the words of the allegorical character Comedia, the original Toledo of the chronicles is displaced to that other city, Seville, chosen for theatrical reasons to develop the play:

> His conversion took place in Toledo,
> and it will not be right for you to get upset
> if, recounting the truth,
> it is told in Seville.
> In Toledo he became a cleric,
> and here, in Mexico, where discourse has now
> brought us through the air, he was a monk. (vv. 1277–1284)[43]

The three places only have the authenticity granted by the discourse that names them. The play speaks about dramatic conventions rather than real cities. Thus, to substitute one for the other also implies telling the truth; that of the scene, from whose context the conversion extracts its logic.

The character is problematic from the very beginning and, although the decisive change of heart and behavior occurs at the moment in which the protagonist takes charge of his own destiny ["I am alone, and I wish / to search only within myself / even if the waves should impede it / the waves where I am afraid to shipwreck" ("solo quedo, y quiero entrar / en cuentas conmigo a solas, / aunque lo impidan las olas / donde temo naufragar")], that change is the culmination of a process of doubt concerning his social and moral condition.

From the beginning Lugo is propelled toward action by a desire to "be someone," by a yearning for independence from the yoke to which he has been subjected by the circumstances of his infamous genealogy. Lugo's rejection of the social role of servant that has been assigned to him by a society of orders and estates marks a desire for self-assertion which manifests itself first through deviant or antisocial behavior and, later, by a movement toward spiritual integration carried out through the exercise of his own free will. The Cervantine character of Lugo moves away from both historical sources and the hagiographic plays that are in vogue in the Spain of his time. His salvation is due less to his devotion and penance,[44] or to the intervention of Divine Grace, than to his solitary and rational decision to take away the burdens of his fellow man without a previous promise of spiritual growth.

This disinterested decision implies a new attitude of the character vis-à-vis charity, which is no longer used as a "marketable commodity," or as an object of investment or exchange. The new man now differs from the former ruffian who had counted on a hundred-to-one return:

> The souls [of purgatory] take from me what I have,
> but I hope that some day
> they will have to return to me one hundred to one. (vv. 646–648)[45]

In the same manner, Lugo has realized that his former devotion to the souls of purgatory and to the rosary functioned as a mere pretext for appeasing his conscience.

When he assumes responsibility for his own actions he also internalizes the implicit suggestions of his master, Don Tello de Sandoval, concerning the need to couple devotion with good deeds:

> Tell me, simpleton, don't you see
> that your silver and copper
> is like giving beggars for alms
> the feet of a stolen pig?
> You offend God a thousand ways,
> as you ordinarily say,

and by reciting the rosary,
and nothing else, you aim to go to heaven? (vv. 822–829)[46]

Lugo's internalization of that lesson distances him from most of the protagonists of the hagiographic plays of his time and establishes the Cervantine text within the Erasmian line of thought.[47] Lugo's spiritual transformation responds to latent inclinations. Thus, unlike the extraordinary conversion of the ruffian of the chronicles—a conversion attributed exclusively to divine intervention—or the "false miracles [that] they feign" in "the divine comedies" (*Don Quijote I*, 48), Lugo's conversion goes through a process of dramatization. That is, the audience of *El rufián dichoso* witnesses the articulation of each link in the protagonist's inner drama. The first step, or act, of that individual drama in Seville is connected with the two others that develop in Mexico, where the now ex-ruffian, known by the spiritual name of Fray Cristóbal de la Cruz, ends the drama of his salvation. That drama revolves precisely around a charity undertaken without previous promises, a type of "never imagined" charity.

That extraordinary act is realized in the form of a contract that Fray Cristóbal initiates with a sinner and unbeliever:

_____ I say:
that the soul of Doña Ana de Treviño,
who is present, I give gladly
all the good deeds that I have performed
in charity and grace from the time
that I left the race of death
and I entered that of life . . .

_____

and, in exchange, I assume her sins
_____ (vv. 2119–2131)[48]

That innovative proposition is followed by the incredulous reactions of the two witnesses who function as a chorus: Fray Cristóbal's friend and ex-ruffian, Lagartija, now transformed—without the slightest explanation—into Fray Antonio, and an anonymous clergyman:

FRAY ANTONIO: His case has never been heard, Father!
CLÉRIGO: And a charity never imagined (vv. 2140–2141)[49]

The protagonist's actions in Mexico are diametrically opposed to his past actions in Seville. Now charity is no longer understood as a ritualistic, selfish, and ordinary act, but rather as a challenge to the imagination, a challenge that each individual must resolve "alone," in conversation with his or her own conscience. Seen in this light, *El rufián* is considerably estranged from its historical sources and the outlandish hagiographic plays that employed miracles as mere tricks in order to attract the common, undiscerning audience to the *corrales*, or, as the Priest says in *Don Quijote*, "so that ignorant people become mesmerized and come to the plays; that all of this prejudices truth and undermines the histories" ["para que la gente ignorante se admire y venga a la comedia; que todo esto es en perjuicio de la verdad y en menosprecio de las historias" (I, 48)].

In *El rufián*, the miracle is used as a dramatic element, insofar as it is a function of a movement that foretells Cristóbal's conversion from "his serious life" to "his saintly death," and, eventually, to "his great miracles" (vv. 1294–1296). The miracle refers to Doña Ana's conversion and to the appearance of leprosy on the friar's face at the very moment in which the terms of the contract that was established with Doña Ana are met. From that perspective, we can see how leprosy is a consequence of Lugo's charity; it is the result of the new role that the innkeeper's son has assumed in the theater of the world. This miracle is announced by a citizen in an ironic speech that could be characterized as having a religious-erotic ambiguity:

> From the clutches of eternal death
> he took away her soul, and she returned to life,
> and he makes her forget her thoughts,
> and she, finding herself enriched
> with the holy present that the blessed father
> gave her in abundance,
> immediately let out a pious shrill
> to heaven, and, crying, asked for confession. (vv. 2191–2198)[50]

According to the same citizen, at the very moment of the sinner's conversion the friar's physical transformation takes place:

> And as soon as in the transparent airs
> the contrite sinner's soul flew
> to the shining regions,
> at the same happy hour, Father Cruz's face
> was covered with leprosy,
> where repugnance itself dwells. (vv. 2215–2220)[51]

We have seen how Lugo's conversion in Seville is confirmed in Mexico, when Fray Cruz voluntarily sacrifices himself for the "blessed sinner" (Act II, v. 2178), Doña Ana de Treviño. That confirmation, exemplified by a "charity never imagined," succeeds in maintaining the dramatic interest of the text.[52] Thus, for example, throughout the third act, the dramatic movement is focused on the protagonist's daily difficulties in his constant struggle to maintain the integrity of his new behavior. Afflicted by leprosy and physically exhausted, Fray Cruz must defend himself from his pride; from the possibility that his new reputation, which is now scattered throughout Mexico, will transform him into a kind of Lucifer. Celebrated by the ecclesiastical authorities for his "saintliness" (v. 2228), and by the people who have observed his work in "God's vineyard" (v. 2245), he tries to convince them— and to convince himself at the same time—of his humility, appealing to his lowly social origin: "Gentlemen, I am the son of an innkeeper" ("Señores, hijo soy de tabernero" v. 2247). Later on, when they propose that he be a prior, Lugo attempts to dissuade them, alluding not only to his physical infirmities and lack of mental clarity—"Consider that physical pains upset the senses" ("Consideren que los dolores turban los sentidos" v. 2594)—but also to his low lineage and his former life among the rabble in Seville. Cruz himself seeks to keep his connection with his ignoble past alive by means of his friend Lagartija, now known in Mexico as Fray Antonio:

> Brother Anthony, my friend, tell the priests
> my life story, of which you were a good witness;
> tell them about my insolences and pastimes,
> expose the immensity of my sins,
> tell them of my lowly lineage,
> tell them that I am the son of an innkeeper,
> so that all of this together will let them
> change their minds . . . (vv. 2598–2605)[53]

Initially, Fray Antonio appears to carry out the role assigned to him by Cruz:

> God blinded them
> for if they knew you
> as I have known you
> they would opt for another party,
> and would elect another prior. (vv. 2515–2519)[54]

He soon makes it clear, however, in a dialogue with another friar, that what he has said does not correspond to what he thinks:

> Brother Angel, I speak truthfully,
> but this is convenient here.
> This saint likes to see himself
> vituperated by all
> and flees all ways that could lead him to pride.
> Look how confused he is
> by the news you have given him. (vv. 2526–2533)[55]

It is clear that the "discerning" receiver of *El rufián* will not have the same notion of dramatic movement gathered by the "undiscerning audience" that frequented the public theater of the early seventeenth century. The receiver that Cervantes appeals to will be able to distinguish between *El rufián* and those extravagant hagiographic plays that were standard fare at the time, that is, plays that stretched the limits of verisimilitude. In his intertextual reading, Cervantes's imagined spectator will have an opportunity to differentiate between the Cervantine dramatization of Cristóbal de Lugo's life and the official versions of the life of the saint that circulated as stories; between the fantastic elements incorporated in those chronicles and the utilization of those same elements in Cervantes's dramatic fiction.

In our opinion, the ironic stage directions of *El rufián*, which are aimed at the "discerning" reader, represent an invitation to that kind of reflection, suggesting in an implicit way that supernatural episodes told by the official story of the saint may indeed prove likely within the verbal scheme of a stage text. Cervantes's irony vis-à-vis the chronicles could not be more cutting: "All of this is the truth of history" (195) ("Todo esto es verdad de la historia"); "All about this masque and vision was true, for the saint's history tells it this way" (200) ("Todo esto desta máscara y visión fue verdad, que así lo cuenta la historia del santo"); "All of this was so, for it is not a supposed, apocryphal, or lying vision" (201) ("Todo esto fue así, que no es visión supuesta, apócrifa ni mentirosa"); "This vision is true, for this is how it is told in his history" (222) ("Esta visión fue verdadera, que así se cuenta en su historia"); and so on.

In *El rufián* the supernatural episodes of the historical sources become dramatic mechanisms that allow for the characterization of the protagonist as someone who is constantly engaged in a struggle to control his own destiny. Moreover, the apparitions play a symbolic role, for Visel, Saquel, Lucifer, the dancing maidens, the bear, and so on, come to represent "the hidden thoughts of the soul: the weaknesses, bad inclinations, and improper and imprudent preoccupations of the character, against which the latter must continually struggle in order to be able to win salvation" (our translation; Zimic 1980: 153–154).

In transforming those "visions" into dramatic mechanisms, and thus endowing them with a symbolic charge, Cervantes's text meets the indispensable requirements of verisimilitude.[56] In the final analysis, for the "discerning" receiver, the stage directions turn into burlesque references that connect a theme common to nearly all of Cervantes's writings: theoretical commentaries about the art of writing fiction (narratives, dramas, and so on).[57] All of them take for granted that the artist operates within a specific space and that his or her freedom dissipates as soon as it clashes with the limits of verisimilitude in the receiver's horizon of expectations.

In *El rufián* the role of the imagination is reaffirmed and an invitation is extended for an active, critical reception of the text in its twofold dialogue: (a) with the new comedy (especially hagiographic plays), and (b) with hagiographic narratives, especially those dealing with Cristóbal de Lugo's conversion. That dialogue is not limited to matters of theory and dramatic practice, but also embraces moral and social topics that place Cervantes within the Erasmian humanistic tradition. Cervantes's "discerning" reader would not have missed the great irony of the drama of Cristóbal de la Cruz in his thirteen years of continuous struggle to reach the path of glory:

> You have been struggling for thirteen years,
>   in order to become charitable,
> beyond the human condition. (vv. 2748–2750)[58]

That struggle, which is a consequence of a "charity never imagined," far from becoming a model to be imitated, manages to trigger a new cult whose propagation is fostered by the state and the church, institutions interested in maintaining the structure of an estatist system. The people's cult is not anchored in the imitation of an extraordinary act of charity toward one's fellow man, but in the belief in the power of empty symbols, relics, and magic formulas. Hence, the plundering of Father Cruz's body invites the "discerning" receiver to a demystifying reading:

> For the entire city is in the convent,
>   and they throw themselves

on his body, and they strip it
with such swiftness. (vv. 2792–2795)[59]

The citizens' struggle over the saint's "relics" affects the reader as
does the intervention of the ecclesiastic and civil authorities in the
spectacle of his burial ["The viceroy and the monks carry him on their
shoulders" ("El virrey le trae en hombro, y sus frailes" v. 2814)]. These
actions, coupled with the lack of imitation of Lugo's extraordinary
behavior, allow the reader to examine the text or "view slowly" ("ver
de espacio") what on stage would "transpire quickly" ("lo que pasa
apriesa"). The reader is thus invited to bring to the reception of *El
rufián* his or her own codes for the production of meaning.

VI

Pedro de Urdemalas takes in and multiplies the process of deconstruction
stated above, integrating the very notion of theatricality as an ordering
principle of the play. The way in which the theatrical reveals itself in
this particular dramatic text is inscribed not only in the utterance, but
in the enunciation itself, in what we earlier referred to as "structure
as narrator *in absentia*."

Written during the last years of Cervantes's life,[60] *Pedro de Urdemalas*
assumes, among other functions, that of contextualizing the other eight
comedies published in *Ocho comedias y ocho entremeses, nunca representados* (1615). At the same time it manages to make explicit its theoretical underpinnings as theatrical discourse.

Already in the Prologue of this volume, which also traces a personal
history of the theater of his time, Cervantes indicates where one can
situate his own position as a playwright, a position halfway between
Lope de Rueda's school in the middle of the sixteenth century and the
new art of writing plays, which was made popular by Lope de Vega,
who managed to capture the "comic monarchy." We do not believe,
however, that the intermediate stage that Cervantes attributes to his
own work should be understood in terms of value, as a conscious
acceptance of his transitional position, but as a simple chronological
statement. The irony with which he alludes to the triumph of Lope de
Vega, called "the Phoenix" ["He made vassals of and placed under his
jurisdiction, all of the *scoundrels/comic playwrights*" ("Avasalló y puso
debajo de su jurisdicción a todos los *farsantes*"; our emphasis)], refers
rather to the conscious awareness of his difference and of the alternative nature of his proposal.

Cervantes's comedies incorporate colloquies in the form of eclogues among two or three shepherds, and the interludes, or *entremeses*, are generally conceived to be intercalated between the acts, or *jornadas*, in a public performance. Yet these disruptive elements cannot be seen as avoiding or delaying the continuous action proposed by Lope de Vega. Cervantes merely conceives theater in a different way. Thus, the episodic fragmentation of the dramatic utterance does not correspond to the parallel fragmentation of theatrical enunciation. There exists in the latter a solid unifying structure that transforms Cervantes's so-called *comedias a fantasía* or *comedias de costumbres* into a kind of comedy of comedies, that is, a comedy that stages the theatricality of comedy.

Pedro de Urdemalas hinges upon the convergence of two parallel intrigues: one, which is seemingly unconnected, relates some diverse vicissitudes linked by a common protagonist called Pedro; the other, which is more concise and structured, narrates the odyssey of Belica, who ascends from her humble position as a gypsy to the level of royalty. Thus, she manages to achieve the higher status that she had willed for herself and in which she had always believed (Canavaggio 1977: 122). This second story differs from the disparate episodes that Pedro protagonizes in that it constitutes a coherent whole and a closed totality. Canavaggio hypothesizes that the compact structure of Belica's episodes would arise from the influence in Cervantes's comedy of an entire cultural tradition, of which *La gitanilla* represents the highest degree of elaboration:

> The story of a young woman of noble lineage, whose disappearance and metamorphosis affect neither her beauty, nor her virtue, nor her grace, and who, at the end of many tribulations, one day finds her loved ones. (Our translation)[61]

This may certainly be the case, but what is relevant here is not the genetic explanation, but what arises from the dramatic functionality of such a topic in relation to the way both parallel stories intersect and complement one another. Pedro, to whom Maldonado has offered Belica in marriage, does not accept her hand in marriage and in so doing becomes instrumental in bringing about the encounter of the young gypsy woman with the king. Pedro's renunciation of marriage carries out two different functions. On the level of utterance, it allows the very existence of the second story, as a story with a complete development. At the same time, on the level of enunciation, it explains its closed nature, that is, the way in which its structure adapts itself to the conventions of the new art. Belica's story thus acquires the feeling of a play within another play, one that is more realistic and is ultimately performed, supported, and, in a symbolic sense, almost written by Pedro, the player. In short, the idea of theater within theater shows that a traditional and rather unlikely plot—the story of a gypsy who in fact is not a gypsy, a story as old as the Turkish-Barbaresque tradition in which it is inserted—can only be acceptable within the conventions of a theatricalized rhetoric. Pedro de Urdemalas, and his fragmentary becoming throughout the play bearing his name, would be from that perspective the counterpoint that underscores the falsity of the new theater as developed by Lope de Vega and his school. For that reason, although both intrigues may appear superimposed, and in fact on the level of utterance they are, one must look for their relationship in the metatheatrical functioning of the whole.

In effect, Cervantes's borrowings from folklore and from the tradition of literature dealing with gypsies, and the incorporation of concrete historical and personal references,[62] operate an important change of perspective on the text. On the one hand, they expose both the possibility and the limits of relating literature to life. On the other, they invert the referential character of discourse from within the very discourse: the world of the errant or wandering gypsy ("andante gitanería") becomes literaturized, inasmuch as it explicitly produces the effect of rhetorical fiction; Pedro, a folkloric character, produces, in contrast, the effect of reality.

We recall, in this connection, the well-known ballad of Lagartija in *El rufián dichoso*:

It was the year fifteen
hundred and thirty-four,
the twenty-fifth of May,
Tuesday, a wretched day,
something notable happened
in the city of Seville,
worthy of being sung by blind men
and written by poets.
From the Corral of Los Olmos
where ruffians stay,
comes Reguilete, the scoundrel,
dressed to kill.
He is not headed toward Cairo,
or Cathay, or China,
or Flanders, or Germany,

much less Lombardy;
he is headed toward the plaza
blessed by Saint Francis,
where bullfights are held
on the [feast] days of Saints Justa and Rufina,
and no sooner had he entered the plaza,
than all eyes
were upon him,
to glance at his good demeanor.
Suddenly, out came a raging bull,
Saint Mary help me!,
and charging him,
threw him up in the air.
He left him dead and lifeless,
drenched in his own blood;
and here the ballad ends
because his life ended as well. (vv. 196–227)[63]

In this ballad Cervantes comes back to an ironic reflection regarding the relationship between real life and narrative. The poem seems to suggest that without reference to someone living in the real world, the very existence of a narrative has no meaning. The same issue was dealt with by Cervantes in *Don Quijote*'s episode of the galley slave Ginés de Pasamonte (I, 22), when the latter first tells the mad Don that he could not possibly have completed his own autobiography (*The Life of Ginés de Pasamonte*) because he is still alive and later goes on to contradict himself, by remarking that he knows the end of his own story. Similarly, the opposition Belica/Pedro, as set forth in our earlier discussion, underlines the weakness of an approach that presupposes the metaphorically "true" character of discourse.

It has frequently been mentioned that, except for Pedro, and Belica to a lesser extent, who possess a certain degree of complexity, the rest of the characters of this play do not have a role and lack an identity of any kind. This is evident when reading Cervantes's play. Moreover, the utter falsity or lack of verisimilitude of those characters is made clear by the text itself. For example, in the first scene of the first act, Clemente addresses Pedro, reproaching him for his excessively high-flown language:

Since you know that I am a shepherd,
lower your rhetoric,
speak more plainly. (vv. 41–43)[64]

Yet, a few moments later, upon addressing Clemencia, Clemente manages to employ the very language that he claimed he did not understand, and speaks in two royal octaves in a fashion that a lowly and ignorant shepherd could not even have articulated:

Clemencia, if I have said something
that does not have service as its goal,
may I go from the most prosperous fortune
to the most fallen and disastrous one;
if always on the halo of the moon
you have not been raised by my tongue,
when I wish to tell you my complaint
may heaven imbue it with a mute silence.

If I did so, may the faith in which I put my thoughts
in order to be saved through love's law,
when life will come to end,
come in law's name to condemn me;
if I said so, may love never find in the quiver
arrows of lead to shoot at me,
if not at you, and to me with the golden ones,
destined to freeze you and to burn me. (vv. 151–166)[65]

The resolution of the problem of Hornachuelos's debt to Lagartija and that of the marriage of Clemente to Clemencia are given without any kind of dramatic structuration; rather, these resolutions appear to be nothing more than a pretext to underscore, in an indirect way, Pedro's intelligence.

The rest of the characters who accompany the protagonist in the different episodes play a similar secondary role. Such is the case with Martín Crespo, the mayor, Sancho and Tarugo, the governors, and even Maldonado. The latter's role is limited, in the first place, to allowing Pedro to renounce Belica, and, thereafter, to give an account of his life.

The sentimental problems of Benita and Pascual play an explicitly anecdotal role. Considered as a whole, however, in all cases the same underlying referentiality exists: that of the peasant world as it had been approached by the comedy of rustic inspiration. Noël Salomon (1965: 644–662) has analyzed with exemplary clarity the three types of peasants that influence *Pedro de Urdemalas*: (a) the naive peasant (Clemente, Martín Crespo, and the dancers rejected by the king); (b) the exemplary peasant from whose typology Martín Crespo and the two lovers take on certain traits—the former his rectitude and generosity; the latter, their purity; and (c) the lyrical and colorful peasant.[66]

As in the *Quijote*, it seems that the reflexive subversion of a genre needed to have an impact not only on that genre, but in every discursive manifestation related to it. In that sense, the playwright Cervantes does not insert himself in the theatrical tradition, but merely uses this tradition as working material. In this manner, the schematic and fragmentary nature of the elements used in his plays acquires its true function.

What is important in *Pedro de Urdemalas* is not for the characters to be constructed as countertypes of existing models, by means of the manipulation of their traditionally constitutive elements (which would bring his proposal closer to the Lopean model), but rather the function that the characters fulfill in relationship to Pedro, *metteur en scène* of their vicissitudes. Pedro is the one who manages to get Martín Crespo's consent for a wedding that he previously did not approve of; Pedro is also the one who, rejecting Belica, makes possible her meeting with the king; it is Pedro who, retrospectively, gives coherence to the whole story in defining himself as a dramatic entity in the closing lines of the play. He not only appears on stage as a student, gypsy, or hermit, but articulates these masks around the final one: that of a player or actor. He assumes the latter as a necessary conclusion to his vital trajectory, thus fulfilling the prophecy of the wizard Malgesí.

It is not accidental that in the third act, in the scene of the farmer and his two hens, Pedro has as privileged spectators the actors who must later perform a comedy before the king and his retinue. This comedy is strikingly similar to the tale of Belica as a victim of the monarch's lust. The success of his deception and that of his parallel performance before that improvised audience is what convinces him to become a player:

> Let the rescue strip
> its feather, and let us see later,
> as a summary and conclusion,
> if there is a hut or a tavern

where everything can be consumed:
that I swear, as a good buddy,
from now on that I prefer
giving all to the adherent . . .
Oh, Adlants of my joy,
ridges of my Potosí,
giants of my smallness!
You offer me
everything that my desire
fancies strongly. (vv. 666–673, 678–683)[67]

From this perspective, Pedro is not so much a *rogue*, as he has often been defined, but an *actor*, who performs and assumes the multiple and unending mobility of the *attrezzo* and stage theatricality.

The attribution of a past to the hero (let us recall the ballad with which Pedro relates his life to Maldonado, vv. 600–767) supposes an important innovation with respect to the tradition (Canavaggio 1977: 127) inasmuch as it separates Pedro from the type that serves as a model. Moreover, from a theatrical perspective, what is important is that tradition is transformed into something different from what it was when used by the new comedy. For the latter, tradition is a realm in which to take root in order to grow and establish oneself as character; for Pedro, on the other hand, it is a trunk where one goes in search of disguises. The traditional elements underscore Pedro's very nature as an actor who lives the false life of his diverse and varied characters, fully conscious of performing his role on a stage. They do so by disembodying his protean personality. As José María Díez Borque has written (1972: 121): "the sum actors of farces + farce makes those actors seem real and alive to us, vis-à-vis the other characters who are fully integrated into and justified by the comedy" ("la suma farsantes + farsa hace que los farsantes se nos antojen reales y vivientes, frente a los otros personajes que están plenamente integrados en la comedia y justificados por ella").

The seemingly parallel nature of Pedro and Belica, both of whom desire to transform their dreams and wishes into reality, becomes neutralized by the different function they have in the development of the play. Her true origin known, following Marcelo's confession, Belica assumes the new position as an integral part of her nature, and rejects Maldonado and Inés, her old companions:

I have another position
which does not require my being here. (vv. 992–993)[68]

Pedro, on the other hand, does not assume the existence of a supposedly true nature, but the very fact that everything is settled in the interminable play of performance. Thus, Belica's happy ending—to which Pedro de Urdemalas alludes ironically and indirectly in the final verses of the play—is not only rhetorical sarcasm, but the statement of something that the new comedy symptomized to perfection: the existence of an ideology that proposed from the stage the need to accept a given hierarchical social structure, understood as a result of a so-called "natural order."

VII

Cervantes's theater, then, is directly opposed to the prevailing stage model of its time, as far as the notion of the world and the role of the artist is concerned. The aforementioned model tended to reflect social myths "on which the established reality was ideologically anchored" (Maravall 1972: 37). What is important to underline here is that the place in which that reflection is inscribed was not defined as much by the themes, argumental anecdotes, or typologies of characters, but by the specific way in which the contract of communicative exchange between emission and reception was established, that is, in terms not of message, but of performance. It becomes problematic to accept, as some critics have (Wardropper 1978: 235), that "the message of comedy is that individuals have rights which exceed those of society. This message was and is revolutionary. It is the exigency of an adjustment on the part of man (and woman) to biological need before social need."

It is possible to read the dramatic utterance along those lines, but it is also true that the spectacular enunciation neutralized such whims, redirecting things toward a more controllable and adequate order for the purpose of supporting the privileges of those groups that were in power. Against this conservative program of the new theater, which was directed toward an undiscerning "mass" receiver, Cervantes seeks to dismantle those contrivances and, in so doing, produces with his comedies and *entremeses* a new kind of discourse. This discourse would be capable of inscribing in the space of the written text what in his time seemed not to be materializable as a performance on stage. It is here that Cervantes's proposal differs as much from that of Lope de Vega as from that which underlies Shakespearean production, although for different reasons. With regard to Lope de Vega, what is at stake in Cervantes's theater is an antithetical vision of the world and of the intellectual function that art as social practice must fulfill. As far as Shakespeare is concerned, the difference lies in the means used to carry out the proposal. One might say that between the respective dramatic proposals of Cervantes and Shakespeare there is a difference similar to that which we may find between Valle-Inclán's and Brecht's. Shakespeare and Brecht worked directly with real actors in stage productions, thus both were able to operate in performance terms, but Cervantes and Valle-Inclán, marginalized from the stage, had to inscribe the performance in the writing. They were thus forced to produce a tour de force that entailed describing with *words*, in the solitary place of reading, what can only exist as a live and collective *presence*. Hence, the abundant Shakespearean or Lopean excursuses are absent in Cervantes, who could resolve problems in strictly discursive terms, without any kind of conditioning on the part of the stage production.

Comedia attributed some freedom to itself in its dialogue with Curiosidad at the beginning of the second act of *El rufián dichoso*:

> I have left some of them [the precepts]
> and I have also kept some,
> for usage which does not follow art
> wants it to be so. (vv. 1241–1244)[69]

This freedom thus acquires, in Cervantes's comedies, and especially in *Pedro de Urdemalas*, a new dimension. On the one hand, by showing the theatricality of performance it underscores to what extent theater is not life and cannot work as a false, realistic metaphor of it; on the other hand, it reveals how the systematic concealment of this dazzling truth on the part of the new comedy, coupled with the ignorance and lack of awareness of the authors and actors who made it possible, had elaborated, by inverting the equation, a model of life in imitation of art. As one of the performers of farces tells Pedro in the third act of *Pedro de Urdemalas*, "Sir, all that you are saying / is enigma and gibberish / for us" ("enigma y algarabía / es cuanto habláis, señor / para nosotros"). This model, which had already been ridiculed in *Don Quijote*, was, ideologically, projected onto the "undiscerning audience" of the public theaters, which, in that way, received as reflection what was nothing more than pure and simple manipulation. This is how the new comedy worked, a "mass"-oriented genre whose primary spokesman was Lope de Vega, who is ironically defined by Cervantes as "a freak of nature" and/or "by nature, a freak" ("monstruo de naturaleza").

CHAPTER 4

Narrativity and the Dialogic: The Multiple Eye

The history of the novella in romance literature has been defined by Walter Pabst (1972) as the history of an antinomy, one that brings about a confrontation between the necessity of obeying the strict rules of classical rhetoric and a writer's explicit will to break them. Theory and practice would not, therefore, be two sides of the same coin, but divergent elements whose fusion's only role would be to enmask, through a totally orthodox, theoretical cloak, a narrative practice that was generally alien to the dictates of the norm. For Pabst, that divergence was usually resolved through irony. His thesis reduces this confrontation to those he calls "great authors," the only ones in his opinion who by their very nature as *individual creators* refuse to follow the theorist's dictates. It happens, however, that the same antinomy can be found through a cursory reading of texts by writers such as María de Zayas y Sotomayor, Alonso de Castillo Solórzano, Gonzalo de Céspedes y Meneses, Camerino, and Mariana de Carvajal, none of whom belongs to the rank of *great author* in line with Pabst's scheme.

We do not propose to enter here into a discussion of the concept of antinomy, nor are we going to deal with the notion of *greatness* as a prior space of analysis. Without denying, for example, that in a hierarchical historical perspective of values, Cervantes occupies a more prominent place in the institutionalized history of narrative than any of his numerous epigones, it is clear that the problem of artistic practice also applies to the latter. Moreover, it is often in the so-called mediocre texts that the *hand* and *craft* of the artist are most clearly evident, precisely because of the failure to reach the desired goals. The problem with Pabst's thesis is to be found in its ambiguous formulation, for in opposing *theory* to practice he calls theory what is, in fact, a *program*.

Theory presupposes certain lines of action that, while guiding practice, do not impose themselves on it in an inescapable way. Practice rectifies and reelaborates what theory proposes in accordance with results. In that respect, the relationship between theory and practice is a dialectical one; it is dynamic and interinfluential. A program acts in a different manner: it imposes criteria that cannot be separated from practice. It is like a corset that represses rather than a guide that directs the relationship between theory and practice. Practice can never enrich the other term of the opposition, which remains unalterable and unverifiable. In fact, what justifies the correction or lack of correction of theory is its existence as practice. In the second case it is practice that achieves the statute of correction by submitting itself to the program, always self-sufficient and always imposed as truth without being questioned. The traditional *Rhetorics* to which Pabst alludes are, in fact, programs rather than theories. Their strength came from the unquestionable prestige of those who drafted them. The principle of authority is related to the social exchange value of the "programmers," not to the use value of their proposals. They were a manifestation like any other of a system of ideological control.

In the history of the analysis of the seventeenth-century novel, what marks the persistence of the antinomy registered by Pabst is the incongruence between what might be called objective theory of narrativity—understood as a specific form of social practice—and literary narrative practice as a rhetorical one; it is not the incongruence between a rhetorical program and its corresponding narrative practice. This forces us to deal with the concept of "frame," redefining it in light of its generic use as an "empty" rhetorical element, as a kind of skeleton that arbitrarily ties one tale with another. In this manner the frame will, on the one hand, have a supporting, rhetorical function—an integrating or instrumental one from a syntactic standpoint—and, on the other, it will be a place where the social practice called "literature" is inscribed within narrative discourse.

No rhetoric is neutral, so the instrumentality or nonintegrating character of the frame refers to a specific way of confronting the problem of the relationship between art and reality. Of course there could well be, initially, an "empty" rhetoric. Thus, for example, the fact that various people gather in Boccaccio's *Decameron* has implications only to the extent that the author wishes to justify through a verisimilar artifice that some tales connect with succeeding ones in his book. What is initially an "empty," meaningless procedure ceases to be so when there is the example of someone who has been able to fill its emptiness with meaning, assigning it a specific role. Such is the case of the post-Cervantine novella.

We are not interested in analyzing here whether the frame of the Castilian novella of the 1600s is a mere rhetorical artifice, or whether it fulfills a clear syntactic function in the organizational structure of the whole. Our basic interest lies in looking at the implications that such a function, or the lack thereof, has. In other words, the idea is to face the problem of *genre* as something that goes beyond the literary as structure and brings us to literature as a differentiated social practice.

Historical Antecedents of the Genre

In principle we know that the task of delineating the theme or narrated materials against the relentless pursuits of the problematic postulates was incumbent upon a *Preface*, a *Dedication*, a descriptive exposition of the cycles of narration, or even upon isolated narrations. In that sense the antinomy between *theory* (or *program* strictly speaking) and *practice* can be located in the disagreement between *proemium* and *narratio*. On the other hand, when we are dealing with a series of novellas with a frame, the antinomy can be situated not in the opposition *preface/narration* but in the opposition *frame/narrations*.

There is no general law that could apply in all instances. It cannot be said that the *frame* exists in view of the antinomy, among other reasons because at times the *frame* does not imply any incongruity or antinomy. We are referring to the so-called *generic narrative frame*—such as, for example, the story of the sultan and his young wife who seeks to escape death in *The Thousand and One Nights*, or the plague in Boccaccio's *Decameron*, or the relation between master and servant in Don Juan Manuel's *Conde Lucanor*—which in some instances does not exist (we are thinking of Cervantes's *Novelas ejemplares*) even though the antinomy, in terms of Pabst's postulates, is retained.

The undertakings of Italian and French Renaissance theoreticians to revitalize and maintain the aesthetic orientations inherited from the Greco-Latin classics had in fact a secular tradition. The laws that governed literary genres and the consequent norms of poetic art rose to the category of unquestionable authority during the Renaissance. One need only look at Marcelino Menéndez y Pelayo's *Historia de las ideas estéticas en España* to see the extent of the presence of Aristotle and Horace in the theoretical apparatus of the sixteenth and seventeenth centuries. Since there was a sense that the doctrines of Aristotle and Horace contained the working recipes of the poets of antiquity—and in the Spanish Golden Age the imitation of the ancients was the highest aim—the drive to theorize became paramount.

As we mentioned earlier, writers did not easily follow those precepts. In his *Estetica come scienza dell'espressione e linguistica generale*, Benedetto Croce cites the case of Giambattista Marino, who, in a letter to Girolano Petri, affirmed with lucidity:

> I propose to know the rules better than all of the pedants together; but the true rule is knowing how to break rules in time and place, accommodating oneself to the common custom and to the taste of the time. (Cited by Pabst 1972: 14, n. 6)[1]

As far as the novel is concerned—a genre unknown to Aristotle—many of the elements learned from Horace or Scaliger were considered Aristotelian. Such was the case with the law of moral utility, which the seventeenth-century poet Scarron admired in the Spanish novella of the seventeenth century. The independence of Spain from a strict Aristotelianism was known since the seventeenth century, and Luzán's *Poética* attests to this fact.

In the first phase of this movement there had already been an attempt to extract the novel as a *modern narrative form* from the field where the doctrines inherited from antiquity were still in force, and there was an attempt (we are thinking for example of Giraldi Cinthio) to separate it from the precept of *unity of action*. In the long run, however, the novel could not escape other precepts: those dealing with the unities of *time* and *place* and, above all, the principle of *verisimilitude*.

The followers of dogmas paid attention only to the major genres such as tragedy, epic poetry, and so on, but their programs were also applied to what were then considered minor genres. In fact, it was practically impossible for writers of novellas to overlook such doctrines. Yet although the theories of great genres could be approached following well-developed treatises, the study of the novella implied going to the texts of the novellas themselves. As we indicated earlier, in the majority of cases, prefaces, introductions, and secondary stories have to be read as forms of programmatic exposition of a doctrine and, in a parallel way, as an indirect manner of attaching themselves to the *superior* value of those *great* genres that had been worthy of the attention of rhetoricians.

It is not clear that as a new genre the novella possessed from the beginning its own program, at least if one thinks of the Renaissance as a point of departure. There is, of course, the possibility of some antecedents that were not written or that have disappeared, of which the novella would be a logical continuation. Curtius (1957) cites an observation by Johann of Salisbury that seems to point to the existence of these stories as well as to their comic character. Also, in his *Novelas a Marcia Leonarda* Lope de Vega speaks of nonwritten narratives as antecedents of the genre that was then emerging.

We are interested here in pointing to two medieval "genres": the *exempla* and the *novas*, whose origins are religious and troubadour-esque, respectively. Both have in common a didactic function. The first reduced the general to each concrete case, and explained the importance and meaning of universals through a comparison with the exemplary or censurable conduct of the individual; the second was a vehicle for educating a troubadour's lady through stories that contained a moral. The didactic end anchored in narrative ended up displacing its center from exemplarity to pleasantness; the moralizing and the educational goals became secondary to the act of narration. It is understandable, therefore, that the novellas that emerged from these medieval forms would seek to dress themselves with a moralizing garb, since within a tradition of a fundamentally Christian sign such as the Occidental, the criteria for judging stories related to whether they were morally edifying or damaging to the receiver. This is one reason, among others, why the double function "narrative material"/"didactic horizon" continues and forms the basis of the existing genre. At the same time it also explains why these stories are made into narratives that are fictionally truthful (one thinks, for example, of Ginés de Pasamonte's reflection on *Lazarillo de Tormes* in *Don Quijote I*, 22). Generalizations were asserted through examples taken from real life so that proverbs and even plots acquired an exemplary, living content by the mere fact that they referred to contemporary or remembered people. In that manner the *novelle antiche* and the *lives of the troubadours*, while formally removed from the *ejemplos*, came close to them in view of their function.

The feigning of a biography confirmed by a verifiable historicity (we are thinking of María de Zayas y Sotomayor, for example) was a way of rebelling against the dictates of rhetoric. It is precisely in this area, in the relation between narrative structure and exterior reality—the latter understood as a complex system of norms of conduct, codes of reading, and so on—that the problem of the decadence of the Spanish novella of the seventeenth century is posed. In relation to Cervantes's model, moreover, it is done in the first and only case in which the genre as such functioned fully: Cervantes's *Novelas ejemplares*. That also explains why the term *novela* was in principle more closely related to the idea of news (*noticia*) and novelty (*novedad*) than to that of narration (narración). Also, the distinctions that are drawn today in literary history between genres did not then exist along clearly demarcated lines. Such is the case of the novella and the *comedia*, which are linked to the extent that Avellaneda refers to Cervantes's *Novelas ejemplares* as "prose comedies" (*comedias en prosa*). And it is not by chance that Cervantes's works culminate in dialogism. The discrediting of the comic witnessed in the Middle Ages would drag along everything that was connected to it. Such was precisely the case with the novella, which would arrive at the threshold of the Renaissance in traditional oral form.

When Cervantes published his *Novelas ejemplares* (1613), he wrote in his prologue:

> There is none [of the novellas] from which some fruitful example could not be extracted; and were it not for drawing out this subject I would, perhaps, show you [the reader] the delicious and honest fruit that could be gathered from all them together as well as from each one individually.[2]

The pedagogical intention that in Italy would probably have caused readers to turn away from the material, was utilized ambiguously in Spain. One could point to the repressive post-Tridentine period, but the fact remains that since the twelfth century the tradition of the *exemplum* in its original sense was more pervasive in Spain than in the rest of the romance-language world. We could mention the prologue to the thirty-four *exempla* contained in Pedro Alfonso's *Disciplina Clericalis* (ca. 1110), a prologue that underscores the markedly pedagogical character of the whole, a character that by any reckoning was not attained in the book. The antinomy between program and practice was already emerging at that time.

An important fact to keep in mind (pointed out by Pabst) is the particular nature of that antinomy in the Spanish case, where the opposition between *prologue* and *text* is less important than the association between the *prologue* and the censor's report. Spanish writers do not struggle so much against the impositions of a dogmatic, and largely sterile, aesthetic doctrine as against the censorship of the ecclesiastical authorities whose favor they seek to gain. That is, the antinomy is not established in the artistic sphere, but in the relationship between *art* and the *reality of everyday life*. For this reason the Spanish *ejemplo* and the Italian *novella* are not synonymous concepts. A simple comparison of the translations of Italian novellas with their respective originals shows the extensive transformation undergone by the latter. Along these lines W. Krauss, in "Novela, Novelle, Roman," cites the case of Torquemada who, in his *Coloquios satíricos*, talks about relating a story that was told to him as a child, and how, upon examining the *ejemplo* to which Torquemada refers, we see that it deals with the manipulation of a text by Boccaccio.

What signifies in a text is not the place where the text originated, but the function that it has in its new reality. It is not in Italy, therefore, where the origins of the Spanish novella must be sought, for the novella does not surface in Spain as a foreign import. Although it shares plots, themes, and even characters with the Italian novella, it is ultimately defined by its own historical specificity. Thus, *Il Cortegiano*'s theory of story appeared in Rodríguez Lobo and later in Cervantes and envisioned two types of narration: those that stressed the narrated story and those that focused on the gracefulness of the narration. The split into two types of narration, which in Castiglione was simply a double definition, was used by Menéndez y Pelayo to underscore what was authentic (*castizo*) in Lobo and later in Cervantes, since those that focused on the gracefulness of the narration supposedly originated in popular oral tradition. What Menéndez y Pelayo did not see, but what Spanish writers of novellas seemed to recognize, was that the hypothetical innate capacity of the common people to narrate is only a literary artifice, a pretext to make plausible the idea that the writer did not tell the stories, but merely repeated what everyone (that hypothetical *everyone* of the anonymous oral tradition) knew how to do. In that manner, the narration was like life itself, a faithful copy of what really occurred. It was therefore a way of producing *ejemplos* without being explicit. Cervantes himself laughs and implicitly criticizes Lope's *Novelas a Marcia Leonarda* when he alludes to the possibility that ordinary people could tell stories as evidenced by Sancho Panza's inability to follow a story line without stumbling and deviating from it (*Don Quijote I*, 20).

What made Spanish narrative authentic was its exemplary character rather than the existence of a narrativity that was autochthonous and peculiar to the Spanish soul (*castizo*). That is, originality was rooted in the objective history of a way of seeing reality that exposed the false exemplary character of the narrative. In fact, what makes Spanish narrative original is the specific worldview of Hapsburg Spain. But that reality is in *the text* and is part of its structure. The reality in the text defined the genre's originality in Spain, and this is precisely what the object of our analysis ought to be. Since this kind of inscription is changed throughout the history and development of the genre, one must locate within it the causes of its decline. Spain was indeed a different world—as Pabst himself argued—with its own social and political circumstances, its own customs, aesthetic-literary traditions, and people. But it also had its own traditions of reading. The novella incorporates the concrete, that is, the individual and personal existence of the reader, in its most immediate context.

The lack of existence of a defined concept of novella prior to the appearance of Cervantes's *Novelas ejemplares* usually converts Cervantes into a paradigm and point of departure for the study of this genre. If we assume the same here, it is for a different reason: we are now dealing with a block of novellas, encased within a larger structure or narrative frame. That frame can lean on a story, on a narrative (María de Zayas y Sotomayor's *Novelas amorosas y ejemplares*), on a prologue (Tirso de Molina's *Cigarrales de Toledo*), on the expressed will of the author—even if it is given as a false moral obligation to serve a lover's petition (Lope de Vega's *Novelas a Marcia Leonarda*), or on the manner of organizing materials (Cervantes's *Novelas ejemplares*). What we call narrative frame, therefore, is an element of structure that has its own signifying entity. What traditionally has been defined as "frame" is only one of the forms that it can adopt as a way to structure narrative. The relationship between the frame and the individual parts that comprise the global structure is at the heart of the problem of the novella as genre. It is in the frame as a form of relating the whole with the parts where Cervantes *invented* a genre, and it is there that one ought to look for the causes that led later novelists to allow the genre to elude them.

Some time ago, in a solid introduction to Spanish literature of the 1600s, Emilio Orozco Díaz (1970) touched in an illuminating way on the problem of narrative, opposing what he called mannerist to baroque structure. The first was said to be based on accumulation, with plurithematic and disintegrating features, and the second was seen as hinging on the existence of an integrating center capable of distributing hierarchically all of its elements within a homogeneous whole. Orozco points out that books of *miscelánea*, collections of stories, anecdotes, sayings, proverbs, and even books that gathered works of different genres with no relation to one another, had in common a predominance of the mannerist aesthetic. Orozco locates the predominance of mannerism in the second half of the sixteenth and beginning of the seventeenth century, a time when foreign works, especially those of the Italianate type, are adapted to Castilian. Thus, Melchor de Santa Cruz's *Floresta española* (1574), or Rufo's *Seiscientos apotegmas* (1596), shows an orientation toward orderliness rather than fusion. The same happens with Timoneda's *El Patrañuelo* (1567), the most direct antecedent, in a chronological sense, of the Cervantine adventure.

Against this mannerist model, the baroque structure—of which Cervantes's *Novelas ejemplares* and *Don Quijote II* are paradigmatic examples—integrates and confers unity to what is dispersed. What formerly was merely juxtaposed is now transformed into an organic whole. If Cervantes's invention of the modern novel is to be found in this area (let us not forget that *Don Quijote II* represents a culmination of the method that was initiated in the *Novelas ejemplares*), one might ask how it is possible that baroque writers of novellas (we are thinking of María de Zayas y Sotomayor, Alonso de Castillo Solórzano, Gonzalo de Céspedes y Meneses, Mariana de Carvajal) represent a step backward. This question cannot be answered simply by pointing to Cervantes's genius, but must be posed instead in terms of the problem of integration: how are the various elements integrated? Around what axis? What role does this axis play within what we earlier called antinomy—not between program and practice, but between writing and reality? As we have indicated from the beginning of this chapter, the fundamental problem stems from the antinomy that opposes literature and reality or, better still, two distinct forms (*metaphorical* and *symbolic*) of integration of reality in literature.

Cervantes's *Novelas ejemplares* have been the object of intense study among Hispanists, so much so that both the volume and the quality of such criticism have begun to rival what is written on *Don Quijote*. This is not surprising, for it is becoming increasingly evident that those same "modern" or experimental designs observable in *Don Quijote* can also be extrapolated from a reading of Cervantes's *Novelas*, most especially, though not exclusively, from *El casamiento engañoso/El coloquio de los perros*.

In this central part of our essay we also intend to examine how the notion of "exemplarity" is invoked and how it is displaced from the strictly conventional realm of the ethical (where an author assumes the responsibility for conveying a conventional moral lesson), to one in which the reader plays a central role in the construction of meaning. We believe that in this context the gaps and silences of the *Novelas* can be filled most productively through the act of reading (see Iser, Macherey, and Talens and Company). Our contention is that by moving away from the traditional notions of exemplarity one can enter Cervantes's novelistic world, a universe that highlights the problem of language and communication, one that manages to register the cleavage between words and things while directing one's attention to the relation between word and self (Forcione 1984: 188–190).

In this respect, the Prologue to Cervantes's *Novelas ejemplares* stakes out a strong claim for the semiautonomy of the text, which, nurtured by the technology of printing, is now accessible to a reading public that is becoming increasingly differentiated:

> For I am the first to have novelized in the Castilian language, for the many novellas that are printed in it are all translated from foreign tongues, but these are my own, neither imitated nor stolen; my mind conceived them, and my pen gave birth to them, and *they are growing up in the arms of printing*. (Emphasis added)[3]

Cervantes does away with the power exercised by traditional models in the reading process by renouncing the private property of the signifieds—what is said or told. In so doing he destabilizes the canonical interpretation and exposes its rhetorical character. Werner Krauss (1940) believes that the essential characteristic of Cervantes's art stems from the voluntary renunciation of the contents of relation prevailing in his society. Those contents were largely Italianate. To some degree Krauss's thesis had been advanced by Menéndez y Pelayo in his *Orígenes de la novela*, where he showed that Boccaccio's influence on Cervantes was not overly important. This thesis was also subscribed to by Emilio Alarcos García (1950) and Gonzalo de Amezúa y Mayo (1956–1958).

Because Cervantes is not simply engaged in breaking a rhetorical relation, but approaches the palpable, "real" problem of the implications of such a relation—the problem of the relationship between art and reality—it may be worthwhile to consider this issue briefly.

Amezúa y Mayo pointed to five characteristics that distinguish Cervantes from the Italian tradition:

a. amplification and expansion of the limits of the story;

b. nationalization of plots and characters (the exceptions are *El amante liberal* and *La señora Cornelia*);

c. the importance given to dialogue;

d. the attempt to moralize;

e. the elimination of the supernatural and the marvelous.

Leaving aside the formal classification of Cervantes's twelve exemplary novellas, it is clear that they have a common unifying element: characters are propelled by an unknown force over and above the ideal base of the character's own being. That base is a state of calm and equilibrium, the country (*la patria*). Characters go through a blundering, incessant search, finding order in their return to the base rather than in the spaces that they traverse.

The Italian *novellieri* strove for the final denouement, but Cervantes's ending needed to be simultaneously a place to stop, a place to rest, and a point of arrival [Lucas Gracián Dantisco, *Galateo español* (1599); cited by Menéndez y Pelayo, *Orígenes de la novela*]. The structure of the *Novelas ejemplares* is thus undermined by the pull between the anxiety and restlessness of the route and the world of order to which that route leads. The roads traveled by the protagonists usually crisscross (on some occasions they are even cut), and only at the end of the novella do they take a parallel or convergent course to flow into a *common stopping place*. This can be seen even in *El celoso extremeño*, where the young wife's withdrawal from the world and the death of her jealous old husband symbolize for the first time a spiritual attitude that is common to both. This type of symmetry is also evident in other novellas. One thinks of the dissimulation and cunning of the lovers in *La gitanilla* and *La ilustre fregona*; or how Cornelia's bad action is balanced by the uneven marriage of the duke.

Neither marriage nor passion is the central element that instigates the amorous passion that may spring from other motives, such as a felony (*El casamiento engañoso*), an accident (*El Licenciado Vidriera*), destiny (*El coloquio de los perros*), and so on. Moreover, the restoration of order in the novellas does not occur through the elimination of these motives, but through a complex link of circumstances that often lack plausibility (because of the lack of evolution of the protagonist as a supporting element in the development of the action) and show the presence of a governing, all-powerful and invisible hand—what might be called destiny or providence. While some elements turn out to be plausible from a human and novelistic standpoint, their accumulation or "casual" concentration on a decisive point demonstrates that for Cervantes an individual is responsible for his or her conflicts. This common thread runs through many of Cervantes's novellas and culminates in *El coloquio de los perros*.

The nonverisimilar aspect of the *Novelas ejemplares* (José Ortega y Gasset, 1914 and 1922) is not a casual trait but an artistic proposal, a conscious way of showing *exemplarity*, on the one hand, as a conviction that the individual's conflict is of his or her own doing, and, on the other hand, as a discursive procedure used to define. As Casalduero saw years ago (1974) the *Novelas'* recurring motifs reinforce the unifying character and flow ultimately into a common stopping place: *El coloquio de los perros*, a novella that may be seen as the end of a thread formed by Novelas 3, 7, and 11 (*Rinconete y Cortadillo, El celoso extremeño*, and *El casamiento engañoso*, respectively) where realistic elements are intercalated among the other, nonverisimilar ones. *El coloquio* manages to unify both lines: (a) what is not verisimilar (a dog that speaks), and (b) the realistic character of what is narrated, thus distancing the novel by having it surface ambiguously from the ensign Campuzano's dream. *El coloquio*, therefore, serves as a frame and, at the same time, as a satirical unmasking—through the distancing that comes from the first glance of Berganza as well as from the ironic commentaries of his interlocutor Cipión—of a multicolored world of gypsies, aristocrats, students, and so on, who appear in a fragmented manner. Their world comprises only parcels of a reality, but that reality appears in *El coloquio* in a global way, as Berganza does not simply speak of one case but of human reality as a whole.

The Problem of Exemplarity

The notion of exemplarity inscribed (and gathered by the reader) in Cervantes's novellas would seem to be tied to two interrelated factors: a new way of writing fiction in the Castilian language and the idea that meaning ultimately depends on the role assumed by the reader in its construction:

> If you [reader] look at it carefully, you will see that there is none [of the novellas] from which some fruitful example could not be gained.[4]

The burden of shaping or harvesting the "provecho" is placed on the discerning eye ("bien mirar") of the receiver whose imagination becomes the very instrument for turning an activity—reading—that was traditionally associated with idleness, leisure, and passivity into a productive enterprise connected to an exploration of the self in the world.

Today, at the present juncture in literary studies, when the reader has gained what amounts to a new privileged status as a producer of meaning, the exemplarity of Cervantes's novellas cannot be seen exclusively in traditional ethical terms. Let us examine this issue.

Even a cursory reading of what is probably Cervantes's most sophisticated novella—*El casamiento engañoso/El coloquio de los perros*—provides a window into exemplarity as a play of perspectives; exemplarity of an aesthetic or artistic kind, and of a sociological kind. Thus one sees that as in *Don Quijote*, the *Coloquio*'s fictionalization of linguistic problems allows one to witness the drama of the "decentering" of language; the turning away from absolute authority and the consequent opening of a greater interpretative space for the reader. Such a drama has been perceptively diagnosed by Forcione (1984), who views it as the reflection of "a radical alteration in man's linguistic consciousness," while pointing out that "in its background we can detect the affirmative attitudes toward the plurality of languages working the most innovative of the humanist writings on the subject" (193).

The *Coloquio*'s exemplarity, then, is tied instead to the problem of language, an issue that is dealt with in terms of major traditions of humanist thought (Forcione 1984: 195). At the same time, it is important to keep in mind that the play of perspectives in the *Coloquio* is less a formalistic game than a reaffirmation of the value of linguistic fragmentation (Forcione 1984: 188–190). Such a value implies that the relation between word and thing is no longer as important as the relation between word and self. Everywhere, says Forcione, attention is drawn to the "destructive powers in language"; to the potential of words to conceal, deceive, and perpetrate violence. We would add here that Cervantes's texts dramatize what has been called the economy of linguistic exchanges, which compels one to go beyond the linguistic properties of discourse to discover its performative aspects (Bourdieu 1982).

In the *Coloquio*, Berganza and Cipión are observed in their role as speakers and readers who are struggling with the ambiguities of their text. Berganza is charged by his companion dog, Cipión, with telling his own story first, which he proceeds to recount in linear fashion, following the model of picaresque, autobiographic "Lives." But the dialogue with the conventions of those narratives begins immediately as Cipión, one of several listeners or "readers" of Berganza's account (a story invented or recorded by the ensign Campuzano, the protagonist of the frame novella *El casamiento engañoso*), stakes out his own position in the communicative process: he will not be content to listen passively to Berganza's representation of his own life. Instead, as a listener or "reader" he intervenes actively in the dialogue, thus producing systematically his own version of his friend's story; his own interpretation.

Cipión has a theory of what a good story ought to sound like and judges Berganza's tale according to his own evaluative system. He also reminds Berganza that, on aesthetic grounds, he himself practices what he preaches:

> And I should like to tell you something that you will see in practice
> when I will relate to you the happenings of my life; and it is that some
> stories hold and contain charm within themselves; others in the manner
> in which they are told. What I mean to say is that some are pleasing
> even if they are told without preambles and flowery words, while others
> need to be dressed up in words; and with gestures of face and hands and
> a change of voice there is something made out of nothing so that stories
> that were loose and faint become sharp and pleasurable.[5]

In Cipión's neo-Aristotelian scheme, stories are divided into two categories: those that are self-contained or envelop properties that please ("dan contento") in and of themselves, and those that need to be charged with kinetic signs by the storyteller. What emerges at this stage of the *Coloquio* is that Cipión judges his companion's story negatively. His view of art does not admit disorderly digressions, long-winded moralizing, or philosophizing of any kind. His dogmatism blinds him to the possibility that such wanderings "are not the result of [Berganza's] lack of capacity to narrate but an intrinsic necessity to produce a discourse on the world" (Nerlich 1988: 93–94). Significantly, such a discourse is framed in a manner that sets it apart from other categories or types of texts that were in vogue during Cervantes's time. Thus, against the monologic structure of picaresque narratives—especially the kind whose archetype is *Guzmán de Alfarache* (1599, 1604)— where an attempt is made to totalize experience for the reader, the *Coloquio* registers the impossibility of such a totalization as a plurality of voices surface *within the text* to focus on the uncertainty of language and on the fragmentary nature of reading and writing. A recurring issue in the *Casamiento/Coloquio* is the propriety of language in relation to its use by speaker(s). At the end of the *Casamiento*, for example, Peralta, the friend to whom Campuzano has entrusted the reading of *El coloquio de los perros*, says to the ensign:

> Although this dialogue may be feigned and may never have transpired, it seems to be so well composed that Sir Ensign may proceed with the second [Cipión's story].[6]

The reference to the "feigned" (*fingido*) character of the *Coloquio* relates directly to the problem of verisimilitude, which, ultimately, in Cervantes is connected not only to the "attitude of the narrator" (El Saffar 1976: 21) but also with the experience and expectations of readers (Spadaccini, "Writing for Reading" 1986). Thus, the reader Peralta is less concerned with whether or not such a dialogue could have transpired in the world outside of the text than with its poetic truth and beauty of composition. One might argue, therefore, that Peralta is not the kind of reader who "would reject any fiction that was untrue to the facts of the material world" (El Saffar 1976: 20), but a critic who measures the story that he has just read against an interpretative model of the verisimilar that is grounded in Plato and Aristotle. That model also views the verisimilar as "the agreement of a particular text with that general and diffuse other text that one calls public opinion" (Genette 1968: 3; our translation).

In Cervantes's *Novelas ejemplares*, as in *Don Quijote*, questions of theory as well as other issues are dealt with fragmentarily within a complex range of narrative voices and shifting perspectives. One of the results of such a fragmentation is that readers—within and outside of the text—are compelled to assess and, perhaps, redefine experience as they go on discovering that perceptions are generally shaky and unstable (Forcione 1984: 173). Moreover, a recurring lesson of the *Casamiento/Coloquio* seems to be that language is an instrument with a potential for deception (*engaño*), a tool that, in the hands of evildoers, can perpetrate dislocation and violence.

Within this context, reading as a critical act becomes paramount (Scholes 1985). If language has the potential for deception, that potential is only realized to the extent that the reader is unable to decode the signs that language projects. Ultimately a "reader-critic" has the capacity to go beyond the simple linguistic properties of discourse to discover that those properties "announce the authority and social competence of speakers" (Bourdieu 1982: 65; our translation).

The issue of authority and competence of speakers and listeners (of narrators and narratees) is at the heart of the problem of communication dramatized in the *Coloquio*. The ongoing dialogue between Berganza and Cipión deals with such an issue as their bartering revolves around the emblem of an octopus with its many arms. Cipión as listener or "reader" of Berganza's text constantly questions the latter's storytelling skills, his inability to focus on the main threads of his story and bring it to conclusion without first entering into gossip and self-serving interpretations. Cipión questions Berganza's authority as storyteller to the extent that his use of language for moralizing purposes—his constant assumptions about the intentions and moral values of others—gets in the way of a carefully crafted and pleasure-inducing narrative. To Berganza's self-serving circumlocutions and resistance to operate within established, that is, neo-Aristotelian narrative norms, Cipión attempts to provide a corrective:

> What I mean is for you to stick to it [your story] and not make it seem like an octopus with all the tails you keep adding to it.[7]

That corrective is nothing less than an attempt to draw qualitative distinctions between different kinds of discourses or domains of thought (Nerlich 1988: 92); it is, ultimately, an attempt to censor the production of a new kind of text that, to follow Ricardou's definition of literary modernity, is "less the writing of an adventure than the adventure of a writing" (see Nerlich 1988: 83–89). Such an adventure also envelops the reader of the *Casamiento/Coloquio*.

Clearly, the reader-critic brings to the reception of stories his or her own horizon of expectations while interpretations are at least partially shaped by the conventions used in reading and by the assumptions made about those conventions (see Wallace Martin 1987: 161). Thus, within the text of the *Coloquio* and its frame novella (*El casamiento engañoso*) we witness Peralta's critical, that is, literary, reading of *El coloquio de los perros*—a reading that reaches beyond the directional comments of the ensign Campuzano. We also listen to Cipión's dogmatic assessment of Berganza's convoluted tale; to Berganza's criticism of Cipión's own inability to practice what he preaches; and, of course, to Berganza's own interpretation of Cañizares's tale of witchcraft and deception. In all instances there is a recurring lesson: that things are not always what they seem to be, that communication is problematic as long as speakers and listeners are not aware of their respective positions of authority and competence in the production/reception of discourse.

An analysis of Cervantes's novellas, and most especially of the *Casamiento/Coloquio*, shows that exemplarity is to be sought in the pragmatic effect on the reader who must cope with the fragmentary nature of language (and communication) and the discovery that the connection between words and things is illusory. What is remarkable is that although these lessons are drawn by readers in the text (Peralta, Berganza, Cipión, and, of course, Campuzano), only recently have they begun to be highlighted by professional critics. (In addition to the pioneering work of Carlos Blanco Aguinaga, there are now a number of excellent studies that have focused on the many innovative or experimental features of Cervantes's *Novelas ejemplares*. One thinks especially of Alban Forcione and Ruth El Saffar, among others.)

Let us follow the main threads of our line of argumentation through a reading of *El coloquio de los perros* and its frame novella, *El casamiento engañoso*. In the process of doing so, we might keep in mind that the text contains gaps and silences, conflicts and contradictions, which shift to the reader-critic the obligation of investing it with meaning. In this sense, Cervantes's texts are always "de-centered" and succeeding generations and types of readers are presented with the challenge of making them speak. Therein resides the most important aspect of their exemplarity.

The *Casamiento engañoso* functions as a frame for the *Coloquio* and is, therefore, part of its structure of meaning. The reader enters the world of the *Coloquio* through a series of filters, the first of which is provided by Campuzano, a soldier who recounts to an old friend, the licentiate Peralta, how, in seeking to arrive at a profitable marriage through deception, he is left instead deceived and with a bad case of venereal disease. The stage for their exchange is set by an omniscient narrator who tells us that the two friends meet as Campuzano leaves the Hospital of the Resurrection in the city of Valladolid, where he most likely has spent some twenty days sweating out his diseased humors.

The initial exchange between the soldier and the licentiate centers on Campuzano's physical appearance and on the reasons for his predicament. Thus, to Peralta's query about his sickly complexion ["What is such color and such frailty due to?" ("¿Qué color, qué flaqueza es esa?")], Campuzano's answer is both forthright and titillating:

> From sweating out fourteen loads of buboes that were laid on me by a woman I chose for mine and should not have.[8]

When the listener Peralta begins to inquire about Campuzano's marital status ["Well then, did you get married?" ("¿Luego casóse vuesa merced?")] and speculates on the reasons for his unhappy outcome ["it must have been for love, and such marriages bring with them the execution of repentance" ("sería por amores, y tales casamientos traen consigo aparejada la ejecución del arrepentimiento")], Campuzano's magical powers as storyteller and his artistry as a creator of fictions come to light:

> For, since I am not in condition to have long discussions in the street, you must excuse me sir; that another day, with more comfort I shall give you an account of my happenings, which are the newest and most unusual that you must have heard in all the days of your life.[9]

Campuzano's apparent reticence in going on with his story until another day and in another space serves to awaken his listener's curiosity. He not only manages to captivate Peralta with the promise of novelty but, more important, he awakens in him a desire, a yearning of entering the world of his imagination and dreams. Such is precisely what happens when Campuzano gingerly introduces the idea that he has other, more interesting and unbelievable stories to tell, stories that stretch the limits of plausibility:

> Other happenings are left for me to relate that exceed all imagination for they go beyond the limits of nature . . . In the hospital I saw what I will now recount, which is what you will neither now nor ever be able to believe, nor will there be any person in the world who would believe it.[10]

The story of Campuzano's own deceitful marriage is thus a (pre)text for that other, more elaborate story—the *Coloquio*—whose reading is, according to the narrator, undertaken by Peralta in order to mock it while the licentiate also admits to the ensign that he has thoroughly enjoyed it because of its inventiveness and artful composition. The *Coloquio* is, therefore, a story within a story; a tale "written" by an imaginative soldier after having "listened" to it while in a state of stupor. Framed by the *Casamiento engañoso*, the *Coloquio* proceeds to incorporate two other autobiographical tales, the story of the dog Berganza and that of the witch Cañizares. The "Life" of Berganza in particular connects the reader-critic with picaresque narratives and above all with the manner in which Cervantes distances himself from them. For, unlike the norm in traditional picaresque fiction, these autobiographical accounts are themselves modified by the interventions of readers or listeners within the text; by a series of filters that bypass the customary and predictable dialectical relationship that is common between the narrators of picaresque tales and the readers of their life stories (see Rey Hazas 1983: 126+; Blanco Aguinaga 1957).

The *Coloquio* is organized around eleven interrelated episodes with two major clusters revolving around the central episodes of the drummer and the witch, respectively, who, "at the center of that world show how deception and greed operate both consciously (the drummer) and unconsciously (the witch) to undermine spiritual values" (El Saffar 1976: 39–40). Berganza's discourse on the world, his report to Cipión, goes beyond the boundaries originally set by the latter ["tonight you tell me the story of your life and the steps by which you have reached the point where you now find yourself" ("que esta noche me cuentes tu vida y los trances por donde has venido al punto en que ahora te hallas" 301)] to philosophize about, and provide an assessment of, a whole range of issues: social, spiritual, political, and literary. While Berganza's discourses are wide-ranging, in the "oral" style of a dialogue, and to some extent directed or redirected by the interlocutor Cipión, they are always permeated by an awareness of the power of language and the necessity of exercising that power through speech:

> Brother Cipión, may Heaven grant you everything your heart desires if you will just let me philosophize a little without taking it amiss; for if I omit saying the things that happened then which just this moment came to my mind, it seems to me that my story would be incomplete and of little profit. (18–19)[11]

If Berganza asks Cipión's indulgence in allowing him to philosophize, it is because without the latter's participation in the communicative process he would be reduced to virtual silence. That is, speaker and listener are mutually dependent, so that Berganza's text is not complete without Cipión's active intervention in its construction. Speaker and listener are both invested with authority.

In line with traditional picaresque narratives, Berganza begins his story with an account of his genealogy—he was born of mastiffs in the lowly world of the slaughterhouse of Seville—and proceeds to comment on the moral qualities of his master—a butcher called Nicolás el Romo (Flat-Nosed Nicholas)—and the depraved environment in which he moved. His master thinks nothing of killing and stealing, and enlists him (then called Gavilán) in ferrying stolen meat to his mistress. Berganza recalls how he stayed with this first master until the day when a beautiful lady stole the meat that he was carrying in a basket to the mistress's house. Fearing for his life, he moves on to the countryside where he comes upon a flock of sheep and rams and is taken in by shepherds. In their service, and known now as the dog Barcino, he experiences a profound disillusionment as he discovers that these shepherds and their lowly life-styles have no connection with the aristocratic and refined shepherds of the pastoral books that had captivated his imagination and that of a large reading public:

> They [the shepherds] spent most of the day picking fleas off themselves. . . . All of which convinced me of what all should realize: that those [pastoral] books are thought up and designed for the entertainment of idlers, and there is not a word of truth in them. (10)[12]

The shepherds he serves are common thieves who use their office in order to butcher sheep and steal their meat; they are "wolves" disguised as shepherds:

> I saw two shepherds take hold of one of the best rams of the flock and kill it in such a way that the following morning it really seemed as though the wolf had been its executioner. I was amazed and confounded when I saw that the shepherds were the wolves and that the very ones who were supposed to watch over the flock were destroying it.[13]

Here Berganza not only gives the reader a glimpse into his former state of dejection, but also alludes to the reasons for such pessimism: he had no power to remedy the observed transgressions, he had no way of making them known. In short, he lacked the power of the word:

> All this filled me with wonder and distress. "God help us," I said to myself, "and who can remedy this evil? Who has the *power to make it known* that the defenders are the offenders, that the sentinels sleep, that the trusted steal and those who should protect kill?" (12; emphasis added)[14]

If words can deceive, conceal, and oppress, silence too can be an accomplice to evil so that those who have the word, who are invested

with the gift of speech and the authority to speak, have the responsibility to awaken consciences and, if need be, raise their voices in the
wilderness. Berganza's philosophizing, then, cannot be taken as digressions but is, instead, part of a larger narrative, one that resists the
narrow parameters of the neo-Aristotelian model that Cipión had tried
to impose.

The reading of the *Casamiento/Coloquio* is indeed an adventure that
entails the discovery of the rhetorical structure of our perceptions of
reality; an exciting encounter with a world constructed out of a con-
fluence of discourses through the "magical" tricks of language. Those
discourses fall within the realm of the moral, social, political, and literary, and encompass a whole range of topics: the practice of good
and evil, the social playing out of illusion/disillusion (*engaño-desen-
gaño*), the seamy side of city life, the constraints and brutality of the
rural world, the escapism of pastoral books, the limitations and re-
petitiveness of picaresque literature, the values of well-to-do merchants, the role of the Jesuits in the education of certain social groups,
the corruption of some individuals who administer justice, the dis-
honesty of some bureaucrats and the honesty of others, the craftiness
of those who live through unproductive activities, the power of sorcery
and witchcraft, the marginality of social groups such as gypsies and
moriscos, the resourcefulness of theatrical troupes, and the foolish ways
of certain types such as bad poets, alchemists, mad mathematicians,
wacky political advisers, and so on. To eliminate Berganza's philosophizing on these issues is to strip Berganza of his voice; it would be
tantamount to putting an end to his and the reader's adventure. Cipión
understands as much at some point in the dialogue, for, commencing
with the sixth episode or the story of Cañizares, he begins to intervene
more sparingly in his companion's narrative and, in fact, agreements
between the two become common. In short, there is a shift in the
attitude of Cipión, who becomes less dogmatic and more flexible, more
attuned to his companion's discourses on the world. Similarly, Berganza begins to display a more accommodating attitude toward the
preoccupations of his interlocutor, realizing as well that narrative is
also limited by consideration of time and space:

> BERGANZA: Oh, Cipión, if only I could tell you all I saw in this and two
> other companies I joined up with! But as it is impossible to encompass it
> in a brief, succinct narration, I'll have to leave it for another day, suppos-
> ing that there will be another day in which we can converse. You see
> how long my tale has been? You see the many and diverse incidents? Do
> you realize how many roads I have traveled, how many masters I have
> had? Well, what you have heard is nothing compared with what I could

tell you of all that I observed, learned, and saw among these people, their behavior, the life they led, their habits, their pastimes, their work, their laziness, their ignorance, their sharp-wittedness, and an infinite number of other things, some to be whispered in the ear, others to be bruited aloud, and all to be engraved on the memory to disabuse the many who worship feigned shapes and beauties of artifice and illusion.

CIPIÓN: I can see clearly, Berganza, the vast horizon that stretches before you to prolong your narration, and it is my opinion that you should leave it to be told on another occasion with more leisure. (55–56)[15]

Cipión has come a long way from that authoritarian moment when he likened Berganza's story to an octopus and explained to him that philosophy is love of knowledge rather than pernicious gossip. From that moment of tension, when communication was on the verge of breaking down, we see the progressive affirmation of Berganza's discourses on the world, discourses that acquire increasing coherence as readers—within and outside of the text—are challenged to question the neo-Aristotelian conventions used in reading and—to follow Ricardou's definition of literary modernity—to focus less on the writing of an adventure than on the adventure of a writing. The adventure of Berganza's writing is connected to making things known by engaging the reader in moral, social, political, and literary issues. Since we have commented on some of the early episodes of the novella, let us now turn to other parts of the story in order to focus on some of those other discourses.

When Berganza reminisces about his experiences and observations at the service of the drummer and his company of marauding ruffians, he ventures a comment that, far from being a frivolous digression, connects with a larger social-political discourse, one that had engaged *arbitristas*, moralists, and literary figures in the early 1600s:

My master [says Berganza] was in clover with all he took in, and supported six comrades in kingly fashion. Greed and envy aroused in the ruffians the idea of stealing me, and they waited for an opportunity, for this business of earning one's living without turning a hand has many addicts and admirers. That is why there are so many jugglers in Spain, so many puppeteers, so many sellers of pins and ballads whose entire stock, even if they sold it all, would not keep them for a day . . . All these people are lazy, worthless, wastrels, wine sponges and bread weevils. (34)[16]

We know of the resistance to manual labor in the Spain of Cervantes, of problems of unemployment and underemployment, of the perceptions of crisis and instability on the part of intellectuals and politicians, of the various diagnoses of the problems at hand, of proposals to remedy them, and so on. We know of the pessimism implied in González de Cellorigo's reflection that Spain is "a republic of enchanted men who live outside of the natural order of things" ("una república de hombres encantados que vivan fuera del orden natural"); or Sancho de Moncada's assertion that Spain is a backward country and that Spaniards are "the Indians of Europe." It is also common knowledge that some of these liberal *arbitristas* saw part of the remedy to the crisis in the export of manufactured goods and in the training of people to assume productive jobs.

Berganza's discourse, then, is hardly an aside and, when read in conjunction with his comments on the driving ambition of merchants who display status and station in their children, whom they regale with the best that a Jesuit education has to offer, or when read in conjunction with his comments on the practices of some minorities in Spain—specifically gypsies and *moriscos*, the reader is challenged into adopting a position on the issues. Thus, for example, after Berganza comments on how he stayed in a fruit farm in Granada at the service of a descendant of the Moors for over a month "not because my life was so pleasant, but for the sake of learning about that of my master, and through it, that of all the Moriscos of Spain" ("no por el gusto de la vida que tenía, sino por el que me daba saber la de mi amo, y por ella la de todos cuantos moriscos viven en España" 349) and after talking about how the "moorish rabble" was fond of hoarding money, of not spending any of it, not even on the education of their children, and of multiplying and thus endangering the very patrimony of Spain, Cipión is no longer concerned about digressions as he enters into a biting sociopolitical commentary:

> CIPIÓN: A remedy is being sought for all the evils you have mentioned and touched upon. I know very well that those you have not listed exceed those you have set forth, and as yet the necessary solution has not been found. But our republic has wise guardians who, knowing that Spain breeds and has in its bosom as many vipers as there are Moriscos, will, with the help of God, find sure, swift and certain relief from such harm. Go on. (51–52)[17]

These commentaries are charged with irony and it is up to the reader-critic to connect them to the adventure of a writing through his or her discerning eye or "bien mirar"; it is the reader who must harvest some kind of profit or "provecho" through reading, interpreting, and criticizing. The power of the word is ultimately measured in its effect on the receiver. For the reader-critic the task is to "complete" the text:

to reconcile its conflicting strands and disparate meanings, understanding with Macherey that "it is in the significant *silences* of a text, in its gaps and absences that the presence of ideology can be most positively felt" (cited by Eagleton 1976: 34–35; emphasis in the original).

As the *Coloquio* draws to a close, the whole issue of authority and social competence of speakers is brought to the foreground. It is not sufficient—we are told—to raise one's voice and to bring forth coherent phrases, for language operates within a social, economic, and political context:

> The advice of the poor [says Cipión] however good it may be, is never taken into account, nor should the humble have the presumption to advise the mighty . . . The wisdom of the poor is beshadowed, for need and poverty are the dark clouds that shadow it, and if perchance it reveals itself, it is regarded as nonsense and treated with contempt.[18]

If the *Coloquio* ends on an apparent note of pessimism and resignation as the interlocutors believe that nothing can change the social structure and that their dialogue has fallen on deaf ears, the reader knows otherwise: that their words have been heard and transcribed for the world outside of literature. So it is that "when the unnamed narrator intervenes and Campuzano wakes up . . . we realize that the very act of reading the story has released the dogs from their solitude and estrangement and that we have participated in their liberation" (El Saffar 1976: 83).

El coloquio de los perros as Narrative Frame

El coloquio is clearly important as an isolated work, but it acquires its full significance only upon gathering the themes previously introduced in the other *Novelas ejemplares* and readdressing them from a realistic perspective. To elaborate his stories Cervantes sought out the fantastic and the marvelous, elements that were to play a role similar to that of the narrative frame in Boccaccio: distancing the narrated from reality. Yet there was a fundamental difference between Boccaccio and Cervantes: whereas in Boccaccio reality appears reflected in the framed stories and the frame serves as a distancing element, in Cervantes the realistic stems from the frame. The distancing that results from it is, therefore, of the reverse order: not from reality to fiction but from fiction to reality.

The Italian narrative frame played a role that was fundamentally literary, but in Cervantes the frame dealt with the relationship between art and reality. In Cervantes the narrative frame is not rhetorical but has instead an explicitly signifying functionality. In this sense the frame is a way of inscribing the conception of the world of the individual who produces the text through narration. The narrative frame resides, thus, in that "extra text" that, through its dialectical relationship with the text, produces the space of narrative production as such, that is, the reality in which the writer Miguel de Cervantes is integrated as a writer and from which his writing stems. This explains why the syntactic *parataxis* is in fact a semantic *hypotaxis* and why the structure of the *Novelas ejemplares* is baroque rather than mannerist. In this sense the novellas are a first step toward the total organizational integration that one finds in *Don Quijote II* (1615), which introduces within the narration of the life of Don Quijote not only the adventures narrated in *Don Quijote I* (1605), but also the real existence of Avellaneda, the writer who published an apocryphal biography of the Knight of La Mancha. The two characteristics mentioned—an integrating frame (implicit and exterior) and the inversion of the Boccaccio model—distinguish Cervantes from other writers of novellas in his own time. Let us touch upon the respective cases of Lope de Vega and María de Zayas y Sotomayor (Talens 1977).

The first characteristic is not understood by Lope de Vega, for although using nonverisimilar elements in his novellas and distancing himself in the frame, he locates this new frame not in the relation literature/reality but in a space that is, properly speaking, literary. The matter thus refers to the dichotomy art/aesthetic theory, that is, to individualized production/rules for production. As a result, in Lope de Vega the idea of "truthful happenings" ("sucesos verdaderos") is but another of the many literary topics that plague his texts. It is not by chance then that what characterizes the Cervantes of the *Novelas ejemplares* is an individual's disillusionment (*desengaño*) toward life while the Lope of the *Novelas a Marcia Leonarda* is characterized by a disconcerted feeling toward a literary genre to which he is not accustomed. Ultimately it is a question of art as *praxis*, as in Cervantes, versus art as a frivolous, stylistic exercise in Lope.

In the second characteristic, that is, in the inversion of the Boccaccio model, María de Zayas y Sotomayor could have tied in with Cervantes's proposal. Her *Novelas amorosas y ejemplares*, however, interweave realistic and nonverisimilar elements to such an extent that this reaches not only the frame but the framed narratives as well. As a result, the entire frame is marked by a literary (rhetorical) character, one that was earlier reinforced by the symbolic role of the last novella of the series—*El jardín engañoso*—narrated by Doña Laura.

What made the degeneration of the genre ever more palpable was the lack of understanding of the global nature of Cervantes's proposal on the part of his contemporaries and continuators. For, if it can be said that a novelist is someone who looks at life from the perspective of death, and that Cervantes is one who questions the implications of such a proposal, it can also be argued that the novella of Cervantes's contemporaries and continuators is the narration of reality without death. It is so because it was previously without life since it surfaced from a referent and with a function that were fundamentally literary in their alienating sense—an alienated relation with reality.

The erroneous understanding of the Cervantine practice has causes and reasons that are historically localizable. Just as the confrontation *culterano-conceptista* often hid problems of caste, of purity of blood (see André Collard), of struggle among social classes, the same occurs here. What was at stake was not a problem of styles or schools but the question of art and literature as tools of ideological control of a culture such as the baroque, which had to tackle the objective contradiction (even if it was not assumed as such) of pretending to be useful for the collectivity when in fact it was guided, produced, and *massified* by and for the benefit of the structures of institutionalized power.

A Guided Culture: Writing as Alienated Theatricality

In a fundamental book for the study of the Spanish 1600s, José Antonio Maravall defines the culture of the baroque as a guided culture:

> The culture of the baroque is an instrument to achieve effects (i.e., the product of a conception such as we have just articulated) whose object is to act upon human beings. Human beings are the object of a determinate conception (to which the culture must be conditioned) that is designed to ensure that they behave, among themselves and with respect to the society of which they are a part and the power that controls it, in such a manner that the societies' capacity for self-preservation is maintained and enhanced according to the way they appear structured under the political primacies in force at the moment. (*Culture of the Baroque* 58)

The implementation of a guided culture implies knowledge, on the practical level, of the human material upon which one would later act. From this comes the attempt to elaborate more than a human science, a technique to manipulate conduct. Of course this attempt to *guide*, to have things seen in a particular way, is not the exclusive domain of the society of the Hapsburgs. The very existence of the state presupposes the necessity to have people act in a controlled and controllable manner. If the political situation is one of crisis, this guidance (*dirigismo*) becomes all-powerful. Such is the case of absolutisms and dictatorships, and it is also the case of the Spanish 1600s. The *guidance* of conduct does not function as it did in the Middle Ages by the simple *presence* of the real, but through *action*. To the extent that truth in the Middle Ages was considered something that existed above and beyond man (even if one had access to it) it was enough to show it. Now, however, there was a need to *convince*. The disappearance of absolute truth as an immovable norm brought with it the possibility of having to elect among relative truths. This choice was in fact *ideological* since each truth was connected with the interests of the class or group that had produced it. Thus each group's tendency to attract from an ideological point of view the greatest possible number of sympathizers was due to the influence that each choice ultimately had on the political play of the contending forces. According to Giulio Carlo Argan (cited by Maravall, *Culture* 1986: 70), because "ideological persuasion can determine the shifting of the masses and compromise the equilibrium of political forces, such persuasion, whether religious or political, becomes an essential mode of the exercise of authority."

That *persuasion* manifested itself in various ways, depending on whether it dealt directly with apologetic or artistic texts. Here we are interested in how ideological persuasion is manifested in the latter; specifically, how it is channeled through the narrative formula of the novella.

Social culture may well have been constituted to keep people occupied and in a state of self-forgetfulness in order to have them obey norms alien to them, and it may be true that when people had free time they were urged to *entertain themselves* with games and diversions (Leo Löwenthal 1971), but it is also the case—following Maravall—that in baroque Spain the attempt on the part of the monarcho-seigneurial segments of society to exercise control encompassed the control of idle time:

> In conformity with this last observation [Leo Löwenthal's] let me add that in the seventeenth century—and in this the "enlighteners" of the eighteenth century differed very little—there was an attempt, in principle and beyond, to control the moments of leisure and all those moments in which a public or group of individuals could be placed in contact with a work, or better with a human creation, and feel in experiencing it a call to freedom. (Maravall, *Culture* 1986: 72)

In this scenario, literature and art in general would be linked to the maintenance of power.

From a rhetorical standpoint, one of the techniques used by art and literature to persuade was to implicate the reader/spectator in the work itself. Yet there is a fundamental difference between the kind of involvement proposed by a medieval writer such as Juan Ruiz, for example, and what is normally proposed within the framework of baroque culture: for the Archpriest of Hita it is a *real* collaboration between text and receiver within the *performance*, achieving its textuality in the pragmatic sphere, but in baroque culture the collaboration between text and receiver is illusory to the extent that the power of interpretation is "given" to the reader/spectator in order to make the manipulation (and the persuasion) more viable.

Talens (1978) has dealt with the problem of fictionality as a procedure of manipulation. The specificity of art—as a process of signifying production—resides in the manner in which a work already conceived and elaborated in a specific way is assumed as something that communicates connotatively through the use of the base elements, but when fiction exists, the only function of these base elements is to support its connotative use. A real history or a natural language used to narrate that real history through a conversation always refers to a reality that is exterior to both of them. Of course, if one approaches such a history as a literary text, what will make the discourse signify from a literary standpoint is not the language utilized but the *secondary* language constructed upon it. A reader who does not have access to the meaning of that language (because of a lack of knowledge of the corresponding codes) will always be left with the signifying level of the base elements (natural language). In this case, reading may be incomplete, but it is nevertheless useful. If, however, those elements refer not to reality but to a fiction, the reading will be absolutely useless, for not only the "artistic content" will have been lost, but any other content as well.

In Juan Ruiz the involvement of readers/spectators in the work made possible their effective participation in something connected to their daily lives. In the case of baroque culture, however, their participation in the work was illusory to the extent that the material to which they were given access was fictitious and illusory. Despite points of identification on the level of the base elements (fictional characters who *looked like* spectators, with problems similar to those that occurred in reality), literature is not life. In the case of baroque culture the reader/spectator is implicated in pure fiction, shrouded, of course, with the attributes of reality.

In Cervantes the separation of reality from literature occurs within fiction, and the involvement of the reader occurs in a space that is different from the literary. In Lope de Vega, Tirso de Molina, and María de Zayas y Sotomayor (to mention just a few examples), the separation is itself literary so that the participation inherent in the theatricality of writing is an unreal, alienated participation. As such, it is a way of having the mechanism of conduct and behavior permeate through the directives of power. For good reason, then, what has been called in an ambiguous way *novela cortesana* was precisely that, but in a different sense: it was the result of what Arnold Hauser has defined as the "authoritarian culture of the court."

The Multiple Eye

It is safe to say that the image of Cervantes as "untutored wit" has been discredited once and for all. For if there is a lucid writer in the period called the Golden Age of Spanish literature, it is Cervantes, who is constantly engaged in the task of problematizing and rethinking his activity as a writer. Although Cervantes did not reveal his thoughts in the form of a treatise, his reflections on literature are numerous. Suffice it to say that what interested him was not the separation of the theoretical from the practical visions of literature, but the emergence of a discursive consciousness from the practice of writing. In Cervantes, the goal of narrative is the investigation of the novel.

During the sixteenth century and in the beginning of the seventeenth there was no theory of the novel in a strict sense. The most modern of genres (let us recall that it was practically nonexistent before the Middle Ages), the novel's prestige was negative. Many moralists deplored the reading of novels, especially by young maidens, a proof that the genre enjoyed great popularity even if not legitimized by canon law. The lack of classical models and the misgivings of moralists help to explain the critical disregard of the novel in Cervantes's time as well as its lack of theorization. Most of the works on the latter are more or less fortuitous adaptations of treatises on poetics. In this context, Cervantes is the first to engage in a theorization of the novel with considerable amplitude. The theoretical thought of Alonso López Pinciano (*Philosophia antigua poética*, 1596) is usually considered to be the basis for Cervantes's own theorizations although the evidence for this is not clear.

If one were to disregard what in Cervantes's reflections on the novel may be a product of his own experience as a novelist or reader of novels, his points of departure may be said to be the very ones found in the poetic or rhetorical treatises of the time, which in turn were dependent upon the literary theory of antiquity, especially the Aristotelian, with certain neo-Platonic incrustations. Cervantes's ideas about the novel seem to have been firmly established, without further change, between the first part of *Don Quijote* (1605) and the *Persiles* (1617). This lack of change may even be observed by going back to the very beginning of his narrative work (*Galatea*, 1585). Cervantes remained true to his ambivalence throughout his work, which shows clearly, from the very beginning, his love-hate relationship—of respect-mockery—with the romances of chivalry and pastoral mythology.

The first truly important nucleus of Cervantes's theory of the novel is the postulation of the author's lucidity and control of the work. The writer must be totally aware of what he or she is doing, and authorial intention appears as a determinant value in the text. Cervantes's main reproach of the romances of chivalry consists precisely of his rejection of their lack of intentionality and control of materials used in the narration. The justification of the text for its intention is extremely important, for even the most improbable follies are legitimated when they take on the function of a given intention that is manifested by the text. This issue is broached in the Prologue to his *Novelas ejemplares*, where he says: "I have opened a path in my novels / through which the Castilian language may / express folly with propriety" ("Yo he abierto en mis novelas un camino / por do la lengua castellana puede / mostrar con propiedad un desatino").[19] The distinction between deliberate and unforeseen nonsense is a central point of Cervantes's narrative theory.

The novel is a form of art and, as such, must be controlled through the use of classical "rules." Yet, those "rules" never paid attention to the novel, a modern genre. This tension between acceptance of the regulating power of classical canons and the proclamation of the freedom of the novel defines a new Cervantine ambivalence. In general terms, the rules deemed important by Cervantes for the novel are plausibility (in the face of inverisimilitude), harmony (vis-à-vis disparity and heterogeneous accumulation), and a pleasant and peaceful style. These three norms are subordinate to two greater principles, which form the essence of his critical thought: (1) art controlled and directed by reason; (2) the text justified and articulated by a creative intention. The violation of any of these norms has repercussions on the others. For Cervantes, then, the novel is a delicate framework of relationships. Consequently "form" and "content" do not exist as separate entities but as functions that are codependent upon one another: a lack of credibility (a question "of content") either provokes or is provoked by an imperfection of harmony or style (a matter "of form").

Situated in a classical theoretical tradition, Cervantes needs to justify the novel, framing it within one of the classical genres. Thus appears his conception of the novel as an epic written in prose. Cervantes will attempt to justify his own work giving it that air of legitimacy by apparently patterning it after classical models, insisting on the fact that the epic is possible not only in verse, but also in prose. While such a theoretical posture was destined to legitimize his *Persiles y Sigismunda,* eighteenth-century criticism was to extend it to *Don Quijote* (the comic epic), leaving out *La Galatea* and the *Exemplary Novels.* By applying theories of the epic to the novel, Cervantes manages to outline a model for the new genre. Such a model encompasses the following:

1. An extensive field in which to describe: (a) a variety of events; (b) an exemplary hero; (c) tragic and joyful events (changes in fortune); (d) a society of characters; (e) a thematic variety that represents different branches of knowledge; and (f) a variety of exemplary human qualities and situations.

2. The means used to describe such a field are: (a) a pleasing style; (b) ingenious invention; and (c) verisimilitude.

3. Cervantes's objectives, which are (a) to achieve an aesthetic harmony of the heterogeneous while (b) entertaining and teaching.

4. The possibility of including (a) features of the four main literary genres and (b) the best qualities of poetry and oratory is allowed.

From this model one can deduce important theoretical positions. In the first place, there is "invention." Since contemporary theory understood the mission of art as the representation of nature through the imitation of the same, where, one might ask, did the faculty for invention lie? We know that in his own time Cervantes is perhaps the writer who most values invention and who feels the proudest of his imaginative power. This privileging of invention, however, does not imply a complete break from contemporary theory, as the artist must create in a way that parallels the manner in which nature creates or invents while not imitating it blindly. Moreover, if there is to be a guarantee that the result will be a representation of nature, such a guarantee is given especially by the principle of verisimilitude of the text. Thus, Cervantes's art supposes a major effort of synthesis between the capacity of art to reflect the world and of world to be a creation or invention of art.

The dichotomy invention-imitation gives rise to a new binomial: history (reality) and fiction (imagination). Aristotelian poetics defined the difference between history and poetry as a difference between what is real and specific (history or what actually takes place) and what is possible and general (poetry or what should or could happen). Yet, in spite of this difference of level between both concepts, Cervantes's era gives moral precedence to history (what is true) while unconsciously connoting fiction as falsehood. Cervantes was unable to escape this prejudice from the point of view of theory.

Some of the theoreticians of Cervantes's time (López Pinciano, for example) exhibit the need to distinguish what is required of history (veracity) from what is required of fiction (verisimilitude). The latter means that the development of the story has to be justified by the logical coherence of the text itself. This distinction was not assimilated by Cervantes along theoretical lines, but he was to take it into account in the practice of writing. In his theoretical manifestations, Cervantes reproaches the romances of chivalry for their lack of faithfulness to reality, whereas he is more forgiving with the pastoral novel, the epic, and lyric poetry, because for him these are self-proclaimed, fictitious genres—unlike the books of knight-errantry, whose missions seem more chronistic (or close to the chronicle) and, hypothetically, attached to reality.

Don Quijote is a formidable investigation of the limits between the real and the fictitious. The hero goes mad in trying to make the fictitious real; in his attempt to transfer to history what belongs to fiction (the books of chivalry). Instead of resigning himself to picking up a pen and writing romances of chivalry (his first temptation), Don Quijote tries to transform the romances into action and to create a work of fiction with his own life. Within this framework Cervantes points to the difference between history and fiction and implies that madness resides in that inability to differentiate between them. It is also clear that, in a parallel manner, the mad hero becomes his own historian: he imagines what the chroniclers are bound to say about him in the future and, in imagining it, he gives life to the adventures written by them (Cervantes is forced to write what is dictated by his character). For if author creates fiction from reality, the character creates reality from fiction. Thus, in the second part of Cervantes's novel, there are numerous characters who have read the story of Don Quijote, a story that becomes a topic of discussion among them. Don Quijote and Sancho even attempt to embody the truth of their own existence vis-à-vis the falsity of the homonymous characters that appear in the apocryphal *Quijote* of Avellaneda. In this manner, it is shown that characters not only may reflect on the work in which they are written or inscribed, but also may decide its veracity.

This situation points toward the capacity of fiction to bring reality into being. But this conclusion is a partial one. For although it is true that the book is generated by Don Quijote's exploits (fiction generates reality), it is also the case that Don Quijote's feats are written by someone who lives in the real world (reality generates fiction, which in turn generates reality). Between reality and fiction an infinite degree of transitions exists. Thus, between himself and his hero, Cervantes inserts a series of intermediate authors, such as Cide Hamete Benengeli and the chroniclers of La Mancha, so that one must go through a series of intermediate stages to arrive at fiction (Don Quijote) from reality (Cervantes); one does not proceed directly from Don Quijote's exploits to the book that relates them. In the first place, the book that Don Quijote imagines that is written about him (an encomiastic book, a book of knight-errantry) differs from the one that is in fact written (a farcical epic, a parody of the novels of knight-errantry). Second, the book is not received directly by the reader (for that would be impossible), but through the impressions drawn from it by the different characters (Sansón Carrasco, the Duke and the Duchess, and so on).

If, on the one hand, Don Quijote is nothing more than the product of a book upon which the author takes pleasure in demonstrating his power (let us recall the interrupted episode of the battle with the Biscayan: with swords held high and horses thrown on top of each other, Cervantes suddenly interrupts the struggle in order to narrate something else, and the battle is not resumed until much later), on the other hand, the characters are almost independent beings (Cardenio admits that Don Quijote's madness is so odd that no one could have invented it; Sansón Carrasco believes that the Sancho of "flesh and blood" is more convincing and amusing than the one he has read about in the book). In this manner, *Don Quijote* becomes a novel of multiple perspectives: that of the reader, those of the characters, and that of the author and/or "authors." The novel comes into being as if through a game of mirrors or prisms. Don Quijote is the deepest formulation of the turbidity of the boundaries that separate reality and imagination, truth and verisimilitude, story and novel.

Cervantes proposes a direct investigation of the possibility of lending verisimilitude to the extraordinary in *Persiles y Sigismunda* and in *El coloquio de los perros*. In these two narratives what is most resolutely fictitious (the extraordinary and marvelous) must be justified as if it were real. Thus in the *Persiles* all of Cervantes's efforts are focused on giving a rational explanation to events that, although natural, seem fantastic, while he places supernatural or excessively marvelous occurrences in either far-off and unknown places or in the mouths of untrustworthy narrators. The fact that dogs speak in *El coloquio de los perros* is justified as a possible dream. Moreover, such a dream is related by a character of dubious integrity and is finally brought forth as a tale within another tale (*El casamiento engañoso*). In Cervantes even the most marvelous occurrences are always structured as possible: the novel cannot be created beyond the limits of history.

Another of the great binomials of Cervantine reflection on the novel is the contrast between unity and variety. Cervantes aspired to create an all-embracing expression of the world from his novels. This means that narration is considered as an instrument capable of encompassing nature and cosmos. This aspiration, however, had to be reconciled with the Aristotelian postulate of unity of the work. The tension between both principles breaks all boundaries in *Persiles* (where heterogeneity is imposed on the unitary), in *Don Quijote I* (in which not all of the intercalated episodes are justified by their connection with the rest of the text), and in some of the *Exemplary Novels* (*La ilustre fregona*, for example), finally reaching a decisive equilibrium in *Don Quijote II*. The tension between unity and variety reaches not only the narrated material and its distribution, but its style as well. In *Don Quijote* the novelist's great ambition is affirmed: "to show oneself epic, lyric, tragic, comic, and with all of those parts that embrace the gentle and pleasing sciences of poetry and oratory" ("mostrarse épico, lírico, trágico, cómico, con todas aquellas partes que encierran en sí las dulcísimas y agradables ciencias de la poesía y de la oratoria").

Cervantes is situated in a tradition that assigns to literature a twofold function: entertainment and instruction. Yet, while accepting this dual function, he nevertheless emphasizes entertainment, placing the burden of instruction on books that could be classified as historical and/or religious. Unlike these books, literature finds its most adequate function in amusement and entertainment, provided that the latter not be morally negative. For Cervantes the moral function of literature is an obligation not to indoctrinate but to liberate the individual from dogmatisms. On the other hand, and related to amusement, one must include the need to provoke some kind of aesthetic admiration in the reader. Entertainment and art thus blend in the concept of delight. Literary admiration may spring forth from the text or from the material dealt with. Cervantes emphasizes the latter in accordance with a demand for imagination and variety. At the same time, when he approaches the problem of morality, his focus is not simple. First, there is the obligation to not produce morally negative works; second, this obligation depends on both the author and the reader, and on the social contract that is established between them. The morality of the text depends on the morality of the author, and simultaneously on a responsible audience, for the undiscerning "common audience"—*el vulgo*—stimulates immoral poets, demanding from them a literature characterized by violence, eroticism, and cheap sentimentalism. Moreover, the work lends itself to various possible interpretations: the uneducated audience (the "common audience" that Cervantes associates not with the lower classes, but with the illiterate mass of society) can grasp only the pleasing dimension of the work, whereas a discerning reader will capture the ethical formulation of reality contained within the work. This means that Cervantes's conception of the morality of the work is not explicit in the form of a moral, but implicit. In fact, his best exemplary novels are not exemplary inasmuch as they provide a moral prescription for living, but to the extent that they reveal individuals who are immersed in limited situations, whose vital solutions imply decisions about life's greatest problems: freedom, oppression, injustice, manipulation and deception, the condition of women, and so on.[20]

The New Novelistic Formula and Its Function: *Don Quijote* (1605–1615)

Cervantes is one of the creators of the modern novel and his *Don Quijote* is not only one of the most complex works ever produced, but the architecture of a genre. It may properly be said that Cervantes assumes the narrative options that preceded him, transgressing and transforming them in order to elaborate a new scheme. Thus, *La Galatea* precipitates the dissolution of the pastoral novel; *Persiles* culminates the tradition of the Byzantine novel of adventure; the *Exemplary Novels* turn their back on the action novels of the Italian Renaissance; and, finally, *Don Quijote* marks a colossal reelaboration where all previous narrative possibilities are endowed with a new functionality. The pastoral novel had discovered the inner side of characters and their capacity for self-analysis, that is, the character's simultaneous capacity to live and feel the experience of living. As Américo Castro (1960) has written:

> The pastoral narrative is where, for the first time, the literary character is shown as a strictly human singularity, as expression of a "within." We have spoken excessively of the abstract and the conventional [traits] of the pastoral, of its ignorance of time and space, and this prevented us from paying attention to the internal projection of its characters, to the only vital space in which they exist. (244; our translation)[21]

The pastoral showed Cervantes the path of psychological introspection. The truly constitutive aspect of the pastoral novel was the presentation of the character, surrendered to self, guarding personal feelings. Cervantes always intended to write a continuation of *La Galatea*; he promised it several times and showed a continuous attraction toward the pastoral genre. This is revealed not only in his own statements, but also in the return on a small scale to the pastoral theme in his work, especially in *Don Quijote*. In light of this attraction, however, one can observe the sarcasm with which Cervantes refers to the pastoral on several occasions. The most famous critique is found in *El coloquio de los perros*, where Berganza says to Cipión:

> Among other things, I thought that what I had heard told of shepherds' lives must not be true . . . that they spent their days singing and playing bagpipes, flutes, rebecs, tabors, and other rare instruments.[22]

The shepherds served by Berganza spend their time grunting instead of singing and "they spent most of the day picking fleas off themselves, or mending their leather sandals."[23] Thus, says Berganza, "All of which convinced me of what all should realize: that those books are thought up and designed for the entertainment of idlers, and there is not a word of truth in them."[24] How does one explain the contradiction of Cervantes's attraction for, and the demystification of, the pastoral? *La Galatea* would respond to the neo-Platonic philosophy of the Renaissance, according to which, concrete reality coexists with its idea; this pure and ideal reality, of which concrete reality would be but an imperfect manifestation, can only be captured through art. In Cervantes's work there is a struggle between a longing to grasp ideal realities and the impulse to confront historical reality. *La Galatea, Persiles,* and some of the *Exemplary Novels* fit within the former, while the impulse to confront historical reality can be seen in a considerable portion of the *Exemplary Novels.* The extremely delicate balance between the two poles would be achieved in *Don Quijote*.

In the pastoral, the character's simultaneous capacity to live and feel the experience of living arose at the expense of an analytical awareness of his or her isolation; at the expense of being placed in an abstract time and an abstract space, cut off from historical and daily life. In contrast to the pastoral novel, the picaresque, from *Lazarillo* to *Guzmán*, had shown the character as an outgrowth of a hostile society. For although the picaresque manages to capture a social-historical space and a story—both of them taken from daily life—it was only capable of finding the exterior side of characters, that is, only their behavior as a product. The novel of chivalry and the Italian novella of intrigue, in turn, had discovered action, the dynamism of human living, and imagination, the power to transform a given reality. The hero of both types of novel, however, exists only as a part of the mechanisms of intrigue, and the space of such novels is abstract and arbitrary.

Cervantes will work in a different way. First, he assumes the pastoral's design of characters, but not their isolation in an abstract space and time. Second, as in the picaresque, his goal is to deal with the real world, but he disagrees with the typology of characters constructed by this genre. From our perspective, Cervantes's solution to this dilemma is clear: he mixes the pastoral's typology of characters with the space and time of the picaresque novel. The characters appear, then, as the crossroad of personal aspirations and social incitations, and the space is no longer that of the impure farce of the picaresque novel but the product of the dialogic interaction between life's material conditions and the ways in which those conditions are assumed by those who live them (in this sense, *Lazarillo* may be seen as the novel that creates modern novelistic space). Moreover, Cervantes eliminates the didactic burden of the novel in the style of *Guzmán de Alfarache*, a burden resulting from a rejection of the world and the need to expose its cruel vanity. Although both the pastoral and the picaresque novels (with the exception of *Lazarillo* and a few later titles) lack action, Cervantes incorporates in *Don Quijote* the throbbing action of the novel of chivalry, no longer as an autonomous element, but as the imaginative creation of the character within the limits and conditions imposed by his circumstance, by his "here" and "now." The union of these narrative elements arises from a new notion of narrative perspective, which we will examine later in this chapter, destined to create an intermediate space between reality and fiction, a space that, on the one hand, leads the reader toward the world of fiction, but, on the other, propels the author time and again toward reality. This new novelistic formula could only appear at the service of a new notion of life. Cervantes confronts reality in historical terms, that is, as a place where both the capacity to transform reality and the resistance of reality to be transformed struggle in search of balance. This confrontation contrasts with the rejection of the world in the picaresque, with the mystic's search for God, and with the escapism that sublimates reality in the pastoral and chivalric romances, or reduces reality to the mechanisms of a game of cleverness in the Italian novella.

The dialectic between the two poles is represented through the struggle of a "madman," a seemingly crazy old gentleman who proclaims his absolute freedom and tries to transform the world. This new knight-errant no longer accepts reality as it is but instead seeks to impose his ideals onto a stagnant, unconscious, self-satisfied, and unproductive society that refuses any change (symbolized in La Mancha and in many of its inhabitants).

The *Quijote* as a Parody of the Novels of Chivalry: The Original Plan

Contemporaries of *Don Quijote* immediately accepted the novel's aim of parodying the romances of chivalry, an extremely popular genre during the 1500s, especially in the first half of that century. Cervantes himself had grown tired of repeating the ostensible objective of his *Don Quijote*, which was to poke fun at the chivalric novels to the point of discrediting them. Very early, nevertheless, the complexity of meanings of *Don Quijote* and its vast semantic richness forced the parodic intention to the background. It seemed too great a work for such a small proposal. The parodic nature of the novel is undeniable, but an accurate interpretation of *Don Quijote* must rely on a shift from the intentions or objectives of the parody to the function that it plays in the structure of the work. The importance of the parodic process during the Renaissance is well known, as one can see in the works of Pulci and Boiardo and in the brilliant example of Ariosto's *Orlando furioso*. In the Renaissance parody justifies itself as yet another form of art for art's sake, but a century later Cervantes transforms that process into a springboard for expressing a vision of a world and of a time, while simultaneously converting the comic epic, which had existed in verse form, into a novel.

The novel to which Cervantes aspires seeks the totalizing expression of a period. But in order to achieve it, he needs not only a broad space but total freedom. He finds that freedom in the parodic structure, for if Don Quijote is mad, everything is possible and able to enter the realm of the verisimilar. As Luis Rosales has written:

> Gingerly, dead people and madmen can say it all. Moreover, if the characters who surround him do not take him for a madman, our hero would have ended up in jail the first time around and, in this case, neither would Don Quijote have been Don Quijote, nor would Cervantes have reached the zenith and realization of the imagined history of his deeds. In the novel's invention there is something of great relief that never seems to be taken into account: *Don Quijote needs an exterior anchor, a social support to maintain for a long time the dangerous and difficult exercise of his errant chivalry.* On this protection depends the miraculous fact that the work can survive in each of its chapters. The resistance shown by the surrounding world to the Don is real; also real and necessary is the help that it provides him. Don Fernando, Cardenio, the Duke and the Duch-

ess, and Sansón Carrasco, the *bachiller*, help him in different ways, and by virtue of this help and complicity—let us not forget it—Don Quijote becomes who he is and in his wanderings manages to free himself from swindlers and from those who are prone to misunderstand him. (1960, 1: 144; emphasis in the original)[25]

The mad Don Quijote defies the most sacred institutions and authorities of his society, while Cervantes, in telling the story of a madman, challenges the norms of narrow realism and offers an unlimited space for imagination. The structure of the parody allows both the writing of a novel and a general reflection upon the genre. Like no other structure, parody makes possible the transformation of the novel into a protean genre, capable of revealing itself epic, lyric, tragic, comic, or rhetorical.

A hypothetical, original plan of *Don Quijote* is related precisely to the problem of parodic structure. It has been said that early in his career Cervantes did not have a clear idea of what he wanted to do, except to parody the romances of chivalry. The division of the *Don Quijote* of 1605 into four parts—that division would later disappear—has been interpreted as a symptom of a project that originally had little scope and limited ambition, and that later was rectified. An entire series of vacillations seems to confirm this hypothesis. Those vacillations are connected to the myth of Cervantes as an "untutored wit": an unconscious Cervantes who did not know what he was doing, a Cervantes who composed his brilliant work through pure improvisation. Even if the project has changed from the first drafts to the final product—something that, in any case, is neither new nor abnormal—one must carefully separate the hypothesis of a different original plan from the interpretation of *Don Quijote* as the improvised work of an "untutored wit." That an original plan existed seems quite likely. Cervantes is very fond of changing the plan for his works as he goes along. *El celoso extremeño* changes completely at the moment when we discover, after following Felipo Carrizales through sixty-eight years of life, that he is terribly jealous. *La ilustre fregona* appears to be a picaresque novel until its structural function is inverted. Don Quijote's first sally also seems to operate in this manner. Nevertheless, as it has been said on numerous occasions, Cervantes's art is an art in motion; it is never a result or an end, but an open process. Yet, while that process aims in all directions, it does not imply the destruction or elimination of the earlier stages of writing or the disappearance of the initial intention. In fact, these earlier stages are assumed and integrated in the final product, which gives them a different meaning. The hero's initial vacillations,

his venturing out and turning back, are retransformed into the symptoms of a man in search of his own definition. As Américo Castro has
stressed, Don Quijote is a never-ending, free character; Don Quijote is
both a will to be and the effort invested to become what he wants to
be.

The interpretation of Cervantes as "untutored wit" is destroyed from
within. The great importance of Cervantes's self-critical activity and
permanent reflection on art has already been shown. *Don Quijote* is a
very clear example of the author's intensely lucid power over his work.
Américo Castro (1972) has revealed the writer's conceptual density.
From our perspective, this self-knowledge is part of the structure of
the novel. If we substitute "Cervantes the real person" for "the discourse called Cervantes," we can assume the following statements of
Leo Spitzer:

> The real protagonist of this novel is not Quijote, with his continual mis-
> representation of reality, or Sancho with his skeptical half-endorsement
> of quixotism—and surely not any of the central figures of the illusionistic
> by-stories: the hero is Cervantes, the artist himself, who combines a criti-
> cal and illusionistic art according to his free will. From the moment we
> open the book to the moment we put it down, we are given to under-
> stand that an almighty overlord is directing us, who leads us where he
> pleases. (69)[26]

Spitzer later adds:

> Don Quijote acquired his immortality exclusively at the hands of Cer-
> vantes—as the latter well knows and admits. Obviously, Quijote wrought
> only what Cervantes wrote, and he was born for Cervantes as much as
> Cervantes was born for him! In the speech of the pen of the pseudo-
> chronicler we have the most discreet and the most powerful self-glorifica-
> tion of the artist which has ever been written. (70)[27]

Novelistic Structure and Technique: Differences between *Quijote I* (1605) and *Quijote II* (1615)

Don Quijote was published in two parts, separated by a period of ten
years (1605 to 1615). The differences between both parts are so great
that the existence of two different novels has been considered by some.
Examined as a whole, they share the external structure of the novel
of chivalry with its accumulation of episodes. The function of those
episodes in *Don Quijote*, however, is completely different. In the romances of chivalry there is an emphasis on the reiteration of the same
kinds of acts. The knights move from one space to another, but they

rarely undergo inner change. Furthermore, they are monolithic characters, established from the first page. The flow of the episodes in *Don Quijote*, in contrast, has a different function: that of exploring from multiple perspectives the self-knowledge of the characters and their search for a self-definition. This is why they are not perfectly stated until the end of the novel. Moreover, the main characters share none of the novelistic archetypes: they are problematic and contradictory beings, who vacillate and hide themselves as they pursue self-realization in accordance with an imposed mission. In *Don Quijote*, nothing is final or necessary: each new episode provokes unexpected, new possible ways to live the world in the spirit of the knight-errant, and these possibilities increase and become involved in the flow of the narration.

Considered as a whole, the book could be structured around the process of progressive independence of its characters. Alvaro Fernández Suárez (1953) emphasizes the process through which the main character is designed in the first chapter. It turns out that the narrator is unaware of something that one would expect him to know perfectly well: he does not know, exactly, the name of his hero—Quijada, Quesada, Quejana. As the novel progresses, the confusion, far from vanishing, increases: Quijana, Quijano. The same thing happens with other characters in the novel (Sancho Panza's wife, for example). All of this is a pretext on the part of the "author" who pretends to create the impression that he finds himself before a serious lack of reliable documents. The reports at his disposal are contradictory and, at times, the historian's difficulties seem insurmountable. By confusing something as fundamental as the names of his characters, the "author" makes use of one of the many methods for persuading the reader that what is being read is not fiction (a novelist who invents knows the names of his characters), but a true story. Similar procedures include the invention of a supposedly Moorish author, Cide Hamete Benengeli, upon whom Cervantes, a mere translator and commentator, depends in order to continue or discontinue his story. Then there are chronological confusions and uncertainties. As the novel progresses and the embroilments and confusions increase, the character becomes even more disconnected from the book, creating the impression that he exists outside of the book rather than within its pages. One assumes that the gentleman (*hidalgo*) from La Mancha is performing and that there is a writer who pursues him and relates his exploits *in whatever way he can*, that is to say, only to the extent that he is familiar with them. Cide Hamete Benengeli becomes the chronicler, and the hero's acts become the story. This goes even further in the second part, where Don Quijote meets characters who have read his story (that of the first part) and therefore know of him. There is no need for introductions. Many of those characters recognize him at first sight from afar. Through them Don Quijote even learns about the existence of Avellaneda's novel—the apocryphal second part—and, indignant about the inauthenticity of that novel's hero, he denies those acts attributed to him by the new chronicler. Fernández Suárez writes:

> As we all know, the two gentlemen invited Don Quijote to have dinner with them, and during their conversation everything was made clear. There had been a supplanting of identities. Let us focus closely on what happened: Cervantes does not attack here the false story of Avellaneda but [he attacks] the falsifier who tried to pass as the true hero, the spurious and mimicking Don Quijote. It turns out, then, that the debate was not polarized between historians but between characters. The author, Cervantes, merely records this debate, this dispute, in the same way he records all of the other events that are in the chronicle. (42)[28]

In order to belie the falsifier, Don Quijote decides to change the route he had announced at the end of part I and bypass Zaragoza where Avellaneda's character had begun his new adventures. Remarkably, then, the character has arrived at such a level of independence that he allows himself to decide which of his historians is the real one and which is the liar and to deny, if necessary, what is said of him. Later on, at the height of his independence, Don Quijote runs into one of the characters of Avellaneda's novel, Don Alvaro Tarfe. As Fernández Suárez writes,

> Don Alvaro Tarfe is thus corroborated by Cervantes as a "real" character, and with this he comes to say that Avellaneda did not altogether lie. For if Don Alvaro Tarfe was "real," was not the other Don Quijote, the falsifier, also real? He must have been, because Don Alvaro Tarfe claims to have met and dealt with him, just as with someone named Sancho, even if he had no resemblance to the real one, the one present during the chat. (49)[29]

Don Quijote petitions Don Alvaro to make a public statement, in the presence of the mayor of the village, to the effect that until then he had never seen the true Don Quijote of La Mancha and Sancho Panza, his squire. It thus became clear that the other Don Quijote and Sancho were nothing but impostors. It is not surprising that Miguel de Unamuno should come to think of Don Quijote and Sancho as being independent of their author. Rather innocently Unamuno had fallen into the extremely subtle Cervantine trap.[30]

In both part I and part II we travel through a fully realistic space: roads, inns, hills, villages, and palaces inhabited by a richly varied human fauna of innkeepers, prostitutes, muleteers, priests, *bachilleres*, canons, barbers, dukes, and shepherds. In their ensemble they trace with great depth an outline of La Mancha, which in turn becomes the symbol of an era. Dustier, more rural, and barren in the first part; more citylike and sheltered in homes and palaces in part II. In both cases we are dealing with a social and human setting that provides a suitable space for Don Quijote's exploits.

Part I is composed of fifty-two chapters, divided into four parts. Its structure, however, lies in Don Quijote's two sallies from his house in search of adventures.

First sally	Second sally
Inn	Adventures
Return	Inn
	Adventures
	Inn
	Return

Each sally or outing brings about a cycle and both cycles are symmetrical, the second being an expansion of the first. It is thus a classical structure, which involves a journey of a circular (or bicircular) nature. The entire first part presents the interaction of three types of episodes: (1) chivalric; (2) literary; and (3) amorous. The three types are imbricated in such a way that they become utterly impossible to disassociate. Don Quijote's chivalric character (he battles windmills and herds) is inseparable from his character as a lover and as untiring reader. In turn, considered neither as episodes nor as the hero's character traits, these three elements constitute three thematic axes that are constantly united. Each one of these axes presents a complexity of strata or layers. The love theme is conceived in the pastoral style (the episode of Marcela), or in the style of the sentimental, or in that of the novel of intrigues (the episodes of Cardenio and Dorotea); there is also the idealized and sublime love (of Don Quijote for Dulcinea), together with the most blatantly sexual love (in the episode of Maritornes), and the simply animalistic kind (in the episode of Rocinante and the ponies); then there is the tragic love of Grisóstomo for Marcela, and the problematic love of Dorotea and Don Fernando, which meets a happy ending. This multiplicity of thrusts on one thematic axis produces a narrative density characteristic of part I. In this book, Cervantes offers us much more than mere episodes of adventure: there are numerous and splendid dialogues between Sancho and his master, and discourses (on arms and letters, and on the Golden Age, for example) as well as readings and commentaries of tales, literary discussions, and so on. One could say that there are very different kinds of episodes and that each type pursues its own autonomy. It is true that each new episode is a Gordian knot of connections or links that lead to other multiple episodes, but the entanglement that runs throughout the novel merely underscores the peculiarity of many of the episodes that are like vignettes with precise limits.

It is not surprising that some of these episodes should acquire such autonomy that Cervantes was accused of inserting them pointlessly in the main thread of the novel. Such is especially the case with the "captive's story," with the pastoral episode of Marcela and Grisóstomo, and, above all, with the Italianate novella entitled *El curioso impertinente*. Although the importance of these interpolations has been acknowledged, as isolated pieces they have been interpreted as symptoms of Cervantes's insecurity regarding his novel, and as a means of his escaping or seeking a respite from a story that disconcerted him. Cervantes was to answer these accusations in the second part of *Don Quijote* (1615) and, from his own statements, one can deduce that in those seemingly disconnected episodes he sought to give variety to the novel (we already know the importance of "variety" in Cervantes's novelistic theory), getting away from the hero's monopoly of the novel. Nevertheless, Cervantes states that in part II he will connect more intimately with the book's plan any episodes that might be viewed as interpolations. Of course Cervantes's response was far too modest, for the text of 1605 presents enough internal reasons to justify the autonomy of the episodes in question. As we have already noted, the structural element characteristic of this text may be defined as an articulation of different levels of narrative density. Cervantes is experimenting with a new instrument, the novel, in order to express the totality of the world. His art achieves the greatest goals when he feels less restricted, but it is also clear that in this experimentation Cervantes assumes and makes use of all types of novels available to him at the time. In order to give shape to the formidable instrument that is the modern novel, Cervantes was forced to create a total expression from this novel through the vertical (not successive) accumulation of different narrative levels. In fact, only a very narrow view of the novel would deem the episode of Marcela and Grisóstomo more autonomous than the tale of the goatherd or the fourfold story of Cardenio, Luscinda, Dorotea, and Don Fernando. As Vicente Gaos (1971) has pointed out, the critical reproaches have only one basis of support: the interruption of the work's main plot. To deem such episodes to be independent from the rest of the novel implies a claim: that the novel's plot is what gives unity to part I. This claim, however, is simply arbitrary, as an entire series of elements has as much, if not more, importance than the plot in the structure of the novel. One might mention, for instance, the importance of dialogue, which is underscored throughout the novel. The astonishing chapter in which the adventure of the rams is related serves as a good example. Cervantes entitles it, "In which are recorded the conversation between Sancho Panza and his master Don Quixote, and other noteworthy adventures" ("Donde se cuentan las razones que pasó Sancho con su señor, don Quijote, con otras aventuras dignas de ser contadas"), and thus highlights the conversation of his heroes rather than the incident itself. He is not so much interested in adventure for adventure's sake than in the way he can provoke the reader's suspense. Perhaps the most convincing evidence lies in the interruption at the climax of the battle between Don Quijote and the Biscayan, to which we alluded earlier. There Cervantes plays with the reader's attention as if trying to demonstrate that it is not in the adventure where one's interest belongs but in narration itself.

Throughout this study we have tried to show that the great guiding force of the novel is neither the action, nor the characters, nor the space of the novel itself. Rather, it is the game of perspectives to which Cervantes submits the world, thus multiplying points of view, giving depth to the narrative, and obscuring the boundaries between reality and fiction. Cervantes in effect makes it possible to narrate the world that one is contemplating, thus contributing to the creation of the modern novel. And if a necessary condition of the novel is someone's self-discovery through narration, then we can say that Cervantes not only discovers this capacity but also manages to problematize it and give it unequaled depth through his games of perspectives. From this ordering principle of superposing heterogeneous and rather delimited (autonomous) levels, the interpolation of these tales is a perfectly legitimate procedure.

Part II contains seventy-four undivided chapters. There are seven chapters of dialogue as well as the constant comings and goings in preparation for the third and final sally, which will last until the end of the novel. This last outing is slow and clear at the beginning [Dulcinea's enchantment, the chariot of death, the Knight of the Wood, the Gentleman in Green, the lions, Camacho's wedding, the cave of Montesinos, Master Peter (maese Pedro), the adventures of the braying and the enchanted boat]. Part II of Don Quijote acquires a certain homogeneity in the long episode in the land of the Duke and the Duchess.

Later on, in the journey to Barcelona and on the return trip, the novel's action is released and is made to race forth, thus multiplying the narrative rhythm.

This second part is characterized by greater narrative unity and by an increased dependence of that unity on the characters. One might say that the prevailing process here is the discursive concatenation, differing from the first part, where action explodes in a multiplicity of directions. In part II, each episode seeks the next one in a linear and direct way. The interest is continually kept alive and heightened as it is completely impossible to predict which turn a thought will take once it has sprung forward in a prodigious succession of associations. At the moment in which the reader is captivated by this articulation of episodes he or she depends completely on the author, and is forced to accept unmercifully his rhythm—be it fast or slow. In part I the tales and stories were told and speeches delivered, but in part II characters speak incessantly.

One of the most characteristic processes of this articulation of episodes is its antithetical parallelism. The second part of the novel begins by introducing us to the knight in his bed, now fully recovered and about to venture out again, and ends in the same room with the knight on his deathbed. In the first adventure of part II, Sancho convinces Don Quijote that Dulcinea is enchanted, and at the end of the novel he fools him once again, making him believe that she is now disenchanted. The same thing happens with Sansón Carrasco's twofold duel: in the first he is conquered and in the second he conquers. Finally, if the episodes in *Don Quijote I* tend toward autonomy, in part II they have a tendency to form a cluster of two or three chapters, and sometimes even very coherent blocks as is the case with life under the domain of the Duke and the Duchess, for example.

In reference to the composition of *Don Quijote*, there have been many discussions over time regarding the major differences between its two parts. We shall now examine some of these differences.

Part I is said to produce a feeling of maximum freedom. Its complicated organization competes with nature in complexity and surpasses it in the sensation of life. Part II, on the other hand, gives the impression of being enclosed within the narrowest of limits. In *Don Quijote I* there is, perhaps, greater imaginative richness, and great vivacity and movement in the episodes, which often happen at a vertiginous pace. In the second part, there is increased psychological complexity and a more equal rhythm. It seems, as Américo Castro has stated, that Cervantes "had familiarized himself with his own genius" ("se había familiarizado con la propia genialidad"), at least as far as regularity was concerned. For if the first part of the novel is deeply dramatic and at times even unrestrained, the tone of the second part tends more toward farce and is more artistically refined and rich in invention. In it, the grotesque becomes quintessential and touches frequently upon the magical. In *Don Quijote II* there is also a resolute predominance of theatrical devices: the chariot of the Parliament of Death, Camacho's wedding celebration, the cave of Montesinos, the braying adventure, Master Peter's tableau, and other spectacles that culminate with Don Quijote's entrance in a city, where he attends a soiree and feels obliged to dance with a few ladies. In 1615, the forests, the plains, the roads, and the inns of 1605 are substituted by inside settings. We enter the respective homes of the Gentleman in Green, of Basilio, and of the Duke and the Duchess; we meet Sancho the Governor, and Don Antonio Moreno. The adventurer (the captive captain) contrasts with the *honnête homme*, the domestic and settled gentleman (the Gentleman in Green). The predominance of nature in part I is opposed to that of a social and cultural setting in part II.

Another fundamental difference lies in the varying treatment of dialogue. Dialogue is Cervantes's great discovery, and *Don Quijote* is perhaps the first novel in which it acquires great extension and all of its human and dialectical value. Cervantine dialogue is characterized by the bareness of the narrator's stage directions, which dramatizes all of his novelistic art. Dialogue is the meeting place for the different characters who reveal and define themselves in the very contrast of their respective opinions. The most disparate theories and positions regarding a given problem are taken on personally and are inserted in the dialogue, which does not reach its qualitative and quantitative fullness until the second part (there is a greater amount of narration in the first part).

Perhaps the greatest differences between the two parts of the novel are semantic in nature and must be sought in the relationship between Don Quijote and his surroundings. For example, in part I Cervantes gives us the objective reality (windmills, inns, herds) on the one hand, and Don Quijote's vision of that reality on the other (giants, castles, armies). The reader finds himself or herself staring in the face of that contrast, and from it there springs forth an irrepressible and violent comicality. In the first part, Don Quijote almost always becomes aware of objective reality; the others are the ones who falsify it in order to fit the hero's madness. It is the *bachiller* Sansón Carrasco and the Duke and the Duchess, for example, who disguise reality and deceive Don Quijote. When Don Quijote confronts the lion he knows perfectly well that it is a lion. His madness is not found in his deformation of reality but in the need to exhibit absurd and gratuitous valor. In part I deception, on the part of the others, is temporary, accidental, and unsystematic (when they find him, they want to make him return home and in order to achieve that aim, they feel obliged to fool him). Don Quijote appears free and without ties; he aims only to wander about in search of adventures. In part II the others deceive him systematically, even when he is on his deathbed. Don Quijote is urged and propelled by others: he is very rarely alone and he almost always has something to do (travel to El Toboso and Zaragoza, for example, or visit the cave of Montesinos). In the first part we see the aggressive Don Quijote and his companion Sancho, grumbling but loyal, challenging and defying the external world, running into or stumbling across a flow of humanity in a series of casual encounters against a changing background of inns and paths in their adventures. In the second part, Don Quijote and Sancho are the ones who are challenged by the world, which is now that of the aristocracy or the big city; a much more fearful and solidly established world. The resistance of the first environment is not enough to cure the mad hero, but it is sufficient in the second, in which Don Quijote is not simply beaten, but becomes the object of mockery.

The final difference may lie in the deepest problematic of the two parts. In part I, there is a struggle between the very drama that touched Cervantes's life and that of Spain as a whole: the dreadful abyss that separated the ideals of Hispanic imperialism and the reality of a society immersed in the profound crisis of its decadence. The disconsolate bitterness with which Cervantes polarizes the two edges of the abyss could not be more tragically comical: on the one hand, a madman who takes on novelistic and anachronistic ideals (as the ideals of his own chivalric youth must have seemed to Cervantes when, upon returning to Spain following his captivity, he was forced to eke out a living as a tax collector); on the other hand, a desolate and barren La Mancha, inhabited by human fauna consumed by stagnation and ignorance. By 1615, his own internal drama transcended, Cervantes seems to devote his efforts to contemplating the society around him and to describing that society through interpretation. *Don Quijote* is, above all, an excuse for recreating an extensive and profound social panorama.

Don Quijote and Sancho Panza as Characters

Don Quijote and Sancho, the two protagonists, attain such an independent existence that they seem to escape from the book and become autonomous myths, not because of the wealth of ideas of each one, or the fact that they embody a passion that they merely bear (like Don

Juan, Faust, Othello, or Macbeth), but because of their personal density. The novel presents them as part of a scheme and develops them as entities possessed by the will to live and to become something. In this effort—one that is completely new in the history of literature—the search for self-definition must be carried out; it is an effort that relies on confrontation with others and with reality (what I am is the result of the interaction between what I want to be and what I am allowed to be), so that the two protagonists function as two poles in this interaction. All personal situations are definable in terms of quixotism, sanchism, and their diverse combinations. But Don Quijote is not the result of quixotism, nor is Sancho the result of sanchism; sanchism and quixotism are simply the two possibilities that arise from two concrete and extremely personalized characters. Nothing in and about them is incarnated a priori. Rather, concrete and personal behavior permits generalization a posteriori. For this reason, rather than the idealism represented by Don Quijote, or the materialism embodied by Sancho Panza, what is important is the complex process through which Don Quijote's conduct comes into being, competing against that of Sancho, and vice versa. In any case, it is impossible to define Don Quijote as a pure idealist or Sancho as a pure materialist. In the process of individualization of the two characters, a series of doubts, vacillations, turnabouts, and mutual contaminations arises, which generate the two polarities (Don Quijote-Sancho) and, more important, a two-headed monster that, in its unity, links the two extreme tendencies of human behavior. In fact, Don Quijote becomes more like Sancho and Sancho becomes more quixotic in an extensive process of osmosis that, in the final analysis, is the nature of the novel.

Salvador de Madariaga has described this process in various stages. Thus, the initial Quijote is to a certain extent a humble and insecure man, who accepts advice and vacillates. Little by little, however, he attempts to feign total security in his convictions even though he has not gained security; his voice becomes more imperious and intransigent. In this phase, as Madariaga writes,

> Don Quijote attacks reality so that reality will not have time to contradict him. He does so with that swiftness of the restlessness of men of action. For, although mad, he was the father of his own chimera, and was unable to subdue that voice within himself that told him that everything was illusion. Hence his longing to avail himself of anything that would confirm his faith. (10)[31]

The end of part I and the beginning of part II represent the culminating period of his security and self-suggestion, although he is never truly free from doubts. His arrival at the home of the Duke and the Duchess incarnates this moment: "And that was the first day that he perceived and believed himself to be a true knight-errant" ("y aquél fue el primer día que de todo en todo conoció y creyó ser caballero andante verdadero, y no fantástico"). In part II Don Quijote is defined by his concessions and by his tendency to come to terms with reality. He travels with money and pays his expenses without demanding his rights as a knight-errant. His departure from the village this time is more provoked by the *bachiller* Sansón Carrasco and by Sancho than decided by himself. Furthermore, from the moment Sancho enchants Dulcinea, Don Quijote will depend more and more—although in a very subtle way—on his squire. He begins to accept some errors, he gives explanations, and he recognizes the reality of many things. He does not even react (at Camacho's wedding, for example) if someone proclaims the beauty of his beloved above all other women (including Dulcinea). The adventure of the cave of Montesinos reveals a Quijote who comes to ironize his own world of chivalric fiction: quixotic idealism gives way to a progressive realism, and the master's superiority over the squire begins to fall apart. The squire disrespectfully doubts what his master claims to have witnessed in the cave, and Don Quijote is reduced to begging Sancho to believe him. In exchange, he will believe what the squire claims to have seen during his journey while riding Clavileño. From that moment the novel shows us "the slow and pathetic decline of the hero's chivalric spirit" ("el lento y patético declinar del ánimo caballeresco del héroe") toward the triumph of realism in his pathetic death. The same process, though of a contrary sign, has been described in Sancho. One must abandon the swarm of clichés that have been assigned to him (his simplicity, materialism, cowardice, and so on); all of these labels are attached to Sancho by Don Quijote, who was forced to reduce his squire for purposes of self-confirmation. What characterizes Sancho is his ambiguous attitude vis-à-vis Don Quijote, his switching back and forth between trust and skepticism, credulity and sarcasm. Moreover, Sancho becomes more like Don Quijote, and the catalyst of this process is none other than the desire for power, embodied in the promised isle. Madariaga writes:

> Power is for Sancho what glory is for Don Quijote. The isle materializes power for Sancho. And thus just as Don Quijote must believe in Dulcinea, in order to believe in himself, Sancho must believe in Don Quijote in order to believe in the isle. In this way the knight's faith will nourish the servant's spirit, after having sustained his own. (135)[32]

For if Sancho does not believe, the isle will disappear, and thus the only possibility of succeeding in life, the only illusion and adventure in his life, becomes absurd. Hence, Sancho also holds on to anything that might strengthen his faith, and he refuses to declare his master utterly mad.

Perspectivism and Significant Complexity of the *Quijote*

As a novel *Don Quijote* finds its unity and ultimate meaning in a plurality of perspectives. If we consider Don Quijote and his exploits as material to be narrated, we find that this material is multirefracted, from two kinds of perspective: an internal one in which Don Quijote narrates himself or is narrated by other characters, and an external perspective in which Don Quijote is narrated by an "author." We shall examine the latter. In *Don Quijote* there are multiple narrators. In theory, several anonymous chroniclers relate the events, albeit in an imperfect manner as they often make mistakes. From what they have written, a "second" author writes, an author who possesses more extensive sources of information and who allows himself to adjust them. At the same time, this "second" author will end up relying on what is written by a "third" author, a Moor named Cide Hamete Benengeli, who places himself on a higher level. Since Benengeli's writings are in Arabic, the "second" author is forced to find a *morisco* to translate them. Now although the "second" author is situated on a lower level than the "third," he nevertheless surpasses the latter in that he updates the story in Castilian, and allows himself to praise, criticize, rectify, or comment on the Moorish historian. Don Quijote's exploits are thus relativized by a plurality of narrators: anything said about him may or may not be true, since no one is certain that a contradictory source does not exist. With this technique Cervantes separates the characters from their narrators. For if the narrators are unaware of certain periods in the characters' lives, or make mistakes and become confused, then surely Don Quijote must exist outside, and independently, of them: in real life. This absence of an absolute and superior narrator who can be trusted is further underscored by the deficiencies of the "second" and "third" narrators. Ultimately, this effort to show the real, independent, and historical existence of Don Quijote clashes with the undeniable fact that he is the character of a novel.

On the other hand, Don Quijote is said to be driven by hopes of achieving fame, and from his first sally he imagines how future historians will tell his story. But his speculations go much further: he imagines the book's words and even tries to articulate them. So, in the manner of a Chinese box—one that includes progressively smaller ones—Don Quijote *says* that his historian *will relate* what Don Quijote *tells* that Don Quijote *said* that his historian *would relate* what Don Quijote *is presently saying.* In other words, if it is true that the different historians relate what Don Quijote says and does, it is no less true that Don Quijote tells what his historians say and do. The author creates his character, but the character also creates his author. (This is also produced with many other characters: Cervantes talks about the priest and the priest talks about Cervantes.) An additional element of complexity comes into play: anything that the historians say about Don Quijote has relative value not only because of the deficiency of the historians but also because of their dependence on the characters. Whatever the historian might say about Don Quijote must be related to what Don Quijote says about himself, or to what the other characters say about him. All affirmations within the book become diluted in a multiplicity of relationships and are immediately relativized. No one is independent from, or superior to, anybody; everyone is interrelated. The book relates only what the book says.

Here Cervantes's methods of perspective become clear as they encompass a multiplicity of authors and circumstantial readers, for example. Many are characters within the book, who write or relate novels, and many are those who read or listen to them. Between the narrators and characters and between the readers and characters different levels of narrators and circumstantial readers are interposed. Even novels are constructed, as happens with the priest who designs an entire novel (that of Dorotea-Micomicona) in order to deceive Don Quijote. The Cervantine novel is constructed and deconstructed in a gigantic game of mirrors or prisms. The narrators include themselves as characters: the "second" narrator creates his own mininovel by relating his search for, and discovery of, Don Quijote's story and how he had it translated.

If we were to consider the irony that governs Cervantes's style, we could understand perfectly the inherent ambiguity of his writings. Irony produces an estrangement whose most immediate consequence is the possibility of uniting two seemingly contradictory ideas. By neither affirming nor denying them, Cervantes opts for both while choosing neither. Irony embraces everything, including the author himself. In irony Cervantes was to discover the novelist's most valuable instrument as the multiplicity of possible perspectives allows for a new and complex vision of things, which, without pointing out with precision the truth of the matter in question, circumscribes the frame of operation. Irony allows Cervantes to criticize, produce, and offer different points of view with remarkable impartiality.

On the level of meanings, the result of such a construction is obvious. One cannot seek the apology of idealism or realism in the *Quijote*. One cannot search for a didactic or logical exposition of a prefabricated thesis. Good and evil do not exist. Rather, there is the interaction among characters and among ideas. What is relevant is the way in which each character takes on the mission of interaction with others. The world is not translatable in a univocal sense but in multiple appropriations and interpretations of the same. Vis-à-vis the basin and the helmet, what the novel gives us is the "basin-helmet," that is, the capacity of each object, through its own peculiarity, for interpretation in accordance with the needs of those who use it. *Don Quijote* is at the same time a rejection of the values of humanism (symbolized in the romances of chivalry) and a cry for lost humanism. The satire of old ideals does not imply the exaltation of current ideals, but the affirmation of their dialectic in search of a synthesis. What is important to Cervantes is the dialectical game, the bringing to light of the multiple aspects of any problem. Hence, the novel seems to be invaded by a series of dualities in search of a synthesis. It is not Don Quijote *and* Sancho but Don Quijote becoming Sancho and Sancho becoming Don Quijote. It is not the sane Don Quijote and the mad Don Quijote but the mad *and* sane Don Quijote. Neither basin nor helmet, but basin-helmet. Cervantes's novel represents a formidable attack on dogmatism, the end of unique and indisputable truths, which, instead of giving way, as has been said, to a wholly relativistic philosophy, leads toward an essentially dialectical philosophy.

Above all the uncertainties and equivocations lies a striking affirmation: the power of writing and of the writer to "re-create" reality and to transform it. A detailed analysis of the dualities of *Don Quijote* would clearly reveal that the decisive element is not the polarization but the process toward the synthesis of that polarization.

Los Trabajos de Persiles y Sigismunda (1617)

This novel was published posthumously in 1617, a year after Cervantes's death. Cervantes had continued to work on it during the last days of his life and in his dedication to the Count of Lemos, he writes some pathetic lines, modifying a popular old ballad:

> With one foot in the grave
> and the anguish of death,
> Great Lord, I write this one for you.[33]

The words that follow reiterate that sense of anguish: "Yesterday they gave me extreme unction and today I write this; there is little time, anguish grows; hopes diminish, and with all of this, I lead my life upon a desire to live, and if I could only preserve it long enough to be able to kiss your excellency's feet . . ." ("Ayer me dieron la estremaución y hoy escrivo ésta; el tiempo es breve, las ansias crecen; las esperanzas menguan, y con todo esto, llevo la vida sobre el deseo que tengo de vivir, y quisiera yo ponerle coto hasta besar los pies a vuessa excelencia . . .").

Cervantes must have worked intensely on the novel during the last days of his life, terrified by the idea of leaving it unfinished. Yet, as may be seen in the last chapters of *Persiles*, he died unable to make final revisions. Perhaps no other work had preoccupied him as much as this one, which he considered his masterpiece. In the dedication to the Count of Lemos in the second part (1615) of *Don Quijote*, Cervantes refers to *Persiles* as a book that "has to be either the worst or the best ever composed in our language. I speak of those of entertainment; and I say that I regret having said the worst because, according to the opinion of my friends, it is bound to achieve the utmost extreme of possible goodness."[34] Cervantes probably devoted a great deal of time to this novel. A reasonable hypothesis[35] is that parts I and II were written between 1599 and 1605, coinciding with the model of the novel outlined by the Toledan canon in *Don Quijote* (I, 47):

> For all that he [the canon] had said against such books [of chivalry], he found one good thing in them: the fact that they offered a good intellect a chance to display itself. For they presented a broad and spacious field through which the pen could run without let or hindrance, describing shipwrecks, tempests, encounters, and battles; painting a brave captain with all the features necessary for the part; showing his wisdom in forestalling his enemies' cunning, his eloquence in persuading or dissuading his soldiers, his ripeness in counsel, his prompt resolution, his courage in awaiting or in making an attack; now depicting a tragic and lamentable incident, now a joyful and unexpected event; here a most beautiful lady, chaste, intelligent, and modest; there a Christian knight, valiant, and gentle; in one place a monstrous, barbarous braggart; in another a courteous prince, brave and wise; representing the goodness and loyalty of vassals, and the greatness and generosity of lords. Sometimes the writer might show his knowledge of astrology, or his excellence at cosmography or as a musician, or his wisdom in affairs of state, and he might even have an opportunity of showing his skill in necromancy. (426)[36]

This monstrous novel, full of action and exoticism, corresponds almost exactly to what is yielded in books I and II of *Persiles*. In books III and IV, however, things happen in a different manner.

A great similarity exists between the outline of *La española inglesa* (1609–1611?) and that of *Persiles*. In fact, one might conclude that the exemplary novel in question is a Byzantine novel in miniature. This would allow us to assume that following the first phase (1599–1605) of composition of the *Persiles*, Cervantes was to concentrate his efforts on *Don Quijote* until the work on *La española inglesa* allowed a re-working of *Persiles*, placing the composition of books III and IV between 1612 and 1616.

Thus, it is possible to explain the striking differences between the first and second halves of the book, the most salient of which is the differing function of the narrator in both parts. For if in books I and II the narrator is scarcely interwoven in the narrative, in books III and IV the narrator's presence is so overwhelming that the latter succeeds, as in some parts of *Don Quijote*, in establishing himself as a veritable protagonist.

The *Persiles* is inscribed within the tradition of the so-called Byzantine novel (distinguished by Heliodorus's classic work *The Aethiopica; or, The Adventures of Theagenes and Chariclea*, considered by critics of the time as an "epic in prose," which is precisely what Cervantes, who was situated in the narrative vanguard of his time, sought to achieve), whose themes were widespread in Spain during the last half of the sixteenth and beginning half of the seventeenth centuries. Just as Cervantes conceived it, the Byzantine novel is above all an adventure novel. The *Trabajos* to which the title alludes are the numerous and varied adventures lived by the two protagonists, the respective son of the queen of Tule and daughter of the queen of Friesland, countries found on the border of the polar areas. The protagonists travel through northern Europe, continuing on to the southern countries (Portugal, Spain, France, and Italy), until they finally reach their destination in Rome, where they are married. The entire novel is an entangled network of vicissitudes, dangers, voyages, shipwrecks, piracies, struggles, kidnappings, duels, captures, and escapes, many of which are of an extraordinary and even supernatural nature, lived out, moreover, by a series of characters who devote themselves not only to carrying out their multiple adventures but to telling and discussing them as well as drawing lessons from and reflecting upon them. The end result is a profusion of action and imagination conveyed in the characteristic fabric of Cervantine writing.

Despite an abundance of imagination and action, one can find a connecting thread as the novel is articulated and organized around the symbol of the pilgrimage. As in the case of *Don Quijote*, the main thread is the protagonists' journey. But the heroes' journey is one of the most characteristic symbols of the Christian tradition, for it alludes to life as a process of perfection and as a path toward God. Once again, Cervantes takes a model (the Byzantine novel, or, as before, the pastoral novel, the chivalric, or the Italian novel of intrigue) and destroys it from within. In making his heroes pilgrims he surpasses, with the stroke of a pen, the dimension of art for art's sake present in the Byzantine novel. The adventures and vicissitudes are not relevant in and of themselves, but as symbols of the pilgrimage toward the City of God. Moreover, he adds a new quality to the ancient symbol of pilgrimage, for now it is not a question of one pilgrim, but of two, and their pilgrimage is one of love. The Byzantine novel is simultaneously Christianized and inscribed in the canons of the Renaissance.[37] The youths' love is perfected during the long process of the pilgrimage. It is a ritual through which they are put to the test, through suffering, danger, and temptation, in order to purify that love and also cleanse themselves. In other words, Persiles and Sigismunda are catechumens, in the religious-erotic sense, until their arrival in Rome. Only after the arrival in the City of God do they achieve total perfection: Catholicism in religion, marriage in love.

The complex narrative structure of *Persiles* is the manifestation of the chain of being, an ideological metaphor characteristic of the Renaissance and perpetuated in the baroque. According to this principle—whose function is that of expressing the abundance, order, and unity of Divine Creation—the latter is a chain whose lowest link is buried in the depths of the inanimate, while the highest link is bound to divinity. All creation is a link in this chain, greater than its predecessor and less important than its follower. The inanimate gives rise to the vegetable; the vegetable to the animal; the animal to the human; the human to the angelic; and, finally, the angelic to the divine. *Persiles* reveals the metaphor of the chain of being from multiple points of view. One such perspective is that of the characters, who appear in an increasing order of perfection: first, the barbarians/savages, the lowest kind of human beings; then those who, like Clodio and Rosamunda, are still full of imperfections but nevertheless are superior to the barbarians; Arnaldo follows, surpassed in turn in physical and moral aspects by Persiles and Sigismunda, who, nevertheless, are intellectually inferior to Mauricio and Soldino. The last link in the chain is the Supreme Pontiff. More than simply a hierarchy of created types, the chain also represents a scale of perfection, which not only Persiles and Sigismunda but also the ex-barbarians Clodio and Ricla, and the Italian Rutilio, ascend. Nevertheless, it is clear that this hierarchy of perfection is viewed ironically, since the differences in the scale of perfection are defined by those who manage the culturally established order (the Pope, for example). In this sense one might say that the metaphor of the pilgrimage is also dealing with social, racial, and cultural status as agency. Another manifestation of the chain is the geographical course of the book—from the mythical Isle of Barbara, where the novel begins, to turbid and imprecise Denmark and Ireland, to Portugal, and through Spain, France, and Italy, finally arriving in Rome, "the heaven on earth." From the Isle of Barbara to the Papacy, or from friendship to marriage, the novel travels through a chain that leads to the apotheosis of the sublime.

Avalle-Arce deduces the novel's powerful ideological content from this structure, finding the true significance of this content in the universalization of human experience. If *Don Quijote* represents the exploration of this experience in its concrete nature and in certain socio-historical parameters, *Persiles* would be its abstraction beyond all conditioning, transforming that experience into a purely symbolic design. *Persiles* thus begins where *Don Quijote* leaves off, and is its culmination. Within this interpretative scheme, however ambitious *Persiles* may have been, a universalizing intention supposedly led it toward an abstraction of all narrative elements. The characters, for example, are (all) deemed to be one-dimensional and artificial, transparent symbols of universal validity. Persiles and Sigismunda would stand as the perfect Christian lovers, Rosamunda would represent lasciviousness, and Clodio slander. The completeness of *Persiles* as a novel was sacrificed to ideological expression. This interpretation undoubtedly leads toward the finding in *Persiles* of the most radical manifestation of the spirit of the Counter-Reformation.

Other possibilities of interpretation of *Persiles* have also been proposed, and not all deal with the culmination of a process—which is emphasized in the *Exemplary Novels* and in *Don Quijote*—or with Cervantes's acceptance of the ideals of the Counter-Reformation. Rather, they would concern another manifestation of the dialectic idealism-realism that is so characteristic in Cervantes's works. The fact that *Persiles* appeared after *Don Quijote,* in which this dialectic is surpassed, would not have any decisive value since *Persiles* was written over many years and cannot be dated with precision. According to this interpretation, Cervantes is torn between the worldview of his youth (Renaissance idealism) and the need to reject it—as an anachronism destroyed by history—in favor of a new interpretation of reality. *Persiles* would represent the final backlash toward an ideological position that begins with *La Galatea*, takes root in several of the *Novelas ejemplares*, and reappears sporadically in *Don Quijote*. While the latter represents the failure of the heroic effort to impose suitable ideals on reality, *Persiles* would have to be read as a triumph of those ideals. Somewhere between the idealism of the Renaissance and the realism of the baroque of the Counter-Reformation, Cervantes's writing would struggle in a multiple and repeated effort to arrive at the possibility of a synthesis.

The recent book by Diane de Armas Wilson (*Allegories of Love*) offers a different and challenging interpretation of *Persiles* and opens a new way of approaching Cervantes's writings from a more complex and fruitful perspective. Her analyses are grounded in the assumption that in his will to problematize the hegemonic discourse of his time Cervantes brings to the foreground the question of gender as an expression of how to give voice to the repressed Other.

It is interesting how, by quoting from Carlos Fuentes's *Old Gringo* ["This would not be only a man's story from now on. A presence (my presence . . .) will alter the story"] Wilson (248) sees *Persiles* as a final statement of Cervantes's interest in marginalized social elements. She remarks that even if Cervantes's sympathy for deviants and marginals has often been pointed out by critics, those groups have normally been cited to include Muslims, thieves, gypsies, Moorish converts, and even Protestants, but not women. Wilson underlines the important role played by gender in the novel and goes on to study "the system of difference in the *Persiles* from multiple angles—from the role of 'Otherness' as a code in Greek romance . . . to its travesty in Renaissance exorcism" (249). She further reflects upon her discovery as a modern "resistant woman reader" of how "Cervantes had opened the Golden Age signifying world to its conventionally absent mothers, that he did not allow them to remain outside representation," even if " 'the name of the Father' requires the repression of the mother" (250).

Wilson's approach highlights how "at the threshold of the *Persiles*, and at the close of his life, Cervantes's primal couple"—a Spaniard called Antonio and a Northern woman called Ricla—"shows readers how men and women can become 'bilingual' " (252). In her opinion, "it is this kind of collaboration that signifies the real 'labors' of Cervantes's title—learning the language of the Other" (252).

Ruth El Saffar (1985) had already underlined how "so long as we are caught in the dichotomies that entangled the Cervantes of 1605, we will not be able to read his late romances. But I think we are arriving at a time when that will be possible" (251). This possibility is at work in Wilson's book. She is not trying to add a particular point of view to the mainstream allegorical-religious approach, but more radically to present "an 'alternative' Cervantes": an interpretation of what has been called his "final statement on the human condition . . . based on the concept of gender as a category of analysis" (xiii).

We have seen in previous chapters how Cervantes's writing activates the reader. This activation is often ascribed to

> a fundamental strategy in the writings of sixteenth-century humanists, with their anti-authoritarian poetics of *serio ludere* and their interest in such literary modes and genres as philosophical and satirical dialogue, intellectual fantasy, and rhetorical paradox (for example, the challenging *Sileni Alcibiadis* of Erasmus) as a means of provoking readers to experience a higher awareness of their individuality, as well as their freedoms, responsibilities, and human limitations. (Forcione 1990: 337)

One must, of course, acknowledge Cervantes's Renaissance heritage (cf. Castro 1972) as it concerns the intimate relationship between the individual and society and, implicitly, the possibility of harmonizing the interests of the former with the ideals and goals of the community. Yet one might also consider that what Cervantes brings to the fore is the illusory character of the representation of "harmony." Thus, while the individual seeks to communicate with society, there also emerges an awareness that language as a means of communication has become an obstacle to knowledge. In Cervantes's dialogical novel, to communicate means to construct a space that allows for the intervention of different discourses. The reader is thus compelled to navigate through the various linguistic and social spheres that are experienced in line with one's interests, desires, and cultural competence. The Cervantine reader or "lector mío" is engaged in a critical activity that involves an exploration of the self in relation to society and its beliefs. This reader, recognizing his or her own ties to those beliefs in the sense of being a part of the society that shares them, also finds those ideas confining in the search for knowledge.

From our perspective, Wilson's book provides an accurate theoretical frame to focus on this specific and definitive "multiple eye" that constitutes the last step of Cervantine writing. If, as she writes, the presence of a woman (Ricla) makes Antonio's story different—as happens in *Old Gringo*, but nearly four centuries earlier—then the lucidity with which Cervantes acknowledges the dead end of Don Quijote's useless idealization of the feminine (Dulcinea) can explain the strong sexuality at work in *Persiles*. From this point of view, this late novel is evidently a follow-up to *Don Quijote* but, at the same time, goes a step beyond. First, the multiplicity of perspectives and points of view that in *Don Quijote* dissolve the unified narrator into multiple single narrators, becomes in *Persiles* a dialogical narrator, that is to say, a system of discursive relations, one which, as Wilson states, has to be "bilingual" in order to be credible and/or real. Second, the apparent lack of realism of this Greek-like romance, by including openly sexual relations into narrative, gives the fictitious world a chance to be closely attached to everyday reality. Thus the place of the subject of discourse will not shift, as in the case of *Don Quijote*, from one point to another. Rather it will now be grounded in the *in-between*, since the acceptance of, and the interrelation with, "Otherness" is the only way for narrator and characters to exist in dialogue with one another.

Epilogue: All That Heaven Allows; or, The Self-Made World

Throughout the pages of this book, we have argued that Cervantes's writing should be viewed not only as an original proposal but also, and fundamentally, as the result of a complex dialogue with the discourses of his own time. In this sense, his interest in writing may be seen as going beyond the production of individual works, to encompass a rethinking and a reshaping of the manner in which those works had to be dealt with. In a way, one could characterize Cervantes's universe as metadiscursive, despite the fact that, until very recently, such a characterization has eluded a large body of critical analysis. Thus, the attention given to Don Quijote as a character rather than to Cervantes as a writing system, or to the sources of *Los trabajos de Persiles y Sigismunda* rather than to its discursive structure has been concerned more with objects than with the epistemological presuppositions that made them work.

Cervantes's criticism of the discursive world of his own time is not limited to matters of art, aesthetics, or literature. Rather, it encompasses the mapping of a new set of parameters as he seeks to subvert the very notions of realism and representation. The idea is that the "real" world, as presented to us, exists only as a construction, one that is shaped through the conventions of perception and interpretation. Things are but things seen, touched, heard, smelled, tasted, in other words, understood; they are the result of a reaccommodation of what exists according to our culturally inherited ideas about how reality works and what reality is. From this perspective, Cervantes's writings aim, simultaneously, toward the production of a new image of the world and toward a dialogue with the very discourses that have constructed the world the way we actually know it. Thus, Cervantes's task as a writer must have been difficult, for he was dealing both with established literary taste—in order to offer a new product for consumption—and with the notion of consumption itself.

One can understand the frustration and parallel pride with which Cervantes justifies a work received from patterns that he is lucidly and constantly trying to question. The irony of some well-known lines from *Viaje del Parnaso* appears quite evident from this perspective, as the Cervantes who is framed within the poem relates poetic "grace" with physical exhaustion and anguish, referring to himself as

> I, who am always out of breath and sleepless,
>> For as a poet I seem to have
>> The grace that heaven denied me.

> Yo, que siempre me afano ye me desvelo
>> Por parecer que tengo de poeta
> La gracia que no quiso darme el cielo. (Ed. Gaos 1974: 54)

The contemporary filmmaker Douglas Sirk, discussing his film *All That Heaven Allows* (1954) with the Spanish filmmaker Antonio Drove in an interview on Spanish television in 1978, stated that the problem is that heaven allows very little, since for good or worse, it has nothing to do with human issues: everything useful for human beings must be constructed from here, with our own means. Along these lines, to be a "poet" does not depend upon having a special body or brain structure, but on the acceptance, by a particular culture, of an individual who writes in a particular way, according to models that are assumed as valid within that culture. For Cervantes, who views writing less in terms of inspiration than as the result of a working process (for inspiration usually comes only after countless hours of hard work), reality is a self-made structure, in the same manner that we can speak of a self-made person; reality is something that exists as a moving and changing construction, depending on the system of values with which one is working. In this sense, Cervantes is stating—however indirectly— the institutional/instructional character of writing.

In this book we have analyzed Cervantes's poetic writings, arguing that the relative lack of importance that is traditionally attributed to this part of his work comes from a misunderstanding of what he was trying to do. In effect, when those writings are approached from a different conception of poetry—Lope de Vega's, for example—Cervantes's verses may seem somewhat rough and lacking in musicality. Yet, does one not face the same problem when analyzing many of the lines of the great playwright Calderón as if he wrote for the page rather than for the stage? The idea here is that different products, made for different "markets," demand different analytical tools; no general and abstract concept of poetry would be valid for all places and for all times. As a cultural construction, "poetry" means different things in different historical and cultural contexts. Cervantes's poems do assume the existence of institutionalized and hegemonic poetic patterns in his medium, but they do so only for purposes of dialogue and discussion; these are never accepted as necessary and immovable rules.

We have seen that something similar happens with Cervantine dramatic works, for neither his comedies nor his interludes belong to the tradition called the "new art of writing plays" ("arte nuevo de hacer comedias"). Cervantes painstakingly attacks this Lopean tradition for its ideological perversion: a propensity to propagate social myths through the manipulation of an undiscerning, and ideologically homogeneous, mass audience. In this sense, Cervantes's well-known reference to Lope de Vega as a "monstruo de naturaleza" ("monster of nature"), which has often been understood as a compliment—as an allusion to his rival's indefatigable energy and productivity, may perhaps be read more accurately as a sarcastic attack on a contemporary playwright who was seen as having "monstrously" sold out his convictions to the exigencies of the marketplace. When Cervantes defines Lope de Vega as a "monstruo de naturaleza" in the very context in which he presents himself as a playwright, he distances himself from the official theater as established and institutionalized by Lope and his school. As a result of that distancing, our critical position in trying to establish a dialogue with Cervantine theatricality must, of necessity, recognize that, far from dealing with a failed playwright, we are confronted with one who, rather than "representing" the world, projects the world itself as a representation. For this reason, it may be said that Cervantes looks for a specific type of receiver ("lector mío" or "my reader"); that he is imagining a "public" in opposition to the undiscerning "mass" audience addressed by Lope de Vega's new theater.

If we may shift the discussion to our time, who can say, for example, that Bertolt Brecht's plays are good theater and that Eugene O'Neill's are not, or vice versa? We know that both wrote for the stage, even though each of them addressed and/or constructed a different typology of spectators and spoke about different worlds, insofar as they were assuming the so-called reality in a different way. As critics, readers, or spectators we can even agree with one or the other, but we cannot assess and evaluate their plays by applying the same rules as if these were universal, just as we cannot use English grammar to judge, linguistically, a Spanish sentence. It is that simple.

The international success of *Don Quijote* is both important and undeniable. One might say, however, that *Don Quijote* is what it is precisely because it belongs to a greater, more complex, and articulated project that encompasses Cervantes's entire discursive production. This project includes his controversial *Persiles y Sigismunda*, whose structure has been viewed recently as constituting "a revolutionary form of writing, one that interweaves the idea of gender with the production of meaning" (Wilson 1991: xiv). It is also becoming increasingly clear that every single discursive practice need not be reduced to narrativity, nor must narrativity be reduced to the institutionalized mode of the novel. In fact, Cervantes's continuous transgression of the limits of traditional genres is precisely what constitutes the central point in his epistemological project. If the world acts as a text, then the relation between reality and literature has to be grounded in this textual character. In the final analysis, neither the novel, nor poetry, nor theater can "double" the world. The metaphor of the mirror that is implied in the theory of *imitatio* has to be substituted for that of the "shattering glass," which, to paraphrase Lewis Carroll, should be able to allow us to dream within the dream when the dream is over. From this perspective, what has been defined as "Cervantian realism" appears to be a problem that goes well beyond the "literary" question. In this sense Cervantes, tired and frustrated as he was at the end of his symbolic journey to Parnassus ["And I threw myself vanquished on the bed / For tiring is a day, when it is long" (Y arrojéme molido sobre el lecho / que cansa, cuando es larga, una jornada)], can establish a living dialogue with our contemporary world. That is, many of the ideas for which he was fighting, within a Spain that was essentially antimodernist and which bore the somber stamp of the Counter-Reformation, are today common currency in our symbolic order.

Notes

Introduction

1. Jacques Dubois, "Pour une critique litteraire sociologique." Critical references to materials that appear in a language other than English are cited in translation. On the question of poetics and discourses we are guided by the insightful work of M. Bakhtin, especially his "Discourses and the Novel."

1. Poetry as Autobiography

1. *Historia y relación verdadera de la enfermedad, felicísimo tránsito y suntuosas exequias fúnebres de la Serenísima Reina de España Doña Isabel de Valois, nuestra Señora.*

2. Quien goza de quietud siempre en su estado,
   y el efecto le acude a la esperanza
   y a lo que quiere nada le es trocado,
   argúyese que poca confianza
   se puede tener dél, que goce y vea
   con claros ojos bienaventuranza. ("Elegía" vv. 133–138)

   No alcanzan perezosos,
   honrados triunfos, ni vitoria alguna,
   ni pueden ser dichosos
   los que, no contrastando a la fortuna,
   entregan, desvalidos,
   al ocio blando todos los sentidos. (*Don Quijote I*, 43)

Quotations from *Don Quijote* follow the edition of Luis Murillo (Madrid: Castalia, 1978). English translations of quotations from Cervantes's writing are our own, unless followed by a page number, which refers to a published translation. For *Don Quijote* we use the translation of J. M. Cohen (Baltimore: Penguin Books, 1950).

3. Desde mis tiernos años amé el arte

   dulce de la agradable poesía

   y en ella procuré siempre agradarte. (Chap. 4, vv. 31–33)

4. See, for example, Ricardo Rojas (1948), or Gerardo Diego (1948) who likewise states that "without divine calling no poet is legitimate. . . . Miguel who was born a poet, died a confessed poet" ("sin la divina vocación no hay poeta legítimo. . . . Miguel que nació poeta, poeta confesado murió").

5. Yo, que siempre me afano y me desvelo

   por parecer que tengo de poeta

   la gracia que no quiso darme el cielo. (Chap. 1, vv. 25–27)

6. Pasa, raro inventor, pasa adelante

   con tu sotil disinio, y presta ayuda

   a Apolo, que la tuya es importante.

   Antes que el escuadrón vulgar acuda

   de más de veinte mil sietemesinos

   poetas, que de serlo están en duda. (Chap. 1, vv. 223–228)

   ¡Cuerpo de mi con tanta poetambre! (Chap. 2, v. 396)

   Dijo: ¿Será posible que en España

   Haya nueve poetas laureados? (Chap. 8, vv. 97–98)

7. See Valbuena Prat (1943), Schevill and Bonilla (1922), or even Alborg (1966), who speak of "painful confession," "bitter realization," and so on.

8. See Blecua (1947).

9. "Con la poca estimación que de ellos los príncipes y el vulgo hace, con sólos sus entendimientos comunican sus altos y extraños conceptos, sin osar publicarlos al mundo, y tengo para mí que el Cielo debe ordenarlo de esta manera, porque no merece el mundo ni el mal considerado siglo nuestro gozar de manjares al alma tan gustosos."

10. "Privilegios, Ordenanzas y Advertencias que Apolo envía a los poetas españoles" (Adjunta al *Viaje del Parnaso*):

   Es el primero, que algunos poetas sean conocidos tanto por el desaliño de sus personas como por la fama de sus versos.

   Item, que si algún poeta dijere que es pobre, sea luego creído por su simple palabra, sin otro juramento o averiguación alguna.

   Ordénase que todo poeta sea de blanda y de suave condición, y que no mire en puntos, aunque los traiga sueltos en sus medias.

   Item, que si algún poeta llegare a casa de algún su amigo o conocido, y estuvieren comiendo, y le convidare, que aunque el jure que ya ha comido, no se le crea en ninguna manera, sino que le hagan comer por fuerza, que en tal caso no se le hará muy grande.

   Item, que el más pobre poeta del mundo, como no sea de los Adanes y Matusalenes, pueda decir que es enamorado, aunque no le esté, y poner el nombre a su dama como más le viniere a cuento, ora llamándola Amarili, ora Anarda, ora Clori, ora Filis, ora Fílida, o ya Juana Téllez, o como más gustare, sin que desto se le pueda pedir ni pida razón alguna. . . .

Item, se advierte que no ha de ser tenido por ladrón el poeta que hurtare algún verso ajeno y le encajare entre los suyos, como no sea todo el concepto y toda la copla entera, que en tal caso tan ladrón es como Caco. (Ed. Gaos, 188–190)

11. Si a militar concierto se reduce

cualquier pequeño ejército que sea,

veréis que como sol claro reluce,

y alcanza las victorias que desea;

pero si a flojedad él se conduce,

aunque abreviado el mundo en él se vea,

en un momento quedará deshecho

por más reglada mano y fuerte pecho.

12.   1. Los conocimientos de tipo intelectual, herméticos, son captados por "ingenios aptos a las cosas divinas e intelectuales y mente conservativa de las verdaderas ciencias y no corruptivas de ellas."

2. En cuanto al "provecho", es asignado a las mentes según tres grados: (a) "las mentes bajas pueden tomar de las poesías solamente la historia con el ornamento del verso y su melodía"; (b) "las otras más levantadas comen, además de esto, el sentido moral"; y (c) "otras más altas pueden comer, allende de esto, del manjar alegórico, no sólo de la filosofía natural, mas también de la astrología y la teología."

13. We are thinking, for example, of the perfection of The Ballad of Jealousy (Romance de los celos):

Where the sun sets

between two boulders split asunder

lies the entrance to the abyss,

I mean by that a cave . . .

Yace donde el sol se pone

entre dos partidas peñas

una entrada del abismo,

quiero decir una cueva . . .

14. See, respectively, the following poems:

Although you think that I am happy

I carry grief within me (The Baths of Algiers)

Aunque pensáis que me alegro

conmigo traigo el dolor (Los baños de Argel)

Child, you spilled the waste water

and did not say: "There it goes." (The House of Jealousy)

Dearramaste el agua niña

y no dijiste: "Agua va." (La casa de los celos)

15. El fruto que fue sembrado

por mi trabajo contino,

a dulce sazón llegado,

fue con próspero destino

en mi poder entregado.

Y apenas pude llegar
a términos tan sin par,
cuando vine a conocer
la ocasión de tal placer
ser para mí de pesar.

Mostróseme a la vista
un rico albergue de mil bienes lleno;
triunfé de su conquista,
y cuando más sereno
se me mostraba el hado,
vilo en escuridad negra cambiado.

16. Vuela mi estrecha y débil esperanza
con flacas alas, y aunque sube el vuelo
a la alta cumbre del hermoso cielo,
jamás el punto que pretende alcanza.
Yo vengo a ser perfecta semejanza
de aquel mancebo que de Creta al suelo
dejó, y, contrario de su padre al celo,
a la región del cielo se abalanza.

Caerán mis atrevidos pensamientos,
del amoroso incendio derretidos,
en el mar del temor turbado y frío;
pero no llevarán cursos violentos,
del tiempo y de la muerte prevenidos,
al lugar del olvido el nombre mío.

17. If, as Gerardo Diego intelligently states, Cervantes had a tin ear that was "not receptive or passive, but active and thunderous" ("no receptiva o pasiva sino activa o entonadora"), how does one account for the fact that through the years he persists in his poetic work and in the orchestration of his prose?

18. "Esta dificultad de las rimas, la cual como saben los que mejor escriben en este género de poesía, disturba muchas y hermosas sentencias; que no se pueden narrar con tanta facilidad y clareza."

19. "Debe el poeta regirse más por el sonido, que por otra ninguna vía; y para esto suelen algunos ir cantando lo que van componiendo . . . Es menester que tenga para cada compostura su sonada . . . Cuando estudiaba me leía mi maestro a Virgilio cantando, porque decía él, que de aquella manera se sentía mejor la suavidad del verso, y que Virgilio al tiempo que los iba componiendo, los iba también cantando."

20. The preoccupations of treatise writers on aspects of tone and time of verse rhythm in the sixteenth century [one of whose most sublime examples is Francisco Salinas (the blind musician immortalized by Fray Luis) in his *De musica libri septem* (1577)] are not documented in the seventeenth century, when the problem of rhythm is reduced to a matter of meter and rhyme, e.g., in Juan Caramuel's *Rhythmica* of 1665.

21. "Pero como la belleza corpórea se divide asimesmo en dos partes, que son en cuerpos vivos y en cuerpos muertos, también puede haber amor de belleza corporal que

sea bueno. Muéstrase la una parte de la belleza corporal en cuerpos vivos de varones y de hembras, y ésta consiste en que todas las partes del cuerpo sean de por sí buenas, y que todas juntas hagan un todo perfecto y formen un cuerpo proporcionado de miembros y suavidad de colores. La otra belleza de la parte corporal no viva, consiste en pinturas, estatuas, edificios, la cual belleza puede amarse sin que el amor con que se amare se vitupere." (II, 44–45)

22. "Y según a mí me parece, este género de escritura y composición cae debajo de aquél de las fábulas que llaman milesias, que son cuentos disparatados, que atienden solamente a deleitar, y no a enseñar; al contrario de lo que hacen las fábulas apólogas, que deleitan y enseñan juntamente. Y puesto que el principal intento de semejantes libros sea el deleitar, no sé yo como pueden conseguirle, yendo llenos de tantos y tan desaforados disparates; que el deleite que en el alma se concibe ha de ser de la hermosura y concordancia que ve o contempla en las cosas que la vista o la imaginación le ponen delante; y toda cosa que tiene en sí fealdad y descompostura no nos puede causar contento alguno. Pues ¿qué hermosura puede haber, o qué proporción de partes con el todo, y del todo con las partes, en un libro o fábula donde un mozo de dieciseis años da una cuchillada a un gigante como una torre, y le divide en dos mitades, como si fuera de alfeñique, y cuando nos quieren pintar una batalla, después de haber dicho que hay de la parte de los enemigos un millón de combatientes, como sea contra ellos el señor del libro, forzosamente mal que nos pese, habemos de entender que el tal caballero alcanzó la victoria por sólo el valor de su fuerte brazo? Pues ¿qué diremos de la facilidad con que una reina o emperatriz heredera se conduce en los brazos de un andante y no conocido caballero?" (1: 564–565)

23. See Vicente Gaos (1971).

24. Mira, Clemente, el estrellado velo

con que esta noche fría

compite con el día

de luces adornando el cielo;

y en esta semejanza,

si tanto tu divino ingenio alcanza,

aquel rostro figura

donde asiste el extremo de hermosura.

25. See Karl Selig (1962).

26. "Despabilé los ojos, limpiémelos, y vi que no dormía, sino que realmente estaba despierto; con todo esto me tenté la cabeza y los pechos, por certificarme si era yo mismo el que allí estaba, o alguna fantasma vana y contrahecha; pero el tacto, el sentimiento, los discursos concertados que entre mí hacía, me certificaron que yo era allí entonces el que soy aquí ahora."

27. For these concepts as used here see Emilio Orozco Díaz (1970).

28. ELICIO: Esle tan fácil a mi corta suerte

ver con la amarga muerte

junta la dulce vida

y estar su mal a do su bien se anida,

que entre contrarios veo

que mengua la esperanza, y no el deseo. (*La Galatea*, vv. 43–48)

SAAVEDRA: En la veloz carrera apresuradas

las horas del ligero tiempo veo

contra mí con el cielo conjuradas

queda atrás la esperanza, y no el deseo. (*Los tratos de Argel*, I)

29. See Alonso Zamora Vicente (1947), who speaks of the "veiled voice" of Cervantes in the poem.

30. See Blecua (1948).

31. Tú que ganaste obrando

un nombre en todo el mundo

y un grado sin segundo.

32. His purpose was not to duplicate what he had already achieved in "Canto de Calíope" ("Calliope's Song") of *La Galatea*. As José Manuel Blecua noted, Cervantes was not merely praising contemporary poets, but was alluding to something much more profound and serious. Nor was it a matter, as Menéndez y Pelayo stated around the turn of the century in"Cervantes, considerado como poeta" (Rpt. 1941) of "an elegant/ ingenious and discreetly critical poem" ("un elegante/ingenioso y discreto poema crítico"). Scholars have usually compared *Viaje* with Lope de Vega's *Laurel de Apolo* (*The Laurel of Apollo*), judging Lope's version to be superior to that of Cervantes. Yet, it is clear that those two works do not have much in common and that *Viaje* should be related to the rest of Cervantes's production.

According to F. Rodríguez Marín, Cervantes conceived his *Viaje* both as escape to a nostalgic past and to celebrate, in passing, his contemporary poets.

33. ¡Oh tú—dijo—que los poetas

canonizaste de la larga lista,

por causas y por vías indirectas!

¿Dónde tenías, magancés, la vista

aguda de tu ingenio, que así ciego

fuiste tan mentiroso cronista?

34. Aquel que de poeta no se precia,

¿para qué escribe versos y los dice?

¿Por qué desdeña lo que más aprecia?

Jamás me contenté ni satisfice

de hipócritos melindres; llanamente

quise alabanzas de lo que bien hice.

35. This autobiographical inscription has been noted by Elias L. Rivers (1970) and Jean Canavaggio (1977). See also Francisco Márquez Villanueva (1990). Jordi Gracia García (1989) points out how the *Viaje* shows the literary and moral abjection as origin of the sad situation of the poets.

36. See Rodríguez Marín (1935).

37. See a brilliant analysis of the poem in Francisco Márques Villanueva (1990), who cites an extensive bibliography on this topic.

38. Ibid.

39. See, for example, Rodríguez Marín (1935), and Schevill and Bonilla (1922).

40. Cantar con voz tan entonada y viva

que piensen que soy cisne y que me muero. (Chap. 4, vv. 564–565)

41. Fuíme con esto, y, lleno de despecho,

busqué mi antigua y lóbrega posada,

y arrojéme molido sobre el lecho;

que cansa, cuando es larga, una jornada. (Chap. 8, vv. 454–457)

2. Theater, Literature, and Social History

1. "El verso es el mismo que piden las comedias, que ha de ser, de los tres estilos, el ínfimo, y que el lenguaje de los entremeses es propio de las figuras que en ellos se introducen." Subsequent quotations from the *entremeses* are from the Spadaccini edition, with page references parenthetically documented; English translations are our own.

2. "La costumbre / de llamar entremeses las comedias / antiguas donde está en su fuerza el arte, / siendo una acción y entre plebeya gente, / porque entremés de rey jamás se ha visto."

3. See Maravall, *La literatura picaresca*.

4. See Maravall, *Culture of the Baroque*.

5. "y por lo menos se debiera prohibir con todo rigor que ninguna mujer de vida notada pudiera andar en coche . . . Parece asimismo conveniente que a los caballeros mozos, que para complir con su estado debieran ejercitarse en la caballería, se le prohibiesen los coches, en que se poltroniza la juventud . . ."

6. "Adviertan los que de Dios / juzgan los castigos grandes / que no hay plazo que no llegue / ni deuda que no se pague" and "Mientras en el mundo viva, / no es justo que diga nadie, / '¡Qué largo me lo fiáis!', / siendo tan breve el cobrarse."

7. "En los reinos y en las repúblicas bien ordenadas, había de ser limitado el tiempo de los matrimonios, y de tres en tres años se habían de deshacer, o confirmarse de nuevo, como cosas de arrendamiento, con perpetuo dolor de entrambas partes."

8. "Todo el mundo ponga demandas de divorcios; que al cabo, al cabo, los más se quedan como estaban, y nosotros habemos gozado del fruto de sus pendencias y necedades."

9. MOSTRENCA: Nacidas somos; no hizo Dios a nadie
   A quien desamparase. Poco valgo;
   Pero, en fin, como y ceno, y a mi cuyo
   Le traigo más vestido que un palmito;
   PIZPITA: Pequeña soy, Trampagos, pero grande
   Tengo la voluntad para servirte;
   No tengo cuyo, y tengo ochenta cobas;
   REPULIDA: Tuya soy; ponme un clavo y una S
   En estas dos mejillas.

10. "¿De qué me sirve a mí todo aquesto, si en mitad de la riqueza estoy pobre, y en medio de la abundancia con hambre?"

11. "¿Yo le tomé, sobrina? A la fe, diómele quien pudo; y yo, como muchacha, fui más presta al obedecer que al contradecir; pero, si yo tuviera tanta experiencia destas cosas, antes me tarazara la lengua con los dientes, que pronunciar aquel sí."

12. "Les daba tantas dádivas que, aunque tenían lástima a su hija por la estrecheza en que vivía [por estar encerrada], la templaban con las muchas dádivas que Carrizales, su liberal yerno, les daba."

13. "¡Si supieses qué galán me ha deparado la buena suerte! Mozo, bien dispuesto, pelinegro, y que le huele la boca a mil azahares!"

14. ESTUDIANTE: La ciencia que aprendí en la Cueva de Salamanca, de donde yo soy natural, si se dejara usar sin miedo de la Santa Inquisición, yo sé que cenara y recenara a costa de mis herederos; y aun quizá no estoy muy fuera de usalla . . . , pero no sé yo si estas señoras serán tan secretas como yo lo he sido.

15. PANCRACIO: No se cure dellas, amigo, sino haga lo que quisiere, que yo las haré que callen; y ya deseo en todo estremo ver algunas destas cosas que dice se aprenden en la Cueva de Salamanca.

16. PANCRACIO: Entremos; que quiero averiguar si los diablos comen o no, con otras cien mil cosas que dellos cuentan; y, por Dios, que no han de salir de mi casa hasta que me dejen enseñado en la ciencia y ciencias que se enseñan en la Cueva de Salamanca.

17. "Aquí le desollaremos cerrado como a gato; y para principio traigo aquí a vuestra merced esta cadena . . . , que pesa ciento y veinte escudos de oro, la cual tomará vuestra merced y me dará diez escudos agora, que yo he menester para ciertas cosillas, y gastará otros veinte en una cena esta noche."

18. "Según he oído decir, andaba muy decaída la caballería en España, porque se empanaban diez o doce caballeros mozos en un coche y azotaban las calles de noche y de día, sin acordárseles que había caballos y jineta en el mundo."

19. "Ese mal nos hagan; porque has de saber, hermana, que está en opinión, entre los que siguen la guerra, cuál es mejor, la caballería o la infantería, y hase averiguado que la infantería española lleva la gala a todas las naciones. Y agora podremos las alegres mostrar a pie nuestra gallardía . . . , y más yendo descubiertos los rostros, quitando la ocasión de que ninguno se llame a engaño si nos sirviese, pues nos ha visto."

20. "Acomoda tu brío y tu limpieza, y tu manto de soplillo sevillano, y tus nuevos chapines, en todo caso, con las virillas de plata, y déjate ir por esas calles; que yo te aseguro que no falten moscas a tan buena miel . . ."

21. SOLDADO: Pues ven acá, sota-sacristán de Satanás.

SACRISTÁN: Pues voy allá, caballo de Ginebra.

SOLDADO: Bueno; sota y caballo; no falta sino el rey para tomar las manos.

22. "Dile una destas cajas de membrillo, muy grande, llena de cercenaduras de hostias, blancas como la misma nieve, y de añadidura cuatro cabos de velas de cera, asimismo blancas como un armiño."

23. SOLDADO: Niña, échame un ojo; mira mi garbo; soldado soy, castellano pienso ser; brío tengo de corazón; soy el más galán hombre del mundo; y, por el hilo deste vestidillo, podrás sacar el ovillo de mi gentileza.

SACRISTÁN: Cristina, yo soy músico, aunque de campanas; para adornar una tumba y colgar una iglesia para fiestas solenes, ningún sacristán me puede llevar ventaja; y estos oficios bien los puedo ejercitar casado, y ganar de comer como un príncipe.

24. "Viene el sotasacristán Pasillas, armado con un tapador de tinaja y una espada muy mohosa; viene con él otro Sacristán, con un morrión y una vara o palo, atado a él un rabo de zorra."

25. "Aunque zapatero, no soy tan descortés que tengo de despojar a vuesa merced de sus joyas y preseas; vuesa merced se quede con ellas, que yo me quedaré con mis chinelas, que es lo que me está más a cuento."

26. "Es Peribáñez labrador de Ocaña, / cristiano viejo y rico, hombre tenido / en gran veneración de sus iguales, / y que si se quisiese alzar ahora / en esta villa, seguirán su nombre / cuantos salen al campo con su arado, / porque es, aunque villano, muy honrado."

27. "el cual fabricó y compuso el sabio Tontonelo debajo de tales paralelos, rumbos, astros y estrellas, con tales puntos, caracteres y observaciones, que ninguno puede ver las cosas que en él se muestran, que tenga alguna raza de confeso, o no sea habido y procreado de sus padres de legítimo matrimonio."

28. "y el que fuere contagiado destas dos tan usadas enfermedades, despídase de ver las cosas, jamás vistas ni oídas, de mi retablo."

29. FURRIER: ¿Está loca esta gente? ¿Qué diablos de doncella es ésta, y qué baile, y que Tontonelo?

30. "El suceso ha sido extraordinario; la virtud del Retablo se queda en su punto, y mañana lo podemos mostrar al pueblo; y nosotros mismos podemos cantar el triunfo desta batalla, diciendo: ¡Vivan Chirinos y Chanfalla!"

31. Y mírese qué alcaldes nombraremos

Para el año que viene, que sean tales,

Que no los pueda calumniar Toledo,

Sino que los confirme y dé por buenos,

Pues para esto ha sido nuestra junta

32. "A tal pueblo podrá llegar el pobre, / Que le pesen a oro; que hay hogaño / Carestía de alcaldes de caletre / En lugares pequeños casi siempre."

33. "Dime, desventurado; ¿que demonio / Se revistió en tu lengua? ¿Quién te mete / A ti en reprehender a la justicia? / ¿Has tú de gobernar a la república? / Métete en tus campanas y en tu oficio; / Deja a los que gobiernan, que ellos saben / Lo que han de hacer mejor que no nosotros."

3. On Theater as Narrativity

1. References are to A. Morel Fatio's edition, reproduced by Federico Sánchez Escribano and Alberto Porqueras Mayo (1965), 125–136.

2. There are some equivalences with Ben Jonson in England. See Stanley Wells (1970: 41–47).

3. As Emilio Orozco Díaz (1978) has shown, Lope's *Arte nuevo* is not a programmatic text in a strict sense, but an academic discourse, a text to be read before an audience, a kind of lecture, subjected to its own restrictions and its own rhetoric. From that perspective, we might even speak of a manifesto, in a modern sense, argumentations, that is, that do not aim to explain as much as to legitimatize a concrete practice.

4. José Antonio Maravall (1975: 220).

5. "Pero lo que más me le quitó de las manos, y aun del pensamiento, de acabarle, fue un argumento que hice conmigo mesmo, sacado de las comedias que ahora se representan, diciendo: "Si estas que ahora se usan, así las imaginadas como las de historia, todas o las más son conocidos disparates y cosas que no llevan pies ni cabeza, y, con todo eso, el vulgo las oye con gusto y las tiene y las aprueba por buenas, estando tan lejos de serlo, y los autores que las componen y los actores que las representan dicen que así han de ser, porque así las quiere el vulgo, y no de otra manera, y que las que llevan traza y siguen la fábula como el arte pide, no sirven sino para cuatro discretos que las entienden, y todos los demás se quedan ayunos de entender su artificio, y que a ellos les está mejor ganar de comer con los muchos, que no opinión de los pocos, deste modo vendrá a ser un libro, al cabo de haberme quemado las cejas por guardar los preceptos referidos, y vendré a ser el sastre del cantillo" (I: 568).

6. "todos ellos [los libros de caballerías] son una mesma cosa, y no tiene más éste o aquél, ni estotro que el otro" (I: 564).

7. "no está la falta en el vulgo que pide disparates, sino en aquellos que no saben representar otra cosa" (I: 569).

8. Mas porque en fin hallé que las comedias

estaban en España en aquel tiempo,

no como sus primeros inventores

pensaron que en el mundo se escribieran,
mas como las trataron muchos bárbaros
que enseñaron al vulgo sus rudezas,
y así se introdujeron de tal modo
que quien con arte agora las escribe
muere sin fama y galardón, que puede,
entre los que carecen de su lumbre,
más que razón y fuerza, la costumbre.

9. Porque considerando que la cólera
de un español sentado no se templa
si no le representan en dos horas
hasta el Final Juïcio desde el Génesis,
yo hallo que, si allí se ha de dar gusto,
con lo que se consigue es lo más justo.

10. Cf. Edward H. Friedman (1981: 10).

11. See Díez Borque (1978: 262).

12. PANCRACIO: ¿Y agora tiene vuesa merced algunas [comedias]?
MIGUEL: Seis tengo, con otros seis entremeses.
PANCRACIO: Pues, ¿por qué no se representan?
MIGUEL: Porque ni los autores me buscan ni yo les voy a buscar a ellos.
PANCRACIO: No deben de saber que vuesa merced las tiene.
MIGUEL: Sí saben; pero como tienen sus poetas paniaguados y les va bien con
ellos, no buscan pan de trastrigo. Pero yo pienso darlas a la estampa, para que
se vea de espacio lo que pasa apriesa, y se disimula, o no se entiende, cuando
las representan. Y las comedias tienen sus sazones y tiempos, como los cantares.
[We quote from Vicente Gaos's edition (1974: 183).]

13. See J. A. Maravall (1972: 36).

14. Cf. Casalduero (1966: 15) and Friedman (1981: 4).

15. Adviértase que sólo este sujeto
tenga una acción, mirando que la fábula
de ninguna manera sea episódica,
quiero decir inserta de otra cosa,
que del primer intento se desvíen,
ni que della se pueda quitar miembro
que del contexto no derriba el todo.

16. no hay que advertir que pase en el periodo
de un sol, aunque es consejo de Aristóteles,
porque ya le perdimos el respeto
cuando mezclamos la sentencia trágica
a la humildad de la bajeza cómica.

17. pues vemos que si acaso un recitante
hace un traidor, es tan odioso a todos
que lo que va a comprar no se lo venden,
y huye el vulgo de él cuando le encuentra;

y si es leal le prestan y convidan,

y hasta los principales le honran y aman,

le buscan, le regalan y le aclaman.

18. See *Memorial de la política necesaria y útil restauración de la república de España,* Part 2, f. 25B.

19. Walter Cohen (1985).

20. See Barthes (1970), White (1972, 1978), Talens (1975).

21. See Jorge Luis Borges, *Otras inquisiciones.*

22. See Blanco Aguinaga (1957).

23. See Talens (1977), and Talens and Canet (1986).

24. Cf. Zumthor.

25. See Pabst (1972) and Talens (1977).

26. See Foucault.

27. The contemporary Spanish playwright Ramón María del Valle-Inclán was faced with the same problem. It is said that during the dress rehearsal of his *Divinas Palabras,* the playwright became furious with the performance of actress Margarita Xirgu, saying: "Had I wanted to write a zarzuela, I would have done so."

28. See Spadaccini (1986) and Talens (1986).

29. Covarrubias cites the double spatial-temporal meaning: "From the Latin *spatium, capedo, intervallum;* it means place . . . It also means time interval . . . or something going slowly or in a hurry" ("Del nombre latino *spatium, capedo, intervallum;* Vale lugar . . . También significa el intervalo de tiempo . . . Ir de espacio o de priessa una cosa").

30.   Séneca, Terencio, Plauto,

y, otros, griegos, que tú sabes.

31.   Ya represento mil cosas,

no en relación, como de antes,

sino en hecho, y assí es fuerça

que haya de mudar lugares:

que como acontecen ellas

en muy diferentes partes,

voyme allí donde acontecen,

disculpa del disparate.

Ya la comedia es un mapa.

32.   Muy poco importa al oyente

que yo en un punto me pase

desde Alemania a Guinea

sin el teatro mudarme;

el pensamiento es ligero.

33. LOBILLO: Yo te daré una baraja

hecha, con que le despojes

sin que le dejes alhaja.

LUGO: ¡Largo medio es el que escoges!

Otro sé por do se ataja.

Juro a Dios omnipotente

        que, si las pierdo al presente,
        me he de hacer salteador.

34. LUGO: Solo quedo, y quiero entrar
        en cuentas conmigo a solas,
        aunque lo impidan las olas
        donde temo naufragar.
        Yo hice voto, si hoy perdía,
        de irme a ser salteador:
        claro y manifiesto error
        de una ciega fantasía.

35. En el acto primero ponga el caso,
        en el segundo enlace los sucesos,
        de suerte que hasta el medio del tercero
        apenas juzgue nadie en lo que para.

36. Dividido en dos partes el asunto,
        ponga la conexión desde el principio
        hasta que vaya declinando el paso,
        pero la solución no la permita
        hasta que llegue a la postrera escena,
        porque, en sabiendo el vulgo el fin que tiene,
        vuelve el rostro a la puerta y las espaldas
        el que esperó tres horas cara a cara
        que no hay más que saber que en lo que para.

37. Una de su vida libre,
        otra de su vida grave,
        otra de su santa muerte
        y de sus milagros grandes.

38. no hay justicia
        que le ose tocar por su respeto.

39. Sin picar nos iremos, y agradézcalo
        a su amo; que a fe de hijodalgo,
        yo no sé en qué parara este negocio.

40. "His desire is . . . to free himself from both. He does not want to be a reflection of the respect owed to his lord (God), nor does he wish to accept his humble origins (dust)" (Casalduero 1966: 106).

41. Que sólo me respeten por mi amo,
        y no por mí, no sé esta maravilla;
        mas yo haré que salga de mí un bramo
        que pase de los muros de Sevilla.

42. See Casalduero (1966: 126): "His devotion, his penitence have saved him."

43. Su conversión fue en Toledo,
        y no será bien te enfade
        que, contando la verdad,

en Sevilla se relate.

En Toledo se hizo clérigo,

y aquí, en México fue fraile,

adonde el discurso ahora

nos trajo aquí por el aire.

44. See Erasmus, *Enquiridion* (252–253): "On the one hand you revere and honor the saints and you receive pleasure in touching their relics . . . no devotion is more agreeable or more proper to saints than to strive to be virtuous in one's works and deeds . . . Doesn't all of your devotion seem to you to be in reverse order and upside down, for what you honor one way you erase in another?" ("Hazes por una parte acatamiento y honrra a los santos y gózate de tocar sus reliquias . . . ninguna devoción tan acepta es a los santos ni tan propia como trabajar por parecerles en las obras virtuosas . . . ¿No te parece que es trastocada y al revés toda tu devoción, pues lo que por una parte onrras luego por otra la borras?"). See also Forcione (1982), especially 395–397: "Erasmus . . . has no intention of denying the miraculous powers of Christ or indeed the 'mystery of the cross,' which, in the *Enquiridion* (184), he contrasts with the wood of its image, but would ever insist that the central miracle for all Christians must remain the miracle of self-transformation, a process that is achieved in large part by the active involvement of the individual in the imitation of Christ's life and the understanding of the spirit that manifests itself through the letter of the Holy Scriptures." Forcione recalls that even in his Life of Saint Jerome, Erasmus "stresses the hagiographer's obligation to record the truths of the daily life of the saint, ridicules traditional chroniclers' distortions of truth and exaggerations of miracles, and points out that a proper reading of a saint's life should lead the Christian to an understanding and an active imitation of the saintly model" (396, n. 136).

45. las ánimas me llevan cuanto tengo;

mas yo tengo esperanza que algún día

lo tienen de volver ciento por uno.

46. Dime, simple: ¿y tú no ves

que de esa tu plata y cobre

es dar en limosna al pobre

del puerco hurtado los pies?

Haces a Dios mil ofensas,

como dices, de ordinario,

¿y con rezar un rosario,

sin más, ir al cielo piensas?

47. See Canavaggio (1977: 297) and Zimic (1980: 124).

48. ———————————————— digo:

que el alma de doña Ana de Treviño,

que está presente, doy de buena gana

todas las buenas obras que yo he hecho

en caridad y en gracia desde el punto

que dejé la carrera de la muerte

y entré en la de la vida . . .

y, en contracambio, tomo sus pecados

---

49. FRAY ANTONIO: ¡Caso jamás oído es éste, padre!

    CLÉRIGO: Y caridad jamás imaginada

50. Su alma de las garras de la muerte
    eterna arrebató, y volvió a la vida,
    y de su pertinacia la divierte,
    la cual, como se viese enriquecida
    con la dádiva santa que el bendito
    padre le dio sin tasa y sin medida,
    alzó al momento un piadoso grito
    al cielo, y confesión pidió llorando.

In the chronicles, Lugo was defined as a womanizer. Cervantes seems to omit explicitly that information. Nevertheless, it is curious to note that, when Antonia refers to Lugo in her conversation with Don Tello (Act I), she describes him as an oaf ("leño") in matters of love. It is not precisely his poetic capacity ("Venus blanda y amorosa") that makes him attractive, but rather his sharp knife and steel dagger ("su aguda ganchosa y su acerado broquel"). As in Shakespeare, the erotic ambivalence of language is evident. It is difficult to believe that Cervantes would overlook the possible dramatic use of something so theatrical as the relationship between religion and eroticism, or between religion and wealth (see the autobiographical ballad of Pedro de Urdemalas in Act I of the play of the same name).

51. Y apenas por los aires transparentes
    voló de la contrita pecadora
    el alma a las regiones refulgentes,
    cuando en aquella misma feliz hora
    se vio el padre Cruz cubierto el rostro
    de lepra, adonde el asco mismo mora.

52. See Zimic (1980: 146–147), where he refutes Canavaggio's thesis (1977: 146), according to which "l'accession du plan de l'éternité signifie ainsi une abolition de la notion même de mouvement dramatique."

53. Amigo Fray Antonio, di a los padres
    mi vida, de quien fuiste buen testigo;
    diles mis insolencias y recreos,
    la inmensidad descubre de mis culpas,
    la bajeza les di de mi linage,
    diles que soy de un tabernero hijo,
    porque les haga todo aquesto junto
    mudar de parecer . . .

54. Cególes Dios los sentidos:
    que si ellos te conocieran
    como yo te he conocido,

> tomaran otro partido,
> y otro prior eligieran.

55. Fray Angel, yo hablo de veras;
    pero conviene esto aquí.
    Gusta este santo de verse
    vituperado de todos,
    y va huyendo los modos
    do pueda ensorberbecerse.
    Mira qué confuso está
    por la nueva que le has dado.

56. On verisimilitude as a base for artistic creation, see Alonso López Pinciano, *Philosophia antigua poética* (1596).

57. See E. C. Riley (1962: 205, 212).

58. Trece años ha que lidias,
    por ser caritativo
    sobre el humano modo.

59. que está toda la ciudad
    en el convento, y se arrojan
    sobre el cuerpo y lo despojan
    con tanta celeridad

60. For Cotarelo y Mori the play was composed, at least in part, before the death of the actor Nicolás de los Ríos, that is, before 1610, "even if finished and retouched in 1611, as we believe" (Cotarelo 1916: 417). Schevill and Bonilla (1922) and Valbuena Prat (1943) accept that date. Buchanan (1938) fixes the date of its composition in 1610 and Astrana Marín (1948–1958) moves it back to 1608. Canavaggio (1977) prefers to speak of the period between 1610 and 1615. We lean toward this last possibility, not only because of the extratextual references enumerated by Canavaggio but above all because of its metadiscursive character, which approximates that of the second part of *Don Quijote*.

61. "La historia de una joven de noble cuna, cuya desaparición y metamorfosis no afectan ni a la belleza ni a la virtud, ni a la gracia, y que al término de muchas tribulaciones, un buen día, encuentra a los suyos."

62. Romera-Navarro (1917) cites, as the most characteristic examples, the cases of the *Comedia Medora* and an anonymous *copla* that predicts for the gypsies the very fate that finally befalls Belica: "Do not speak badly of gypsies, / for they carry the blood of kings / in the palms of their hands" ("No hables mal de los gitanos, / que llevan sangre de reyes / en las palmas de las manos"). See also Amezúa y Mayo (1956–58) and Canavaggio (1977: 141+), among others.

63. Año de mil y quinientos
    y treinta y cuatro corría,
    a veinte y cinco de mayo,
    martes, acïago día,
    sucedió un caso notable
    en la ciudad de Sevilla,
    digno que ciegos lo canten

y que poetas le escriban.
Del gran corral de los Olmos,
do está la jacarandina,
sale Reguilete, el jaque,
vestido a las maravillas.
No va a la vuelta del Cairo,
del Catay ni de la China,
ni de Flandes, ni Alemania,
ni menos de Lombardía;
va la vuelta de la plaza
de San Francisco bendita,
que corren toros en ella
por Santa Justa y Rufina,
y apenas entró en la plaza,
cuando se lleva la vista
tras sí de todos los ojos,
que su buen donaire miran.
Salió en esto un toro hosco,
¡válasme Santa María!,
y, arremetiendo con él,
dio con él patas arriba.
Dejóle muerto y mohino,
bañado en su sangre misma;
y aquí da fin el romance
porque llegó el de su vida.

64. Pues sabes que soy pastor,
entona más bajo el punto,
habla con menos primor.

65. Clemencia, si yo he dicho cosa alguna
que no vaya a servirte encaminada,
venga de la más próspera fortuna
a la más abatida y desastrada;
si siempre sobre el cerco de la luna
no has sido por mi lengua levantada,
cuando quiera decirte mi querella,
mudo silencio el cielo infunda en ella.

Si mostré tal, la fe en que yo pensaba,
por la ley amorosa de salvarme,
cuando a la vida el término se acaba,
por ella entonces venga a condenarme;
si dije tal, jamás halle en su aljaba

flechas de plomo amor con que tirarme,
si no es a ti, y a mí con las doradas,
a helarte y abrasarme encaminadas.

66. See Canavaggio (1977: 124).

67. Despójese de su pluma
el rescate, y véase luego,
en resolución y en suma,
si hay algun rancho o bodego
donde todo se consuma:
que yo, a fe de compañero,
desde agora me prefiero
a dar todo al adherente. . . .
¡Oh de mis dichas Adlantes,
cerros de mi Potosí,
de mi pequeñez gigantes!
En vosotros se me ofrece
todo aquello que apetece
mi deseo en sumo grado.

68. Tengo otro estado
que estar aquí no requiere.

69. He dejado parte de ellos [los preceptos]
y he también guardado parte,
porque lo quiere así el uso
que no se acomoda al arte.

4. Narrativity and the Dialogic

1. Io pretendo di sapere le regole più che non sanno tutti i pedanti insieme; ma la vera regola è sapere rompere le regole a tempo e luogo, accomodandosi al costume e al gusto del secolo.

2. "No hay ninguna de quien no se pueda sacar algún ejemplo provechoso; y si no fuera por no alargar este sujeto, quizá te mostrara el sabroso y honesto fruto que se podría sacar, así de todas juntas como de cada una por sí."

3. "que yo soy el primero que he novelado en lengua castellana, que las muchas novelas que en ella andan impresas, todas son traducidas de lenguas estranjeras, y éstas son mía propias, no imitadas ni hurtadas; mi ingenio las engendró, y las parió mi pluma, y *van creciendo en los brazos de la estampa*" (emphasis added). Quotations from *Novelas ejemplares* are from the edition of Harry Sieber. English translations documented with a parenthetical page number refer to the translation by Harriet de Onís; other translations are our own.

4. "si bien lo miras [lector] no hay ninguna [novela ejemplar] de quien no se pueda sacar algún ejemplo provechoso."

5. "y quiérote [Berganza] advertir una cosa, de la cual verás la experiencia cuando te cuente los sucesos de mi vida; y es que los cuentos unos encierran y tienen la gracia en ellos mismos; otros, en el modo de contarlos; quiero decir que algunos hay que aunque

se cuenten sin preámbulos y ornamentos de palabras, dan contento; otros hay que es menester vestirlos de palabras, y con demostraciones del rostro y de las manos y con mudar la voz se hacen algo de nonada, y de flojos y desmayados se vuelven agudos y gustosos" (2: 304).

6. "Aunque este coloquio sea fingido y nunca haya pasado, paréceme que está tan bien compuesto que puede el señor Alférez pasar adelante con el segundo [Cipión's story]" (2: 359).

7. "Quiero decir que la sigas de golpe, sin que la hagas que parezca pulpo, según la vas añadiendo colas" (2: 318).

8. "de sudar catorce cargas de bubas que me hechó a cuestas una mujer que escogí por mía, que non debiera" (2: 282).

9. "Pero porque no estoy para tener largas pláticas en la calle, vuesa merced me perdone; que otro día con más comodidad le daré cuenta de mis sucesos, que son los más nuevos y peregrinos que vuestra merced habrá oído en todos los días de su vida" (2: 282).

10. "que otros sucesos me quedan por decir que exceden a toda imaginación, pues van fuera de todos los términos de naturaleza . . . En el hospital ví lo que ahora diré, que es lo que ahora ni nunca vuesa merced podrá creer, ni habrá persona en el mundo que lo crea" (2: 292).

11. "Cipión hermano, así el cielo te conceda el bien que deseas, que, sin que te enfades, me dejes ahora filosofar un poco; porque si dejase de decir las cosas que en este instante me han venido a la memoria de aquellas que entonces me ocurrieron, me parece que no sería mi historia cabal ni de fruto alguno" (2: 318).

12. "Lo más del día se les pasaba espulgándose . . . por donde vine a entender lo que pienso que deben de creer todos: que todos aquellos libros son cosas soñadas y bien escritas para entretenimiento de los ociosos, y no verdad alguna" (2: 309).

13. "vi que dos pastores asieron de un carnero de los mejores del aprisco, y le mataron, de manera que verdaderamente pareció a la mañana que había sido su verdugo el lobo. Pasméme, quedé suspenso cuando ví que los pastores eran los lobos y que despedazaban el ganado los mismos que le habían de guardar" (2: 311).

14. "Todo lo cual me traía lleno de admiración y de congoja. ¡Válame Dios!—decía entre mí—. ¿Quién podrá remediar esta maldad? ¿Quién será poderoso a dar a entender que la defensa ofende, que las centinelas duermen, que la confianza roba y el que os guarda os mata?" (2: 311).

15. BERGANZA: ¡Oh Cipión, quién te pudiera contar lo que vi en ésta y en otras dos compañías de comediantes en que anduve! Mas por no ser posible reducirlo a narración sucinta y breve, lo habré de dejar para otro día, si es que ha de haber otro día en que nos comuniquemos. ¿Ves cuán larga ha sido mi plática? ¿Ves mis muchos y diversos sucesos? ¿Consideras mis caminos y mis amos tantos? Pues todo lo que has oído es nada comparado a lo que te pudiera contar de lo que noté, averigüé y vi desta gente, su proceder, su vida, sus costumbres, sus ejercicios, su trabajo, su ociosidad, su ignorancia y su agudeza, con otras infinitas cosas, unas para decirse al oído y otras para aclamallas en público, y todas para hacer memoria dellas y para desengaño de muchos que idolatran en figuras fingidas y en bellezas de artificio y de transformación.
CIPIÓN: Bien se me trasluce, Berganza, el largo campo que se te descubría para dilatar tu plática, y soy de parecer que la dejes para cuento particular y para sosiego no sobresaltado. (2: 354)

16. "Triunfaba mi amo con la mucha ganancia, y sustentaba seis camaradas como unos reyes. La codicia y la envidia despertó en los rufianes voluntad de hurtarme, y andaban buscando ocasión para ello; que esto del ganar de comer holgando tiene muchos

aficionados y golosos; por esto hay tantos titereros en España, tantos que muestran retablos, tantos que venden alfileres y coplas, que todo su caudal, aunque le vendiesen todo, no llega a poderse sustentar un día; . . . Toda esta gente es vagamunda, inútil y sin provecho; esponjas del vino y gorgojos del pan'' (2: 333).

17. CIPIÓN: Buscado se ha remedio para todos los daños que has apuntado y bosquejado en sombra: que bien sé que son más y mayores que los que callas que los que cuentas, y hasta ahora no se ha dado con el que conviene; pero celadores prudentísimos tiene nuestra república, que considerando que España cría y tiene en su seno tantas víboras como moriscos, ayudados de Dios hallarán a tanto daño cierta, presta y segura salida. Di adelante. (2: 350)

18. "Y has de considerar que nunca el consejo del pobre, por bueno que sea, fue admitido, ni el pobre humilde ha de tener presunción de aconsejar a los grandes y a los que piensan que se lo saben todo. La sabiduría en el pobre está asombrada; que la necesidad y miseria son las sombras y nubes que la escurecen, y si acaso se descubre, la juzgan por tontedad y la tratan con menosprecio'' (2: 358).

19. See Nerlich and Spadaccini (1990).

20. See also Alban K. Forcione (1984, 1990), Ruth El Saffar (1976), and Anthony Cascardi (1990).

21. "En el relato pastoril es donde, por primera vez, se muestra el personaje literario como una singularidad estrictamente humana, como expresión de un 'dentro de sí'. Hemos hablado con exceso de lo abstracto y convencional de lo pastoril, de su ignorancia del tiempo y del espacio, y esto impidió atender a la proyección interior de sus personajes, al único espacio vital en que existen.''

22. "Entre otras cosas consideraba que no debía ser verdad lo que había oído contar de la vida de los pastores . . . diciendo que se les pasava toda la vida cantando y tañendo con gaitas, zampoñas, rabeles y chirumbelas, y con otros instrumentos extraordinarios'' (307).

23. "Lo más del día se les pasaba espulgándose o remendando sus abarcas'' (309).

24. "Lo que pienso que deben de creer todos: que todos aquellos libros son cosas soñadas y bien escritas para entretenimiento de ociosos, y no verdad alguna'' (309).

25. "A la chita callando, los muertos y los locos pueden decirlo todo. Pero además, si los personajes que le rodean no le tomaran por loco, nuestro héroe hubiera dado con sus huesos en la cárcel en la primera ocasión y, en este caso, ni Don Quijote hubiera sido Don Quijote, ni Cervantes hubiera dado cima y realización a la imaginada historia de sus hazañas. En la invención de la novela hay un hecho de gran relieve que nunca suele ser tenido en cuenta: *Don Quijote necesita un apoyo exterior, un apoyo social para mantener durante largo tiempo el peligroso y difícil ejercicio de su andante caballería.* Depende de esta protección el hecho milagroso de que la obra pueda sobrevivir en cada uno de sus capítulos. Cierta es, y necesaria, la resistencia que opone al caballero el mundo circundante; cierta es, y necesaria, la ayuda que le brinda. Don Fernando, Cardenio, los Duques y el Bachiller Sansón Carrasco le apoyan, de diferentes modos, y en virtud de este amparo y complicidad—no lo olvidemos—consigue Don Quijote llegar a ser quien es y librarse en sus andanzas de malentendedores y cuadrilleros.''

26. "El protagonista de esta novela no es realmente Don Quijote, con su siempre torcida interpretación de la realidad, ni Sancho, con su escéptica semiaceptación del quijotismo de su amo, ni mucho menos ninguna otra de las figuras centrales de los episodios ilusionistas intercalados en la novela: el verdadero héroe de la novela lo es Cervantes en persona, el artista que combina un arte de crítica y de ilusión conforme a su libérrima voluntad. Desde el instante en que abrimos el libro hasta el momento en

que lo cerramos, sentimos que hay allí un poder invisible y omnipotente que nos lleva adonde y como quiere.''

27. "Don Quijote consigue la inmortalidad gracias exclusivamente a la pluma de Cervantes, como muy bien sabe y reconoce el mismo escritor. Don Quijote, evidentemente, ejecutó sólo lo que Cervantes escribió y había nacido para Cervantes, igual que Cervantes había nacido para él. En el discurso de la pluma del supuesto cronista árabe encontramos la más discreta, la más enérgica y convincente autoglorificación del artista que jamás se haya escrito.''

28. "Como se sabe, los dos caballeros invitaron a Don Quijote a compartir su cena, y en la conversación quedó todo aclarado. Había habido una suplantación de personalidad. Nótese bien lo sucedido: Cervantes no ataca aquí la falsa historia de Avellaneda, sino al falsario que se hizo pasar por el héroe verdadero, el Don Quijote espúreo y remedador. Resulta, pues, que el debate no se polariza entre historiador e historiador, sino entre personaje y personaje. El autor, Cervantes, no hace sino registrar este debate, esta contienda, como registra todos los demás hechos que figuran en la crónica.''

29. "Don Alvaro Tarfe queda así corroborado por Cervantes como personaje real, y con esto se viene a decir que Avellaneda no mintió del todo. Si era real don Alvaro Tarfe, ¿lo sería también el otro Don Quijote, el falsario? Debió de serlo, porque don Alvaro Tarfe declara haberle conocido y tratado, así como a un tal Sancho, si bien nada parecido al verdadero, presente a la plática.''

30. See Anthony Close (1978).

31. "Salta Don Quijote al cuello de la realidad para no dar tiempo a que la realidad le desmienta, con esa rapidez que es la inquietud de los hombres de acción. Pues, aunque loco, era padre de su propia quimera, y no podía matar en su ser la voz que le decía que todo era ilusión. De aquí su ansiedad en acogerse a todo lo que confirmase su fe.''

32. "El poder es para Sancho lo que la gloria para Don Quijote, la ínsula materializa el poder para Sancho. Y así como Don Quijote tiene que creer en Dulcinea, a fin de creer en sí mismo, Sancho tiene que creer en Don Quijote para creer en la ínsula. De este modo, la fe del caballero va a nutrir el espíritu del criado, después de haber sostenido el espíritu propio.''

33. Puesto ya el pie en el estrivo

 con las ansias de la muerte,

 Gran señor, ésta te escrivo.

34. "El cual ha de ser o el más malo o el mejor que en nuestra lengua se haya compuesto, quiero decir de los de entretenimiento; y digo que me arrepiento de haber dicho el más malo porque, según la opinión de mis amigos, ha de llegar al extremo de bondad posible.''

35. See Juan Bautista Avalle-Arce, "Introducción" to his edition of *Los trabajos de Persiles y Sigismunda*.

36. "Con todo cuanto mal había dicho [el canónigo] de tales libros [de caballerías], hallaba en ellos una cosa buena: que era el sujeto que ofrecían para que un buen entendimiento pudiese mostrarse en ellos, porque daban largo y espacioso campo por donde, sin empacho alguno pudiese correr la pluma, describiendo naufragios, tormentas, rencuentros y batallas, pintando un capitán valeroso con todas las partes que para ser tal se requieren, mostrándose prudente previniendo las astucias de sus enemigos, y elocuente orador persuadiendo o disuadiendo a sus soldados, maduro en el consejo, presto en lo determinado, tan valiente en el esperar como en el acometer: pintando ora un lamentable y trágico suceso, ahora un alegre y no pensado acontecimiento; allí una hermosísima dama, honesta, discreta y recatada; aquí un caballero cristiano, valiente y

comedido; acullá un desaforado bárbaro fanfarrón; acá un príncipe cortés, valeroso y bien mirado; representando bondad y lealtad de vasallos, grandeza y mercedes de señores. Ya puede mostrarse astrólogo, ya cosmógrafo excelente, ya músico, ya inteligente en las materias de estado, y tal vez le vendrá ocasión de mostrarse nigromante, si quisiere'' (I: 566).

37. See Avalle-Arce (1977). Also, Alban K. Forcione in his excellent *Cervantes, Aristotle and the Persiles* documents the numerous sources that could justify a reading of Cervantes's last novel as a religious allegory (its orthodox Christian sense).

Works Cited

Alarcos García, Emilio. "Cervantes y Boccaccio." *Mediterráneo*. Special Issue on Cervantes. Valencia, 1950.

Alborg, Juan Luis. "La poesía de Cervantes." *Cervantes*. Madrid: Gredos, 1966.

Alter, Jean. "From Text to Performance." *Poetics Today* 2, no. 3 (1981): 113–139.

Amezúa y Mayo, Gonzalo de. *Cervantes, creador de la novela corta española*. 2 vols. Valencia: Consejo Superior de Investigaciones Científicas, 1956–1958.

Asensio, Eugenio. "Introducción." *Entremeses*. Madrid: Castalia, 1970.

———. *Itinerario del entremés: desde Lope de Rueda a Quiñones de Benavente*. Madrid: Gredos, 1965.

Astrana Marín, Luis. *Vida ejemplar y heroica de Miguel de Cervantes Saavedra*. 7 vols. Madrid: Reus, 1948–1958.

Avalle-Arce, Juan Bautista. "Introducción." *Los trabajos de Persiles y Sigismunda*. By Miguel Cervantes. Madrid: Castalia, 1977.

Bakhtin, Mikhail. "Discourses and the Novel." *The Dialogic Imagination*. Ed. Michael Holquist. Trans. Caryl Emerson and Michael Holquist. Austin: Univ. of Texas Press, 1981.

———. *Problems of Dostoevsky's Poetics*. Ed. and Trans. Caryl Emerson. Intro. Wayne C. Booth. Minneapolis: Univ. of Minnesota Press, 1984.

———. *Rabelais and His World*. Trans. Helene Iswolski. Cambridge, Mass.: MIT Press, 1968.

Barthes, Roland. "El discurso de la historia." *Estructuralismo y literatura*. Buenos Aires: Ediciones Nueva Visión, 1970.

Bataillon, Marcel. *Erasmo y España. Estudios sobre la historia espiritual del siglo XVI*. Mexico City: Fondo de Cultura Económica, 1950.

Benveniste, Emile. "Sémiologie de la langue." *Semiotica* I, no. 1 and I, no. 2 (1969): 1–12, 127–135.

Blanco Aguinaga, Carlos. "Cervantes y la picaresca. Notas sobre dos tipos de realismos." *Nueva Revista de Filología Hispánica* 11 (1957): 313–342.

Blecua, José Manuel (pseudonym Joseph M. Claube). "La poesía lírica de Cervantes." Madrid: *Cuadernos de Insula*, 1947.

———. "Garcilaso y Cervantes." Madrid: *Cuadernos de Insula*, 1948.

Borges, Jorge Luis. *Otras Inquisiciones*. Buenos Aires: Sur, 1952.

Bourdieu, Pierre. *Ce que parler veut dire*. Paris: Fayard, 1982.

Bovadilla, Castillo de. *Política para corregidores y señores de vasallos*. Madrid, 1597.

Buchanan, M. A. "The Works of Cervantes and Their Dates of Composition." *Transactions of the Royal Society of Canada*, Section II, Vol. 32 (1938).

Canavaggio, Jean. *Cervantès dramaturge. Un théâtre à naître*. Paris: Presses Universitaires de France, 1977.

———. "La dimension autobiographique du *Viaje del Parnaso*". *Actes du colloque international de la Baume-lès-Aix*. Aix-en-Provence, 1980: 171–184.

Casalduero, Joaquín. *Sentido y forma de las novelas ejemplares*. Madrid: Gredos, 1974.

———. *Sentido y forma del Quijote*. Madrid: Ediciones Insula, 1949.

———. *Sentido y forma del teatro de Cervantes*. Madrid: Gredos, 1966.

Cascardi, Anthony. "Cervantes's Exemplary Subjects." *Cervantes's Exemplary Novels and the Adventure of Writing*. Ed. Michael Nerlich and Nicholas Spadaccini. Hispanic Issues 6. Minneapolis: The Prisma Institute, 1990. 49–71.

Castro, Adolfo. "Cervantes, ¿fue poeta o no fue poeta?" Intro. to *Biblioteca de autores españoles*, vol. 42. Madrid: Hernando, 1906.

Castro, Américo. *Cervantes y los casticismos españoles*. Madrid: Alfaguara, 1966.

———. *Hacia Cervantes*. 2nd. ed. Madrid: Taurus, 1960.

———. *El pensamiento de Cervantes*. Madrid, 1925. Rpt. Barcelona: Noguer, 1972.

Cernuda, Luis. "Cervantes, poeta." *Poesía y Literatura II*. Barcelona: Seix Barral, 1964.

Cervantes Saavedra, Miguel de. *The Adventures of Don Quijote*. Trans. J. M. Cohen. Baltimore: Penguin, 1950.

———. *Entremeses*. Ed. Nicholas Spadaccini. Madrid: Cátedra, 1982.

———. *La Galatea*. Ed. Juan Bautista Avalle-Arce. 2 vols. Madrid: Espasa-Calpe, 1961.

———. *El ingenioso hidalgo don Quijote de la Mancha*. Ed. Luis Andrés Murillo. 3 vols. Madrid: Castalia, 1978.

———. *Novelas ejemplares*. 2 vols. Ed. Harry Sieber. Madrid: Cátedra, 1985.

———. *Obras completas*. Ed. Angel Valbuena Prat. Madrid: Aguilar, 1943.

———. *Obras completas de Cervantes*. Ed. Cayetano Rosell. Vol. 3. Madrid: Rivadeneyra, 1864.

———. *Obras completas de Miguel de Cervantes Saavedra*. Ed. Rodolfo Schevill and Adolfo Bonilla. Madrid: Gráficas Reunidas, 1922.

———. *Obras menores de Cervantes*. Ed. J. Givanel Mas. Vol. 2. Barcelona: Antonio López, 1905.

———. *Poesía*. Ed. Adriana Lewis. Zaragoza: Ebro, 1972.

———. *Poesías completas II*. Ed. Vicente Gaos. Madrid: Castalia, 1973.

———. *Poesías de Cervantes*. Ed. Vicente Gaos. Madrid: Taurus, 1970.

———. *Poesías de Cervantes*. Ed. Ricardo Rojas. Buenos Aires: Coni Hermanos, 1916.

———. *El rufián dichoso/Pedro de Urdemalas*. Ed. Nicholas Spadaccini and Jenaro Talens. Madrid: Cátedra, 1986.

———. *Six Exemplary Novels*. Trans. Harriet de Onís. Woodbury, N.Y.: Barron's Educational Series, 1961.

———. *Los trabajos de Persiles y Sigismunda*. Ed. Juan Bautista Avalle-Arce. Madrid: Castalia, 1977.

————. *Viaje del Parnaso*. Ed. Vicente Gaos. Madrid: Castalia, 1974.

————. *The Voyage to Parnassus*. Trans. G. W. J. Gyll. London: Alex, Murray and Son, 1870.

Close, Anthony. *The Romantic Approach to* Don Quijote. Cambridge: Cambridge Univ. Press, 1978.

Cohen, Walter. *Drama of a Nation*. Ithaca, N.Y.: Cornell Univ. Press, 1985.

————. "Drama of a Nation: Public Theater in Renaissance England and Spain." *Plays and Playhouses in Imperial Decadence*. Ed. Anthony N. Zahareas. Minneapolis: Institute for the Study of Ideologies and Literature, 1986. 13–23.

Collard, André. *Nueva poesía*. 2d ed. Madrid: Castalia, 1971.

Cotarelo y Mori, Emilio. *Los puntos oscuros de la vida de Cervantes*. Madrid, 1916.

Croce, Benedetto. *Aesthetic as Science of Expression and General Linguistics*. Trans. Douglas Ainslie. New York: Noonday, 1953.

————. "Due illustrazioni al *Viaje del Parnaso* di Cervantes." *Homenaje a Menéndez Pelayo I*. Madrid, 1899.

Curtius, Ernst. *European Literature and the Latin Middle Ages*. Trans. Wilard R. Trask. Princeton: Princeton Univ. Press, 1957.

de Marinis, Marco. *Semiotica del teatro*. Milan: Bompiani, 1982.

de Mauro, Tullio. *Introduzione alla semantica*. Bari: Laterza, 1970.

Descouzis, Paul. *Cervantes a nueva luz*. Frankfurt am Main: V. Klostermann, 1966.

Diccionario de Autoridades. 3 vols. Ed. facsímil. Madrid: Real Academia Española-Gredos, 1963.

Diego, Gerardo. "Cervantes y la poesía." *Revista de filología española* 32 (1948): 213–236.

Díez Borque, José María. *Sociedad y teatro en la España de Lope de Vega*. Barcelona: Bosch, 1978.

————. "Teatro dentro del teatro, novela de la novela en Miguel de Cervantes." *Anales cervantinos* 11 (1972): 113–128.

Dubois, Jacques. "Pour une critique littéraire sociologique." *Le Littéraire et le social*. Ed. Robert Escarpit. Paris: Flammarion, 1970. 56–75.

Eagleton, Terry. *Marxism and Literary Criticism*. Berkeley: Univ. of California Press, 1976.

Eco, Umberto. *A Theory of Semiotics*. Bloomington: Indiana Univ. Press, 1976.

El Saffar, Ruth. El casamiento engañoso *and* El Coloquio de los perros. By Miguel de Cervantes. London: Tamesis, 1976.

————. "The Truth of the Matter: The Place of Romance in the Works of Cervantes." In *Romance: Generic Transformations from Chrétien de Troyes to Cervantes*. Ed. Kevin Brownlee and Marina Scordilis Brownlee. Hanover, N.H.: Univ. Press of New England, 1985.

Erasmus, Desiderius. *Enquiridion*. Ed. Dámaso Alonso. *Revista de Filología Española*, Anejo XVI (1932): 252–253.

Fernández de Navarrete, Pedro. *Conservación de monarquías*. [1626.] Rpt. *Biblioteca de autores españoles*, vol. 25. Madrid: Rivadeneyra, 1853.

Fernández Suárez, Alvaro. *Los mitos del* Quijote. Madrid: Aguilar, 1953.

Forcione, Alban K. "Afterword: Exemplarity, Modernity, and the Discriminating Games of Reading." In *Cervantes's Exemplary Novels and the Adventure of Writing*. Ed. Michael Nerlich and Nicholas Spadaccini. Hispanic Issues 6. Minneapolis: Prisma Institute, 1990. 331–351.

————. *Cervantes and the Humanist Vision: A Study of Four Exemplary Novels*. Princeton: Princeton Univ. Press, 1982.

————. *Cervantes and the Mystery of Lawlessness: A Study of* El casamiento engañoso y El coloquio de los perros. Princeton: Princeton Univ. Press, 1984.

————. *Cervantes, Aristotle and the Persiles.* Princeton: Princeton Univ. Press, 1970.

Foucault, Michel. *L'ordre du discours.* Paris, 1971.

Friedman, Edward H. "Perspectivism on Stage: *Don Quijote* and the Mediated Vision of Cervantes's *Comedias.*" *Plays and Playhouses in Imperial Decadence.* Ed. Anthony N. Zahareas. Minneapolis: Institute for the Study of Ideologies and Literature, 1986. 69–86.

————. *The Unifying Concept: Approaches to the Structure of Cervantes' Comedias.* York, S.C.: Spanish Literature Publications Company, 1981.

Gaos, Vicente. "Cervantes, poeta." *Claves de literatura española.* Vol. 1. Madrid: Guadarrama, 1971.

Genette, Gérard. "Vraisemblance et motivation." *Communications* 11 (1968): 1–21.

González de Cellorigo, Martín. *Memorial de la política necesaria y útil restauración de la república de España.* Valladolid, 1600.

Gracia García, Jordi. "Intención crítica del *Viaje del Parnaso*: en torno a la adulación y la vanagloria." *Anthropos* 88–89 (1989).

Halliday, M. A. K. *Learning How to Mean.* New York: Elsevier, 1977.

Hatzfeld, Helmut. *El* Quijote *como obra de arte del lenguaje.* Madrid: Patronato del IV Centenario del Nacimiento de Cervantes, 1949.

Hauser, Arnold. *The Social History of Art.* 4 vols. Vol. 2: *Renaissance, Mannerism, Baroque.* Trans. Stanley Godman. New York: Vintage Books, 1951.

Herrera, Fernando de. Anotaciones. *Obras de Garcilaso de la Vega.* Edición facsimilar, 1580. Madrid: Consejo Superior de Investigaciones Científicas, 1973.

Hjelmslev, Louis. *Prolegomena to a Theory of Language.* Madison: Univ. of Wisconsin Press, 1943.

Iser, Wolfgang. *The Act of Reading.* Baltimore: Johns Hopkins Univ. Press, 1978.

Jansen, Steen. "L'unité d'action dans *Andromaque* et dans *Lorenzaccio.*" *Revue Romane* 3. 1–2; 16–19 (1968): 116–135.

Johnson, Carroll B. "El arte viejo de hacer teatro: Lope de Rueda, Lope de Vega y Cervantes." *Cuadernos de Filología. Literaturas*: Análisis III, 1–2 (1980): 250–251.

Kenworthy, Patricia. "The Entremeses of Cervantes: The Dramaturgy of Illusion." Diss., Univ. of Arizona, 1976.

Kowzan, Tadeusz. *Littérature et spectacle.* The Hague: Mouton, 1969.

Krauss, Werner. "Novela, Novelle, Roman." *Zr Ph*, 60 (1940): 16–28.

Kristeva, Julia. *Semeiotike. Recherches pour une sémanalyse.* Paris: Editions du Seuil, 1969.

Liñan y Verdugo, A. *Guía y aviso de forasteros que vienen a la corte.* Ed. Edisons Simons. Madrid: Editora Nacional, 1980.

López-Estrada, Francisco. La Galatea *de Cervantes: Estudio crítico.* La Laguna de Tenerife: Univ. de La Laguna, 1948.

López Pinciano, Alonso. *Philosophia antigua poética.* (1595–1596). 3 vols. Ed. Alfredo Carballo Picazo. Madrid: Consejo Superior de Investigaciones Científicas, 1953.

Lotman, Jurij. *The Structure of the Artistic Text.* Trans. Ronald Vroon and Gail Vroon. Ann Arbor: Univ. of Michigan, 1977 (Dept. of Slavic Languages and Literatures). [Original Russian edition, 1970.]

Löwenthal, Leo. *Literature, Popular Culture and Society.* Palo Alto: Pacific Books Publishers, 1971.

Lynch, John. *España bajo los Austrias.* 2 vols. Barcelona: Fundamentos, 1972.

Macherey, Pierre. *Pour une théorie de la production littéraire.* Paris: Maspero, 1971.

Madariaga, Salvador de. *Guía del lector del Quijote.* Madrid: Espasa-Calpe, 1976.

Maravall, José Antonio. *Culture of the Baroque.* Trans. Terry Cochran. Minneapolis: Univ. of Minnesota Press, 1986.

———. *La cultura del barroco: Análisis de una estructura histórica.* Barcelona: Ariel, 1975.

——— "La función del honor en la sociedad tradicional." *Ideologies and Literature* II, 7 (1978): 9–27.

———. *La literatura picaresca desde la historia social.* Madrid: Taurus, 1986.

———. *Poder, honor y élites en el siglo XVII.* Madrid: Siglo Veintiuno, 1979.

———. *Teatro y literatura en la sociedad Barroca.* Madrid: Seminarios y Ediciones, 1972.

———. *Utopía y Contrautopía en El Quijote.* Santiago de Compostela: Pico Sacro, 1976.

Márquez Villanueva, Francisco. "El Retorno del Parnaso." *Nueva Revista de Filología Hispánica* 38 (1990): 693–732.

Marrast, Robert. *Miguel de Cervantes, dramaturgue.* Paris: L'Arche, 1957.

Martin, Wallace. *Recent Theories of Narrative.* Ithaca: Cornell Univ. Press, 1987.

Menéndez y Pelayo, Marcelino. "Cervantes, considerado como poeta." *Estudios y discurso de crítica literaria I.* Madrid: Consejo Superior de Investigaciones Científicas, 1941.

———. "Cultura literaria de Miguel de Cervantes y elaboración del Quijote." *Orígenes de la novela. Obras Completas.* Madrid: Consejo Superior de Investigaciones Científicas, 1961.

———. *Historia de las ideas estéticas en España. Obras completas.* Madrid: Consejo Superior de Investigaciones Científicas, 1961.

Molho, Maurice. *Cervantes: raíces folklóricas.* Madrid: Gredos, 1976.

———. "Sur le discours idéologique du 'Burlador de Sevilla' y 'Convidado de Piedra' ". *L'Idéologie dans le texte.* Actes du Collogue du Séminaire d'Etudes Littéraires. Univ. de Toulouse-Le Mirail, 1978.

Molina, Tirso de. *"El burlador de Sevilla" and "La prudencia en la mujer."* Ed. Raymond MacCurdy. New York: Dell, 1965.

Moncada, Sancho de. *Restauración Política de España* (1619). Ed. Jean Vilar. Madrid: Instituto de Estudios Fiscales, 1974.

Nerlich, Michael. "L'Ombre du Silence. *El coloquio de los perros* ou l'aventure du récit' ". In *Mélanges offerts au Professeur Maurice Descottes.* Ed. Yves-Alain Favre et Christian Manso, Univ. de Pau et des Pays de l'Adour, 1988. 83–103.

———, and Nicholas Spadaccini (Eds.) *Cervantes's Exemplary Novels and the Adventure of Writing.* Hispanic Issues 6. Minneapolis: The Prisma Institute, 1990.

Olson, E., and Bruce W. Wardropper. *Teoría de la comedia.* Barcelona: Seix Barral, 1978.

Orozco Díaz, Emilio. "Introducción." *Historia de la literatura española.* Vol. 2. Ed. José María Díez Borque. Madrid: Taurus, 1973.

———. *Introducción al Barroco.* 2 vols. Ed. José Lara Garrido. Granada: Univ. de Granada, 1988.

———. *Manierismo y Barroco.* Salamanca: Anaya, 1970. 2d ed. Madrid: Cátedra, 1975.

———. *¿Qué es el* Arte nuevo *de Lope de Vega?* Salamanca: Universidad, 1978.

———. *El teatro y la teatralidad del Barroco.* Barcelona: Planeta, 1969.

Ortega y Gasset, José. "Teoría de la inverosimilitud" (1922); *Meditaciones del Quijote* (1914). In *Obras completas.* Madrid: Revista de Occidente, 1963–1983.

Pabst, Walter. *La novela corta en la teoría y en la creación literaria.* Madrid. Gredos, 1972. [Originally published as *Novellentheorie und Novellendichtung. Zur Geschichte ihrer Antinomie in den romanischen Literaturen.* Hamburg, 1953; 2d ed. Heidelberg: Carl Winter, 1967.]

Pagnini, Marcello. "Per una semiologia del teatro classico." *Strumenti critici* 12 (1970): 121–140.

Ponzio, Augusto. *Producción lingüística e ideología social.* Madrid: Comunicación, 1974.

Prieto, Luis J. "Preface" to the Italian edition of *Elementi di semiologia* (orig. *Messages et signaux*, 1966), 1970.

Querol, Miguel. "Cervantes y la música." *Revista de Filología Española* 32 (1948): 367–382.

Quevedo, Francisco de. *La vida del Buscón llamado Don Pablos*. Ed. Domingo Ynduráin. Madrid: Cátedra, 1981.

Rey Hazas, Antonio. "Género y estructura de 'El Coloquio de los perros' ". In *Lenguaje, ideología y organización textual de las Novelas Ejemplares*. Ed. José Jesus de Bustos Tovar. Madrid: Univ. Complutense, 1983. 119-143.

Ricardou, Jean. *Problèmes du Nouveau Roman*. Paris: Minuit, 1967.

Riley, E. C. *Cervantes's Theory of the Novel*. Oxford: Oxford Univ. Press, 1962.

Rivers, Elias L. "Cervantes' *Journey to Parnassus*." *MLN* 85 (1970): 243–248.

Robbe-Grillet, Alain. *Le miroir qui revient*. Paris: Editions de Minuit, 1984.

Rodríguez Marín, F. "Prologue" to *Viaje del Parnaso*. Madrid: C. Bermejo, 1935.

Rojas, Ricardo. *Cervantes*. Buenos Aires: Losada, 1948.

Romera-Navarro, M. "La andante gitanería." *La lectura* 17, no. 3 (1917): 399–407.

Rosales, Luis. *Cervantes y la libertad*. 2 vols. Madrid: Sociedad de Estudios y Publicaciones, 1960.

Ruffini, Franco. *Semiotica del testo. L'esempio del teatro*. Rome: Bulzoni, 1978.

Salazar, Adolfo. "Música, instrumentos y danzas en la obra de Cervantes." *Nueva Revista de Filología Hispánica* 2 (1948): 118–173.

Salomon, Noël. *Recherches sur le thème paysan dans la 'comedia' au temps de Lope de Vega*. Bourdeaux: Feret et fils, 1965.

Schevill, Rodolfo, and Adolfo Bonilla (Eds.). "Introduction." *Obras completas de Miguel de Cervantes Saavedra*. 6 vols. Vol. 4 (1922): 1–158. Madrid: Gráficas Reunidas, 1914–1931.

Scholes, Robert. *Textual Power*. New Haven: Yale Univ. Press, 1985.

Segre, Cesare. "Contribution to the Semiotics of Theater." *Poetics Today* 1, no. 2 (1980): 39–48.

———. "Narratology and Theater." *Poetics Today* 2, no. 3 (1981): 95–104.

Selig, Karl. "Concerning the Structure of Cervantes' *La Gitanilla*." *Romanistisches Jahrbuch* 18 (1962).

Shergold, N. D. *A History of the Spanish Stage from Medieval Times until the End of the Seventeenth Century*. Oxford: Oxford Univ. Press, 1967.

Spadaccini, Nicholas. "Introducción." *Entremeses*. By Miguel de Cervantes. Madrid: Cátedra, 1982.

———. "Cervantes and the Spanish Comedia." *Plays and Playhouses in Imperial Decadence*. Ed. Anthony N. Zahareas. Minneapolis: Institute for the Study of Ideologies and Literature, 1986. 53–67.

———. "Writing for Reading: Cervantes's Aesthetics of Reception in the *Entremeses*." In *Critical Essays on Cervantes*. Ed. Ruth El Saffar. Boston: G. K. Hall, 1986. 162-175.

———, and Jenaro Talens. "Introducción." *El rufián dichoso/Pedro de Urdemalas*. Madrid: Cátedra, 1986.

Spitzer, Leo. "Perspectivismo lingüístico en El Quijote." *Lingüística e historia literaria*. Madrid: Gredos, 1955. Trans. "Linguistic Perspectivism in the *Don Quijote*." *Linguistics and Literary History: Essays in Stylistics*. New York: Russell and Russell, 1962. 41–85.

Talens, Jenaro. *La escritura como teatralidad*. Valencia: Univ. de Valencia, 1977.

———. *Elementos para una semiótica del texto artístico*. Madrid: Cátedra, 1978.

————. "Narrating Theatricality." *Plays and Playhouses in Imperial Decadence*. Ed. Anthony N. Zahareas. Minneapolis: Institute for the Study of Ideologies and Literature, 1986. 87–101.

————. *Novela picaresca y práctica de la transgresión*. Madrid: Júcar, 1975.

————, and José-Luis Canet. "Literature vs. Theatricality: On the Notion of 'Popular' in the Spanish Culture of the Golden Age." In *Literature among Discourses: The Spanish Golden Age*. Ed. W. Godzich and N. Spadaccini. Minneapolis: Univ. of Minnesota Press, 1986.

————, and Juan-Miguel Company. "The Textual Space: On the Notion of Text." *Journal of the Midwest Modern Language Association* 17:2 (1984): 24–36.

Tordera, Antonio. *Teoría e historia de la semiótica teatral*. Diss., Univ. de Valencia, 1979.

————. "Teoría y técnica del análisis teatral." In *Elementos para una semiótica del texto artístico*. Ed. Talens et al. Madrid: Cátedra, 1978.

Valbuena Prat, Angel. "Recopilación, estudio preliminar y notas." *Obras completas de Miguel de Cervantes Saavedra*. Madrid: Aguilar, 1943.

Vega, Lope de. *Arte nuevo de hacer comedias en este tiempo*. Madrid, 1609. Ed. A. Morel Fatio. Rpt. in *Preceptiva dramática española*. Ed. Federico Sánchez Escribano y Alberto Porqueras Mayo. Madrid: Gredos, 1965. 125–136.

————. *Peribáñez y el Comendador de Ocaña*. Ed. Juan María Marín. Madrid: Cátedra, 1987.

Vives, Juan Luis. *De officio mariti* (1528). Spanish trans. Lorenzo Riber. Madrid: Aguilar, 1947.

Vossler, Karl. *Lecciones sobre Tirso de Molina*. Madrid: Taurus, 1965.

Wardropper, Bruce. "Cervantes' Theory of Drama." *Modern Philology* 52 (1955): 217–221.

————. *La comedia española del Siglo de Oro*. Barcelona: Ariel, 1978.

Wells, Stanley W. *Literature and Drama with Special References to Shakespeare and His Contemporaries*. London: Routledge and K. Paul, 1970.

White, Hayden. "The Historical Text as Literary Artifact." *Tropics of Discourse*. Baltimore: Johns Hopkins Univ. Press, 1978.

————. "The Structure of Historical Narrative." *Clio* I (1972): 5–20.

Wilson, Diana de Armas. *Allegories of Love: Cervantes's 'Persiles and Sigismunda.'* Princeton: Princeton Univ. Press, 1991.

Ynduráin, Domingo. "El Gran Teatro de Calderón y el mundo del XVII." *Segismundo* 19–20 (1974): 17–71.

Zamora Vicente, Alonso. "La 'Epístola a Mateo Vázquez.' " Madrid: *Cuadernos de Insula*, 1947.

Zimic, Stanislav. "La caridad 'jamás imaginada' de Cristóbal de Lugo. Estudio de *El Rufián Dichoso* de Cervantes." *Boletín de la Biblioteca Menéndez y Pelayo* 56 (1980): 85–171.

Zumthor, Paul. *Essai de poétique médiévale*. Paris: Editions du Seuil, 1972.

Index

About the Authors

Nicholas Spadaccini is professor of Hispanic studies and comparative literature at the University of Minnesota. He has written on Cervantes, the picaresque novel, and Spanish Golden Age drama, edited several Spanish classics, and coedited numerous books on literary theory and criticism.

Jenaro Talens is professor of literary theory and film at the University of Valencia, Spain, and since 1983 has been regular Visiting Professor at the University of Minnesota. He has published numerous books of poetry, translated a number of European classics in Spanish, and written many books on literary criticism and theory.